# OPCS Classification of Interventions and Procedures, Version 4.6

# Volume II

## Alphabetical Index

**NHS Classifications Service**

London: TSO

information & publishing solutions

Published by TSO (The Stationery Office) and available from:

**Online**
**www.tsoshop.co.uk**

**Mail, Telephone, Fax & E-mail**
TSO
PO Box 29, Norwich, NR3 1GN
Telephone orders/General enquiries: 0870 600 5522
Order through the Parliamentary Hotline Lo-Call 0845 7 023474
Fax orders: 0870 600 5533
E-mail: customer.services@tso.co.uk
Textphone: 0870 240 3701

**TSO@Blackwell and other Accredited Agents**

**Customers can also order publications from:**
TSO Ireland
16 Arthur Street, Belfast BT1 4GD
Tel 028 9023 8451    Fax 028 9023 5401

A Tabular List (volume I) is available separately under ISBN 978 0 11 322866 9
Both volumes can be purchased together at a discounted price, if ordered under
ISBN 978 0 11 322868 3.

First published 2011
Second impression 2011
ISBN 978 0 11 322867 6

Printed in the United Kingdom for The Stationery Office

# TABLE OF CONTENTS

# INTRODUCTION

## Section I: Alphabetical Index of Interventions and Procedures

Welcome to the Alphabetical Index (Volume II) of the OPCS Classification of Interventions and Procedures Version 4.6, April 2011.

The Alphabetical Index (Volume II) is integral to the use of the classification and must be used in conjunction with the primary coding tool – the OPCS-4 Tabular List (Volume I). Reference must always be made to the Tabular List in order to select the code which best represents the nature of the intervention performed.

This latest release also sees the Alphabetical Index (Volume II) of the OPCS Classification of Interventions and Procedures Version 4.6, April 2011 available as an electronic version for the first time.

In addition, changes to the OPCS-4 classification continue to be produced and validated in a more structured and controlled environment. This enables continual improvements to content for future releases of the classification.

As well as including statements indexed to the full four character code, the Alphabetical Index also refers to codes in the format XXX .- e.g. A03.-. This format directs the coder to a variety of qualifying statements at four-character level.

The use of the alpha O carries specific meaning within OPCS-4 because it provides overflow codes to allow interventions to be placed within the correct body system where the chapter has reached capacity. The body system chapter to which the alpha O code relates is represented in the Index by a parenthesis enclosing the chapter prefix. This notation follows the description of the procedure e.g.

*O03.- Embolisation Artery Aneurysmal Coil Stent Assisted Transluminal Percutaneous (L)*

## Guide for Use of the Alphabetical Index

The Alphabetical Index must always be used in conjunction with the Tabular List in Volume I.

The Alphabetical Index has four distinct sections, which are:

1. Alphabetical Index of Interventions and Procedures
2. Alphabetical Index of Surgical Eponyms
3. Alphabetical Index of Surgical Abbreviations
4. Alphabetical Index of Common Surgical Suffixes

The Alphabetical Index includes the following abbreviations:

HFQ However Further Qualified
NEC Not Elsewhere Classified
NOC Not Otherwise Classifiable

It also includes abbreviations and curtailed terms:

| | |
|---|---|
| anast. | = anastomosis |
| cong. | = congenital |
| disloc. | = dislocation |
| endo. | = endoscopic |
| exam. | = examination |
| fibreop. | = fibreoptic |
| gi. | = gastrointestinal |
| mcp. | = metacarpophalangeal |
| mtp. | = metatarsophalangeal |
| prox. | = proximal |
| recur. | = recurrent |
| ugi. | = upper gastrointestinal |

The format of each entry, in general, follows the example below:

ABLATION BRAIN TISSUE STEREOTACTIC:-

| | |
|---|---|
| ABLATION | = ACTION |
| BRAIN | = SITE |
| TISSUE | = SUBSITE |
| STEREOTACTIC | = ACTION QUALIFIER |

## Endoscopic and minimal access operations

The Tabular List of the classification includes a range of categories designated as 'endoscopic' procedures e.g.

### M42  Endoscopic extirpation of lesion of bladder

When the classification was constructed it was intended that these categories would be primarily used for operations carried out through existing anatomical passages.  However, in the past, some of these categories were also expected to be used for operations carried out using minimal incisions through which rigid or fibreoptic scopes were introduced into body cavities, e.g.

### Q37  Endoscopic reversal of female sterilisation

This practice has been maintained in subsequent versions of OPCS-4 and further specific categories have been introduced which differentiate between endoscopic and laparoscopic e.g.

### J17.1 Endoscopic ultrasound examination of liver and biopsy of lesion of liver

### J09.3 Laparoscopic ultrasound examination of liver NEC

Where such specific categories are not available it is recommended that dual coding be used for minimally invasive procedures.  This has the advantage that it can be applied to any existing procedure that may be done via one of these approaches. The preferred form used in the Alphabetical Index is ACCESS MINIMAL.

The primary code is normally that code which is associated with the open form of the procedure. It must be used with maximum clinical detail to identify what was done and on what organ.  A second code in the range Y74–Y76 is used to specify the approach. These can be found under the lead terms ACCESS and APPROACH e.g.

### Y74  Minimal access to thoracic cavity

## Section II: Alphabetical Index of Surgical Eponyms

The Alphabetical Index of Surgical Eponyms includes a brief description of each intervention, principally to distinguish between those of the same name. If the same operation can be done on different subsites e.g. parts of the spine, then the eponym is assigned to the unspecified site and reference to the Tabular List suggests allocation to a particular site. Each eponym also has the corresponding OPCS-4 code listed. This index also includes one abbreviation:

(D) = Device.

The device code is assigned to the normal code for insertion or placement. The Tabular List must be consulted for maintenance, removal etc.

## Section III: Alphabetical Index of Surgical Abbreviations

The Alphabetical Index of Surgical Abbreviations includes the description of the abbreviation in addition to the corresponding OPCS-4 code.

## Section IV: Alphabetical Index of Common Surgical Suffixes

This section of the Alphabetical Index can be used to rapidly identify the meaning of the more common surgical suffixes.

## Training and Advice

The NHS Classifications Service provides a centralised national clinical classifications service with the primary objective of supporting the NHS.

In addition to developing the OPCS-4 information standard, the NHS Classifications Service provides expert clinical classifications knowledge on all coding standards in use in the NHS. This covers all aspects of guidance, advice, maintenance, implementation, cross-mapping, coding audit, data quality, training and accreditation.

The central service makes best use of clinical and classification expertise by providing the national helpdesk for resolution of queries. We also provide a centre of expertise and point of contact for international work in this area.

As the national service for clinical coding, our development of the core suite of clinical coding training materials minimises training development costs for the NHS as well as providing professional development for the clinical coder.

By using NCS training materials, the NHS also ensures they are compliant with current national coding standards and information governance guidelines.

A rigorous development, quality assurance and maintenance programme is followed in all our work. Consequently, all NHS coders can trust the training courses delivered using NCS materials to meet their professional development needs and, more crucially, national data standards.

For more information on our work:
www.cfh.nhs.uk/clinicalcoding

For all clinical coding queries, including the national clinical classifications helpdesk:
Email: datastandards@nhs.net   Tel: 01392 206 248

For more information on OPCS-4:
www.cfh.nhs.uk/clinicalcoding/codingstandards/opcs4/

To access the online web portal to offer requests for change:
www.cfh.nhs.uk/opcs4requestsportal

To download the eBook version of the OPCS-4 Tabular List and Index visit and register for the Terminology Release Update Data Service (TRUD):
www.uktcregistration.nss.cfh.nhs.uk

# Section I

Alphabetical Index
of
Interventions and
Surgical Procedures

# A

|  | Abandoned Operations – refer to Tabular List Introduction |
| --- | --- |
| Y50.- | Abdominal Cavity Approach |
| T45.- | Abdominal Cavity Operations Image Controlled |
| M52.- | Abdominal Operations Support Bladder Outlet Female NEC |
| Z31.- | Abdominal Organ site NEC |
| T31.- | Abdominal Wall Anterior Operations NEC |
| T31.- | Abdominal Wall Operations NEC |
| T39.- | Abdominal Wall Posterior Operations |
| Z53.- | Abdominal Wall site |
| S02.2 | Abdominolipectomy |
| S02.1 | Abdominoplasty |
| M51.- | Abdominovaginal Operations Support Bladder Outlet Female |
|  | Ablation – see also Destruction |
|  | Ablation – see also Extirpation |
|  | Ablation – see also Resection |
| K57.4 | Ablation Accessory Pathway Transluminal Percutaneous |
| K62.2 | Ablation Atrial Wall Atrial Flutter Transluminal Percutaneous |
| K57.5 | Ablation Atrial Wall Transluminal Percutaneous NEC |
| K52.- | Ablation Atrioventricular Node |
| K57.1 | Ablation Atrioventricular Node Transluminal Percutaneous |
| K62.1 | Ablation Atrium Left to Vein Pulmonary Transluminal Percutaneous |
| W35.6 | Ablation Bone Lesion Radiofrequency Percutaneous |
| A03.- | Ablation Brain Tissue Stereotactic |
| Q16.2 | Ablation Endometrium Balloon |
| Q17.7 | Ablation Endometrium Balloon Endoscopic |
| Q17.6 | Ablation Endometrium Microwave Endoscopic |
| Q16.3 | Ablation Endometrium Microwave NEC |
| Q16.6 | Ablation Endometrium Photodynamic |
| Q16.5 | Ablation Endometrium Radiofrequency |
| Q16.4 | Ablation Endometrium Saline Free Circulating |
| K64.1 | Ablation Epicardium Radiofrequency Percutaneous |
| R04.7 | Ablation Fetus Lesion Laser Percutaneous |
| A03.3 | Ablation Globus Pallidus Tissue Stereotactic |
| K62.3 | Ablation Heart Conducting System Atrial Flutter Transluminal Percutaneous |
| K57.2 | Ablation Heart Conducting System Transluminal Percutaneous NEC |
| K57.7 | Ablation Heart Congenital Malformation Transluminal Percutaneous |
| K16.6 | Ablation Heart Septum Chemical Mediated Transluminal Percutaneous |
| M13.7 | Ablation Kidney Lesion Radiofrequency Percutaneous |
| L88.- | Ablation Leg Vein Varicose |
| J12.6 | Ablation Liver Lesion Chemical Percutaneous |

| | |
|---|---|
| J08.3 | Ablation Liver Lesion Microwave Access Minimal |
| J08.3 | Ablation Liver Lesion Microwave Endoscopic |
| J08.3 | Ablation Liver Lesion Microwave Laparoscopic |
| J12.7 | Ablation Liver Lesion Microwave Percutaneous |
| J03.4 | Ablation Liver Lesion Multiple Thermal Open |
| J12.4 | Ablation Liver Lesion Radiofrequency Percutaneous |
| J03.3 | Ablation Liver Lesion Single Thermal Open |
| J03.3 | Ablation Liver Lesion Thermal Open NEC |
| J12.5 | Ablation Liver Lesion Thermal Percutaneous NEC |
| E59.5 | Ablation Lung Lesion Radiofrequency Percutaneous |
| | |
| J66.5 | Ablation Pancreas Lesion Chemical Percutaneous |
| R07.1 | Ablation Placental Arteriovenous Anastomosis Laser Endoscopic |
| R08.1 | Ablation Placental Arteriovenous Anastomosis Laser Percutaneous |
| M67.6 | Ablation Prostate Lesion Radiofrequency Endoscopic |
| M70.7 | Ablation Prostate Transurethral Radiofrequency Needle |
| A03.2 | Ablation Thalamus Tissue Stereotactic |
| X65.5 | Ablation Thyroid Radiotherapy Oral Delivery |
| K57.6 | Ablation Ventricular Wall Transluminal Percutaneous |
| | Access Minimal – refer to Index Introduction |
| Y75.- | Access Minimal Abdominal |
| | |
| Y76.- | Access Minimal Body Area Other |
| Y76.- | Access Minimal Body Cavity Other |
| Y74.- | Access Minimal Thoracic |
| Z75.6 | Acetabulum site |
| O29.1 | Acromioplasty NEC (W) |
| A70.6 | Acupuncture NEC |
| Y33.1 | Acupuncture NOC |
| E20.- | Adenoid Operations |
| Z22.5 | Adenoid site |
| E20.1 | Adenoidectomy |
| | |
| E20.4 | Adenoidectomy Diathermy Suction |
| F63.3 | Adjustment Denture |
| F15.5 | Adjustment Device Orthodontic |
| C35.- | Adjustment Eye Muscle NEC |
| F03.3 | Adjustment Lip Vermilion Border NEC |
| C35.- | Adjustment Muscle Eye NEC |
| F63.3 | Adjustment Obturator |
| | Adjustment Prosthesis – see Prosthesis site |
| Y15.6 | Adjustment Stent NOC |
| | Adjustment Suture – see Suture site |
| | |
| T70.- | Adjustment Tendon Length |
| F17.4 | Adjustment Tooth Crown Dental |
| G48.4 | Administration Activated Charcoal |
| | Administration Chemotherapy Neoplasm – see Delivery Chemotherapy Neoplasm |
| X39.6 | Administration Intraocular Therapeutic Substance |
| X39.- | Administration Therapeutic Substance NEC |
| X39.5 | Administration Transdermal Therapeutic Substance |
| E95.2 | Administration Vaccine Bacillus Calmette-Guerin |
| X44.- | Administration Vaccine NEC |
| B25.- | Adrenal Operations NEC |

| | |
|---|---|
| Z14.4 | Adrenal site |
| B23.- | Adrenal Tissue Aberrant Operations |
| Z14.5 | Adrenal Tissue Aberrant site |
| B22.- | Adrenalectomy |
| C33.- | Advancement Eye Muscle |
| F05.2 | Advancement Lip Mucosa NEC |
| V16.1 | Advancement Mandible & Osteotomy |
| C33.- | Advancement Muscle Eye |
| S39.- | Allograft Amniotic Membrane |
| W32.- | Allograft Bone |
| | |
| W32.6 | Allograft Bone Bulk |
| W32.5 | Allograft Bone Cancellous Chip |
| W34.- | Allograft Bone Marrow |
| W34.6 | Allograft Bone Marrow Unrelated Donor Unmatched |
| Y27.2 | Allograft NOC |
| S37.- | Allograft Skin |
| W99.1 | Allograft Stem Cells Cord Blood to Bone Marrow |
| Y01.- | Alloreplacement NOC |
| W34.- | Allotransplantation Bone Marrow |
| C46.7 | Allotransplantation Cornea Limbal Cells |
| | |
| K01.1 | Allotransplantation Heart & Lung |
| K02.1 | Allotransplantation Heart NEC |
| G68.1 | Allotransplantation Ileum |
| G68.- | Allotransplantation Intestine Small NEC |
| M01.- | Allotransplantation Kidney |
| K01.1 | Allotransplantation Lung & Heart |
| F08.1 | Allotransplantation Tooth |
| F11.1 | Alveoplasty Oral |
| R10.- | Amniocentesis |
| R10.3 | Amnioscopy |
| | |
| R10.- | Amniotic Cavity Operations NEC |
| Z45.5 | Amniotic Membrane site |
| J39.- | Ampulla Vater Operations Endoscopic Therapeutic NEC |
| J36.- | Ampulla Vater Operations NEC |
| Z30.7 | Ampulla Vater site |
| X07.- | Amputation Arm |
| Q01.1 | Amputation Cervix Uteri |
| P22.- | Amputation Cervix Uteri & Colporrhaphy |
| P22.- | Amputation Cervix Uteri & Repair Vagina Prolapse |
| X21.6 | Amputation Finger Supernumerary NEC |
| | |
| X10.- | Amputation Foot |
| X10.1 | Amputation Foot Through Ankle |
| X08.- | Amputation Hand |
| X09.- | Amputation Leg |
| N26.- | Amputation Penis |
| | Amputation Revision – see Amputation site |
| X12.4 | Amputation Stump Bone Revision |
| X12.4 | Amputation Stump Coverage Revision |
| X12.- | Amputation Stump Operations |
| X21.5 | Amputation Thumb Duplicate |

| | |
|---|---|
| X11.- | Amputation Toe |
| X27.3 | Amputation Toe Supernumerary |
| X59.1 | Anaesthetic Death Preoperative |
| Y81.- | Anaesthetic Epidural |
| Y80.- | Anaesthetic General |
| Y80.- | Anaesthetic Inhalation |
| Y80.4 | Anaesthetic Intravenous |
| Y82.3 | Anaesthetic Local Application NEC |
| Y82.2 | Anaesthetic Local Injection NEC |
| Y82.- | Anaesthetic Local NEC |
| | |
| C90.- | Anaesthetic Local Ophthalmology Procedures |
| Y84.- | Anaesthetic NEC |
| C90.4 | Anaesthetic Peribulbar |
| C90.5 | Anaesthetic Retrobulbar |
| Y81.- | Anaesthetic Spinal |
| C90.2 | Anaesthetic Subconjunctival |
| C90.3 | Anaesthetic Subtenons |
| C90.1 | Anaesthetic Topical Ophthalmology Procedures |
| X59.- | Anaesthetic without Surgery |
| H57.- | Anal Sphincter Artificial NEC |
| | |
| Y84.1 | Analgesia Gas & Air Labour |
| E92.4 | Analysis Blood Gas |
| | Anastomosis – see also Bypass |
| | Anastomosis – see also Connection |
| | Anastomosis – see also Interposition |
| | Anastomosis – see also Reanastomosis |
| | Anastomosis – see also Shunt |
| L06.- | Anastomosis Aortopulmonary NEC |
| L07.- | Anastomosis Aortopulmonary Prosthesis Interposition Tube |
| L50.- | Anastomosis Artery Aortofemoral Emergency |
| | |
| L51.- | Anastomosis Artery Aortofemoral NEC |
| L50.- | Anastomosis Artery Aortoiliac Emergency |
| L51.- | Anastomosis Artery Aortoiliac NEC |
| L34.2 | Anastomosis Artery Cerebral |
| L34.2 | Anastomosis Artery Circle Willis |
| L50.- | Anastomosis Artery Iliofemoral Emergency |
| L51.- | Anastomosis Artery Iliofemoral NEC |
| K45.- | Anastomosis Artery Mammary Coronary |
| L09.- | Anastomosis Artery Pulmonary NEC |
| L08.- | Anastomosis Artery Subclavian Pulmonary NEC |
| | |
| L07.- | Anastomosis Artery Subclavian Pulmonary Prosthesis Tube Creation |
| K45.- | Anastomosis Artery Thoracic Coronary |
| J27.- | Anastomosis Bile Duct & Excision Partial |
| J46.- | Anastomosis Bile Duct Attention Percutaneous |
| J30.- | Anastomosis Bile Duct Common |
| J32.2 | Anastomosis Bile Duct Divided End to End |
| A13.- | Anastomosis Brain Ventricle Component Attention |
| A14.- | Anastomosis Brain Ventricle NEC |
| E46.1 | Anastomosis Bronchus & Resection Sleeve |
| H13.- | Anastomosis Caecum |

| | |
|---|---|
| L09.1 | Anastomosis Cavopulmonary Superior Bi-directional |
| H13.- | Anastomosis Colon |
| H09.- | Anastomosis Colon & Excision Left |
| H11.- | Anastomosis Colon & Excision NEC |
| H07.- | Anastomosis Colon & Excision Right |
| H06.- | Anastomosis Colon & Excision Right Extended |
| H33.3 | Anastomosis Colon & Rectosigmoidectomy |
| H33.2 | Anastomosis Colon Anus & Excision Rectum |
| H40.4 | Anastomosis Colon Anus Trans-sphincteric |
| H10.- | Anastomosis Colon Sigmoid & Excision |
| | |
| H08.- | Anastomosis Colon Transverse & Excision |
| G58.- | Anastomosis Duodenum & Excision Jejunum |
| A42.1 | Anastomosis Dura Creation |
| H41.4 | Anastomosis Endoanal & Excision Rectum |
| Q30.3 | Anastomosis Fallopian Tube NEC |
| J19.- | Anastomosis Gall Bladder |
| J29.- | Anastomosis Hepatic Duct |
| A36.1 | Anastomosis Hypoglossofacial |
| H04.- | Anastomosis Ileum Anus & Panproctocolectomy |
| G73.- | Anastomosis Ileum Attention |
| | |
| G72.- | Anastomosis Ileum NEC |
| H05.- | Anastomosis Ileum Rectum & Excision Colon Total |
| G73.- | Anastomosis Intestine Small Attention |
| G72.- | Anastomosis Intestine Small NEC |
| G58.- | Anastomosis Jejunum & Excision Jejunum |
| G61.- | Anastomosis Jejunum NEC |
| C25.- | Anastomosis Lacrimal Apparatus Nose |
| A36.2 | Anastomosis Nerve Cranial NEC |
| Y16.2 | Anastomosis NOC |
| G01.- | Anastomosis Oesophagus & Excision Oesophagus & Stomach |
| | |
| G03.- | Anastomosis Oesophagus & Excision Partial |
| G01.- | Anastomosis Oesophagus & Excision Stomach & Oesophagus |
| G27.- | Anastomosis Oesophagus & Excision Stomach Total |
| G02.- | Anastomosis Oesophagus & Excision Total |
| G06.- | Anastomosis Oesophagus Attention |
| G06.0 | Anastomosis Oesophagus Direct Conversion From |
| G06.3 | Anastomosis Oesophagus Interposition Conversion Direct |
| G05.- | Anastomosis Oesophagus NEC |
| J59.- | Anastomosis Pancreatic Duct |
| H41.1 | Anastomosis Peranal & Rectosigmoidectomy |
| | |
| H33.- | Anastomosis Rectum & Excision |
| H33.- | Anastomosis Rectum & Resection Rectum Anterior |
| L41.1 | Anastomosis Renal Artery End to End & Repair Plastic |
| G28.- | Anastomosis Stomach & Excision Partial |
| G31.- | Anastomosis Stomach Duodenum |
| G58.1 | Anastomosis Stomach Ileum & Excision Jejunum Total |
| G33.- | Anastomosis Stomach Jejunum NEC |
| G32.- | Anastomosis Stomach Jejunum Transposed |
| M21.- | Anastomosis Ureter NEC |
| Q19.1 | Anastomosis Uterovaginal |

| | |
|---|---|
| L77.- | Anastomosis Vena Cava |
| L77.- | Anastomosis Vena Cava Branch |
| L98.- | Anastomosis Vessel Microvascular |
| L33.- | Aneurysmectomy Artery Cerebral |
| L33.- | Aneurysmectomy Artery Circle Willis |
| K63.- | Angiocardiography Heart |
| U10.5 | Angiocardiography Radionuclide |
| | Angiography – see also Arteriography |
| | Angiography – see also Venography |
| C86.5 | Angiography Eye Fluorescein |
| | |
| C87.2 | Angiography Retina Indocyanine |
| U11.7 | Angiography Vascular System Magnetic Resonance |
| L26.- | Angioplasty Aorta Transluminal Percutaneous |
| L39.1 | Angioplasty Artery Axillary Transluminal Percutaneous |
| L66.5 | Angioplasty Artery Balloon Cutting Transluminal Percutaneous |
| L66.5 | Angioplasty Artery Balloon Transluminal Percutaneous |
| L39.1 | Angioplasty Artery Brachial Transluminal Percutaneous |
| L31.1 | Angioplasty Artery Carotid Transluminal Percutaneous |
| L47.1 | Angioplasty Artery Coeliac Transluminal Percutaneous |
| L69.4 | Angioplasty Artery Collateral Systemic to Pulmonary Major Transluminal Percutaneous |
| | |
| K75.3 | Angioplasty Artery Coronary & Insertion Stent NEC |
| K75.1 | Angioplasty Artery Coronary Balloon & Insertion Stent Drug-eluting Transluminal Percutaneous |
| K75.- | Angioplasty Artery Coronary Balloon & Insertion Stent Transluminal Percutaneous |
| K49.- | Angioplasty Artery Coronary Balloon Transluminal Percutaneous |
| K49.1 | Angioplasty Artery Coronary NEC |
| K48.3 | Angioplasty Artery Coronary Open |
| K50.1 | Angioplasty Artery Coronary Transluminal Percutaneous Laser |
| L63.1 | Angioplasty Artery Femoral Transluminal Percutaneous |
| J10.4 | Angioplasty Artery Hepatic Transluminal Percutaneous |
| L54.1 | Angioplasty Artery Iliac Transluminal Percutaneous |
| | |
| L47.1 | Angioplasty Artery Mesenteric Transluminal Percutaneous |
| L63.1 | Angioplasty Artery Popliteal Transluminal Percutaneous |
| L13.- | Angioplasty Artery Pulmonary Transluminal Percutaneous |
| L41.6 | Angioplasty Artery Renal Patch |
| L43.1 | Angioplasty Artery Renal Transluminal Percutaneous |
| L39.1 | Angioplasty Artery Subclavian Transluminal Percutaneous |
| L47.1 | Angioplasty Artery Suprarenal Transluminal Percutaneous |
| L71.1 | Angioplasty Artery Transluminal Percutaneous |
| L39.1 | Angioplasty Artery Vertebral Transluminal Percutaneous |
| J10.4 | Angioplasty Blood Vessel Liver Transluminal Percutaneous NEC |

| | |
|---|---|
| L97.2 | Angioplasty Peroperative |
| L94.7 | Angioplasty Vein Balloon Transluminal Percutaneous NEC |
| J10.4 | Angioplasty Vein Hepatic Transluminal Percutaneous |
| J11.1 | Angioplasty Vein Portal Intrahepatic Transjugular |
| J10.4 | Angioplasty Vein Portal Transluminal Percutaneous |
| L80.3 | Angioplasty Vein Pulmonary Balloon Cutting Transluminal Percutaneous |
| L80.2 | Angioplasty Vein Pulmonary Balloon Transluminal Percutaneous |
| L99.1 | Angioplasty Vein Transluminal Percutaneous NEC |
| K51.1 | Angioscopy Transluminal Percutaneous |
| L72.3 | Angioscopy Transluminal Percutaneous NEC |
| | |
| K34.- | Annuloplasty Heart Valve ( Wound . o peatiu |
| H50.- | Anoplasty |
| G24.- | Antireflux Operations |
| G24.5 | Antireflux Operations & Stomach Operations Plastic |
| G25.- | Antireflux Operations Revision |
| E13.3 | Antrostomy Intranasal |
| H56.- | Anus Operations NEC |
| Z29.2 | Anus site |
| Z96.- | Aorta Abdominal Branch Lateral Other site |
| Z37.- | Aorta Abdominal Branch Lateral site |
| | |
| L25.4 | Aorta Aneurysmal Operations NEC |
| L28.- | Aorta Aneurysmal Operations Transluminal |
| L25.- | Aorta Operations Open NEC |
| L26.- | Aorta Operations Transluminal |
| K33.- | Aorta Root Operations |
| Z34.- | Aorta site NEC |
| Z97.- | Aorta Terminal Branch Other site |
| Z38.- | Aorta Terminal Branch site |
| Z95.- | Aorta Thoracic Branch Other site |
| Z36.- | Aorta Thoracic Branch site |
| | |
| L25.5 | Aortic Body Operations |
| Z40.5 | Aortic Body site |
| L26.4 | Aortography |
| K17.3 | Aortopulmonary Reconstruction |
| L06.1 | Aortopulmonary Window Creation |
| K37.6 | Aortoventriculoplasty |
| K33.6 | Aortoventriculoplasty Autograft Valve Pulmonary |
| X47.1 | Apheresis Low-density Lipoprotein |
| F12.1 | Apicectomy Tooth |
| H01.- | Appendicectomy Emergency |
| | |
| H02.- | Appendicectomy NEC |
| H14.4 | Appendicocaecostomy |
| H03.3 | Appendicostomy |
| Y51.5 | Appendicostomy Approach |
| H03.- | Appendix Operations NEC |
| Z28.1 | Appendix site |
| | Application – see also Implantation |
| | Application – see also Introduction |
| Y82.3 | Application Anaesthetic Local |
| | Application Band – see Banding site |

| | |
|---|---|
| X49.- | Application Bandage |
| U33.2 | Application Blood Pressure Monitor Ambulatory |
| F16.6 | Application Fluoride Topical |
| A70.7 | Application Nerve Transcutaneous Electrical Stimulator |
| X48.1 | Application Plaster Cast |
| | Application Ring – see Ringing site |
| F16.5 | Application Sealant Fissure |
| X49.5 | Application Sling NEC |
| | Approach – refer to Index Introduction |
| Y75.4 | Approach Abdominal Cavity Hand Assisted Minimal Access |
| Y75.2 | Approach Abdominal Cavity Laparoscopic NEC |
| Y75.5 | Approach Abdominal Cavity Laparoscopic Ultrasonic |
| Y75.1 | Approach Abdominal Cavity Laparoscopically Assisted |
| Y75.- | Approach Abdominal Cavity Minimal Access |
| Y50.- | Approach Abdominal Cavity NEC |
| Y75.3 | Approach Abdominal Cavity Robotic Minimal Access |
| Y51.5 | Approach Appendicostomy |
| Y78.- | Approach Arteriotomy Image Control |
| Y79.- | Approach Artery |
| Y79.4 | Approach Artery Aortic Transluminal |
| Y79.2 | Approach Artery Brachial Transluminal |
| Y79.3 | Approach Artery Femoral Transluminal |
| Y79.1 | Approach Artery Subclavian Transluminal |
| Y76.- | Approach Body Area Minimal Access |
| Y76.3 | Approach Body Cavity Endoscopic |
| Y76.6 | Approach Body Cavity Endoscopic Endonasal |
| Y76.4 | Approach Body Cavity Endoscopic Ultrasonic |
| Y76.- | Approach Body Cavity Minimal Access |
| Y76.5 | Approach Body Cavity Robotic Minimal Access |
| Y51.4 | Approach Colostomy |
| Y53.3 | Approach Control Computed Tomography |
| Y53.4 | Approach Control Fluoroscopic |
| Y53.- | Approach Control Image |
| Y53.5 | Approach Control Image Intensifier |
| Y53.7 | Approach Control Magnetic Resonance Imaging |
| Y53.1 | Approach Control Radiological |
| Y53.3 | Approach Control Stereotactic |
| Y53.2 | Approach Control Ultrasonic |
| Y53.6 | Approach Control Video |
| Y47.- | Approach Cranium Contents Burrhole |
| Y46.7 | Approach Cranium Contents Craniectomy |
| Y46.- | Approach Cranium Contents Open |
| Y52.3 | Approach Cystostomy |
| Y53.4 | Approach Fluoroscopic Control |
| Y51.- | Approach Gastrointestinal Tract Opening Artificial |
| Y51.2 | Approach Gastrostomy |
| Y49.4 | Approach Heart Transapical |
| Y49.4 | Approach Heart Transventricular |
| Y51.3 | Approach Ileostomy |
| Y53.- | Approach Image Control |

| | |
|---|---|
| Y53.5 | Approach Image Intensifier Control |
| Y76.7 | Approach Joint Arthroscopic |
| Y50.2 | Approach Laparotomy NEC |
| Y74.5 | Approach Mediastinal Cavity Mediastinoscopic |
| Y71.4 | Approach Minimal Access Failed Converted to Open |
| Y76.1 | Approach Nasal Sinus Endoscopic |
| Y76.2 | Approach Nose Endoscopic |
| Y51.1 | Approach Oesophagostomy |
| Y52.- | Approach Opening Artificial NEC |
| Y53.- | Approach Percutaneous Control Image |
| | |
| Y71.5 | Approach Percutaneous Transluminal Access Failed Converted to Open |
| Y53.1 | Approach Radiological Control |
| Y48.- | Approach Spine Back |
| Y48.- | Approach Spine Laminectomy |
| Y50.1 | Approach Spine Transperitoneal |
| Y49.2 | Approach Spine Transthoracic |
| Y49.1 | Approach Sternotomy Median |
| Y74.- | Approach Thoracic Cavity Minimal Access |
| Y74.3 | Approach Thoracic Cavity Robotic Minimal Access |
| Y74.2 | Approach Thoracic Cavity Thoracoscopic NEC |
| | |
| Y74.4 | Approach Thoracic Cavity Thoracoscopic Video-assisted |
| Y74.1 | Approach Thoracic Cavity Thoracoscopically Assisted |
| Y49.3 | Approach Thoracotomy NEC |
| Y52.1 | Approach Tracheostomy |
| Y53.2 | Approach Ultrasonic Control |
| Y52.2 | Approach Urethrostomy |
| Y50.3 | Approach Vaginal |
| Y53.6 | Approach Video Control |
| A64.1 | Approximation Nerve Peripheral Primary |
| Z89.- | Arm Region site NEC |
| | |
| E20.3 | Arrest Bleeding Adenoid Postoperative Surgical |
| E05.- | Arrest Bleeding Nose Internal Postoperative Surgical |
| E05.- | Arrest Bleeding Nose Internal Spontaneous Surgical |
| | Arrest Bleeding Postoperative Surgical – see also Haemostasis |
| | Arrest Bleeding Surgical – see also Haemostasis |
| F36.5 | Arrest Bleeding Tonsillar Bed Postoperative Surgical |
| F16.2 | Arrest Bleeding Tooth Socket Postoperative Surgical |
| K06.1 | Arterial Switch Procedure |
| L04.- | Arterial Tree Pulmonary Operations Open |
| L39.4 | Arteriography Artery Axillary |
| | |
| L39.4 | Arteriography Artery Brachial |
| L31.2 | Arteriography Artery Carotid |
| L35.2 | Arteriography Artery Cerebral |
| L35.2 | Arteriography Artery Circle Willis |
| L47.3 | Arteriography Artery Coeliac |
| K63.- | Arteriography Artery Coronary |
| L63.4 | Arteriography Artery Femoral |
| J10.7 | Arteriography Artery Hepatic |
| L54.3 | Arteriography Artery Iliac |
| L47.3 | Arteriography Artery Mesenteric |

| | |
|---|---|
| L72.1 | Arteriography Artery NEC |
| L72.5 | Arteriography Artery Pancreas Stimulated |
| L63.4 | Arteriography Artery Popliteal |
| L13.3 | Arteriography Artery Pulmonary |
| L43.4 | Arteriography Artery Renal |
| L39.4 | Arteriography Artery Subclavian |
| L47.3 | Arteriography Artery Suprarenal |
| L39.4 | Arteriography Artery Vertebral |
| L02.- | Arteriosus Ductus Patent Operations Open |
| Y78.- | Arteriotomy Approach Image Control |
| | |
| L75.- | Arteriovenous Operations NEC |
| L70.5 | Artery Aneurysmal Operations NEC |
| L38.4 | Artery Axillary Aneurysmal Operations |
| L38.- | Artery Axillary Operations Open NEC |
| L39.- | Artery Axillary Operations Transluminal |
| Z36.3 | Artery Axillary site |
| O28.1 | Artery Basilar site (Z) |
| L38.4 | Artery Brachial Aneurysmal Operations |
| L38.- | Artery Brachial Operations Open NEC |
| L39.- | Artery Brachial Operations Transluminal |
| | |
| Z36.4 | Artery Brachial site |
| Z36.7 | Artery Brachiocephalic site |
| Z95.2 | Artery Bronchial site |
| L30.4 | Artery Carotid Aneurysmal Operations |
| Z95.6 | Artery Carotid Common site |
| O12.- | Artery Carotid External Branch site (Z) |
| Z95.5 | Artery Carotid External site |
| Z95.7 | Artery Carotid Internal site |
| L30.- | Artery Carotid Operations Open NEC |
| L31.- | Artery Carotid Operations Transluminal |
| | |
| Z36.1 | Artery Carotid site NEC |
| L33.- | Artery Cerebral Aneurysmal Operations |
| L34.- | Artery Cerebral Operations Open NEC |
| L35.- | Artery Cerebral Operations Transluminal |
| Z35.- | Artery Cerebral site |
| L33.- | Artery Circle Willis Aneurysmal Operations |
| L34.- | Artery Circle Willis Operations Open NEC |
| L35.- | Artery Circle Willis Operations Transluminal |
| Z35.7 | Artery Circle Willis site |
| L46.4 | Artery Coeliac Aneurysmal Operations NEC |
| | |
| L46.- | Artery Coeliac Operations Open NEC |
| L47.- | Artery Coeliac Operations Transluminal |
| Z37.2 | Artery Coeliac site |
| Z35.- | Artery Communicating site |
| K48.- | Artery Coronary Operations NEC |
| K48.- | Artery Coronary Operations Open NEC |
| K51.- | Artery Coronary Operations Transluminal Diagnostic |
| K50.- | Artery Coronary Operations Transluminal Therapeutic NEC |
| Z33.4 | Artery Coronary site |
| Z97.4 | Artery Dorsalis Pedis site |

| | |
|---|---|
| L62.4 | Artery Femoral Aneurysmal Operations NEC |
| L62.- | Artery Femoral Operations Open NEC |
| L63.- | Artery Femoral Operations Transluminal |
| Z38.- | Artery Femoral site |
| Z96.1 | Artery Gastroduodenal site |
| Z37.6 | Artery Hepatic site |
| L53.3 | Artery Iliac Aneurysmal Operations NEC |
| Z38.1 | Artery Iliac Common site |
| Z97.5 | Artery Iliac External site |
| Z38.2 | Artery Iliac Internal site |
| | |
| L53.- | Artery Iliac Operations Open NEC |
| L54.- | Artery Iliac Operations Transluminal |
| Z97.6 | Artery Iliac site NEC |
| Z36.2 | Artery Innominate site |
| Z95.1 | Artery Intercostal site |
| Z96.3 | Artery Lumbar site |
| Z36.6 | Artery Mammary Internal site |
| O12.2 | Artery Maxillary site (Z) |
| L46.4 | Artery Mesenteric Aneurysmal Operations NEC |
| L46.- | Artery Mesenteric Operations Open NEC |
| | |
| L47.- | Artery Mesenteric Operations Transluminal |
| Z37.- | Artery Mesenteric site |
| L97.4 | Artery Operations NEC |
| L70.- | Artery Operations Open NEC |
| L72.- | Artery Operations Transluminal Diagnostic NEC |
| L71.- | Artery Operations Transluminal Percutaneous NEC |
| L71.- | Artery Operations Transluminal Therapeutic NEC |
| Z35.2 | Artery Ophthalmic site |
| Z96.2 | Artery Pancreaticoduodenal site |
| Z97.3 | Artery Peroneal site |
| | |
| L62.4 | Artery Popliteal Aneurysmal Operations NEC |
| L62.- | Artery Popliteal Operations Open NEC |
| L63.- | Artery Popliteal Operations Transluminal |
| Z38.6 | Artery Popliteal site |
| Z96.5 | Artery Pudendal site |
| L12.- | Artery Pulmonary Operations Open NEC |
| L13.- | Artery Pulmonary Operations Transluminal |
| Z40.1 | Artery Pulmonary site |
| Z95.4 | Artery Radial site |
| L42.4 | Artery Renal Aneurysmal Operations |
| | |
| L42.- | Artery Renal Operations Open NEC |
| L43.- | Artery Renal Operations Transluminal |
| Z37.1 | Artery Renal site |
| Z40.7 | Artery site NEC |
| Z37.7 | Artery Splenic site |
| L38.4 | Artery Subclavian Aneurysmal Operations |
| L38.- | Artery Subclavian Operations Open NEC |
| L39.- | Artery Subclavian Operations Transluminal |
| Z36.2 | Artery Subclavian site |
| L46.4 | Artery Suprarenal Aneurysmal Operations NEC |

| | |
|---|---|
| L46.- | Artery Suprarenal Operations Open NEC |
| L47.- | Artery Suprarenal Operations Transluminal |
| Z37.5 | Artery Suprarenal site |
| O12.1 | Artery Temporal Superficial site (Z) |
| Z96.7 | Artery Testicular site |
| Z97.- | Artery Tibia site |
| Z95.3 | Artery Ulnar site |
| Z96.6 | Artery Uterine site |
| L38.4 | Artery Vertebral Aneurysmal Operations |
| L38.- | Artery Vertebral Operations Open NEC |
| | |
| L39.- | Artery Vertebral Operations Transluminal |
| Z36.5 | Artery Vertebral site |
| W62.- | Arthrodesis Joint & Fixation Joint |
| W61.- | Arthrodesis Joint & Graft Bone Articular NEC |
| W60.- | Arthrodesis Joint & Graft Bone Extra-articular |
| W60.- | Arthrodesis Joint & Graft Bone NEC |
| W64.- | Arthrodesis Joint Conversion NEC |
| W62.- | Arthrodesis Joint NEC |
| W63.- | Arthrodesis Joint Revision NEC |
| W90.2 | Arthrography Joint |
| | |
| W78.5 | Arthrolysis Joint Elbow NEC |
| W42.6 | Arthrolysis Joint Knee Prosthetic Total |
| | Arthroplasty – see also Hemiarthroplasty |
| W57.- | Arthroplasty Joint Excision |
| X22.- | Arthroplasty Joint Hip Correction Deformity Congenital |
| W56.- | Arthroplasty Joint Interposition Natural Tissue |
| W56.- | Arthroplasty Joint Interposition NEC |
| W55.- | Arthroplasty Joint Interposition Prosthetic |
| W58.- | Arthroplasty Joint Resurfacing |
| V20.- | Arthroplasty Joint Temporomandibular |
| | |
| W87.- | Arthroscopy Joint Knee |
| W88.- | Arthroscopy Joint NEC |
| W81.4 | Arthrotomy Joint NEC |
| E35.1 | Arytenoidectomy Endoscopic |
| E33.1 | Arytenoidectomy External |
| M48.1 | Aspiration Bladder Suprapubic |
| W36.5 | Aspiration Bone Marrow NEC |
| W36.4 | Aspiration Bone Marrow Sternum |
| A10.2 | Aspiration Brain Tissue Abscess |
| A10.3 | Aspiration Brain Tissue Haematoma |
| | |
| A10.4 | Aspiration Brain Tissue Lesion NEC |
| B37.1 | Aspiration Breast |
| E48.4 | Aspiration Bronchus Endoscopic NEC |
| E50.4 | Aspiration Bronchus Endoscopic Rigid |
| E52.2 | Aspiration Bronchus NEC |
| T62.4 | Aspiration Bursa |
| E48.4 | Aspiration Carina Endoscopic NEC |
| E50.4 | Aspiration Carina Endoscopic Rigid |
| V52.5 | Aspiration Disc Intervertebral |
| N15.6 | Aspiration Epididymis Lesion |

| | |
|---|---|
| N34.- | Aspiration Epididymis Sperm |
| Q41.7 | Aspiration Fallopian Tube |
| Y20.4 | Aspiration Fine Needle NOC |
| Y22.1 | Aspiration Haematoma NOC |
| S47.2 | Aspiration Haematoma Skin |
| N11.5 | Aspiration Hydrocele Sac |
| W90.1 | Aspiration Joint |
| M13.3 | Aspiration Kidney Pelvis Percutaneous NEC |
| M13.3 | Aspiration Kidney Percutaneous NEC |
| C71.3 | Aspiration Lens |
| | |
| Y22.2 | Aspiration Lesion NOC |
| J14.2 | Aspiration Liver NEC |
| E48.4 | Aspiration Lung Endoscopic NEC |
| E50.4 | Aspiration Lung Endoscopic Rigid |
| Q51.1 | Aspiration Ovary Cyst Transvaginal Ultrasound |
| J66.4 | Aspiration Pancreas Lesion Percutaneous |
| J67.1 | Aspiration Pancreas Lesion Percutaneous Diagnostic |
| J66.4 | Aspiration Pancreas Needle NEC |
| T12.3 | Aspiration Pleural Cavity |
| P31.3 | Aspiration Pouch of Douglas |
| | |
| M70.1 | Aspiration Prostate NEC |
| E48.4 | Aspiration Respiratory Tract Lower Endoscopic NEC |
| E50.4 | Aspiration Respiratory Tract Lower Endoscopic Rigid |
| N34.- | Aspiration Sperm |
| A48.2 | Aspiration Spinal Cord Lesion NEC |
| A45.6 | Aspiration Spinal Cord Lesion Open |
| E48.4 | Aspiration Trachea Endoscopic NEC |
| E50.4 | Aspiration Trachea Endoscopic Rigid |
| E52.2 | Aspiration Trachea NEC |
| Q11.- | Aspiration Uterus Vacuum Products Conception |
| | |
| U11.6 | Assay D-Dimer |
| U24.2 | Assessment Balance |
| R40.2 | Assessment Cervical Length Scanning |
| R40.1 | Assessment Cervix Maternal |
| E87.4 | Assessment Flight |
| U24.3 | Assessment Hearing |
| X62.- | Assessment NEC |
| E91.1 | Assessment Oximetry |
| E87.- | Assessment Oxygen |
| R40.- | Assessment Physiological Maternal |
| | |
| X60.- | Assessment Rehabilitation |
| X60.4 | Assessment Rehabilitation Team Unidisciplinary Specialised |
| J16.2 | Assistance Liver Extracorporeal |
| K50.4 | Atherectomy Artery Coronary Transluminal Percutaneous |
| L71.7 | Atherectomy Artery Transluminal Percutaneous |
| Z66.1 | Atlas site |
| K05.- | Atrial Inversion Operations Transposition Arteries Great |
| Z33.6 | Atrium Heart site |
| Z33.1 | Atrium Septum site |
| K22.- | Atrium Wall Operations NEC |

| | |
|---|---|
| | Attachment – see also Reattachment |
| D05.- | Attachment Auricular Prosthesis |
| D13.- | Attachment Bone Mastoid Prosthesis Anchored Hearing |
| E11.2 | Attachment Nasal Prosthesis Fixtures First Stage |
| E11.1 | Attachment Nasal Prosthesis Fixtures One Stage NEC |
| E11.3 | Attachment Nasal Prosthesis Fixtures Second Stage |
| E11.6 | Attachment Nasal Prosthesis NEC |
| C54.- | Attachment Retina Operations Buckling |
| V41.4 | Attachment Spine Correctional Instrument Anterior & Posterior |
| D05.4 | Attention Auricular Fixtures Prosthesis |
| | |
| W05.5 | Attention Bone Endoprosthesis |
| W05.4 | Attention Bone Endoprosthesis Massive |
| D13.4 | Attention Bone Mastoid Prosthesis Anchored Fixture Hearing |
| | Attention Connection – see Connection site |
| D05.6 | Attention Ear External Hearing Implant |
| D20.5 | Attention Ear Middle Hearing Implant |
| G48.6 | Attention Gastric Balloon |
| G31.6 | Attention Gastroduodenostomy |
| G33.6 | Attention Gastroenterostomy NEC |
| G33.6 | Attention Gastrojejunostomy NEC |
| | |
| A54.4 | Attention Intrathecal Drug Delivery Device Adjacent Spinal Cord |
| E31.5 | Attention Larynx Voice Box Artificial |
| | Attention Prosthesis – see Prosthesis site |
| | Attention Stent – see also Placement site Stent |
| | Attention Stent – see also Prosthesis |
| Y15.- | Attention Stent NOC |
| | Attention to Shunt – see Shunt site |
| | Attention Tube – see Tube |
| D12.- | Attic Operations |
| Z20.3 | Attic site |
| | |
| D12.7 | Atticoantrostomy |
| D12.2 | Atticotomy |
| U24.- | Audiology Diagnostic |
| U24.1 | Audiometry Pure Tone |
| D08.- | Auditory Canal External Operations NEC |
| Z20.2 | Auditory Canal External site |
| F11.- | Augmentation Alveolar Ridge |
| | Augmentation Labour – see Induction Labour |
| W73.- | Augmentation Ligament Prosthetic |
| M55.- | Augmentation Urethral Sphincter Female |
| | |
| | Autograft – see also Graft |
| W31.- | Autograft Bone Cancellous |
| W31.- | Autograft Bone Cortex |
| W34.1 | Autograft Bone Marrow |
| W31.6 | Autograft Bone Muscle Pedicle |
| W31.- | Autograft Bone NEC |
| W31.5 | Autograft Bone Vascularised Pedicle |
| Y27.1 | Autograft NOC |
| W83.7 | Autograft Osteochondral Endoscopic |
| S36.- | Autograft Skin NEC |

| | |
|---|---|
| S35.- | Autograft Skin Split |
| Y01.1 | Autoreplacement NOC |
| | Autotransplantation – see Transplantation |
| | Avulsion – see also Destruction |
| Q02.1 | Avulsion Cervix Uteri Lesion |
| C22.1 | Avulsion Eyelid Nerve |
| L87.4 | Avulsion Leg Vein Varicose |
| S70.1 | Avulsion Nail |
| A60.2 | Avulsion Nerve Peripheral |
| Z66.2 | Axis site |

# B

| | |
|---|---|
| L74.4 | Banding Arteriovenous Fistula |
| L12.- | Banding Artery Pulmonary |
| H52.4 | Banding Haemorrhoid |
| J72.5 | Banding Spleen |
| G30.3 | Banding Stomach |
| G30.5 | Banding Stomach Maintenance |
| L01.2 | Banding Truncus Arteriosus Persistent |
| U17.4 | Barium Enema |
| U17.3 | Barium Meal |
| U17.3 | Barium Swallow |
| | |
| P03.5 | Bartholin Duct Operations |
| Z44.2 | Bartholin Duct site |
| P03.- | Bartholin Gland Operations |
| Z44.2 | Bartholin Gland site |
| Z94.1 | Bilateral Operations |
| J41.- | Bile Duct Operations Endoscopic Therapeutic Retrograde NEC |
| J52.- | Bile Duct Operations NEC |
| J37.- | Bile Duct Operations Open NEC |
| J76.- | Bile Duct Operations Percutaneous NEC |
| J48.- | Bile Duct Operations Percutaneous Other NEC |
| | |
| J49.- | Bile Duct Operations Therapeutic T Tube Track |
| Z30.- | Bile Duct site |
| Z30.- | Biliary Tract site |
| E54.2 | Bilobectomy Lung |
| R37.3 | Biometry Fetal |
| X55.1 | Biopsy Abdominal Mass |
| T31.1 | Biopsy Abdominal Wall Anterior |
| T31.1 | Biopsy Abdominal Wall NEC |
| T39.3 | Biopsy Abdominal Wall Posterior |
| E20.2 | Biopsy Adenoid |
| | |
| B25.2 | Biopsy Adrenal |
| J36.2 | Biopsy Ampulla Vater |
| J43.- | Biopsy Ampulla Vater Endoscopic Retrograde |
| H56.1 | Biopsy Anus |
| L67.1 | Biopsy Artery NEC |
| J44.- | Biopsy Bile Duct Endoscopic Retrograde NEC |
| J53.1 | Biopsy Bile Duct Endoscopic Ultrasonic |
| J51.1 | Biopsy Bile Duct Laparoscopic Ultrasonic |
| J37.1 | Biopsy Bile Duct NEC |
| J37.1 | Biopsy Bile Duct Open |

| | |
|---|---|
| J50.3 | Biopsy Bile Duct Percutaneous Transbiliary |
| J43.- | Biopsy Biliary System Endoscopic Retrograde |
| M45.- | Biopsy Bladder Endoscopic |
| M45.- | Biopsy Bladder NEC |
| M41.4 | Biopsy Bladder Open |
| V13.3 | Biopsy Bone Face |
| W36.5 | Biopsy Bone Marrow NEC |
| W36.- | Biopsy Bone NEC |
| W36.- | Biopsy Bone Needle Percutaneous |
| W33.1 | Biopsy Bone Open |
| | |
| H25.- | Biopsy Bowel Lower Endoscopic NEC |
| H25.- | Biopsy Bowel Lower Sigmoidoscope Fibreoptic |
| H28.- | Biopsy Bowel Lower Sigmoidoscope Rigid |
| A18.1 | Biopsy Brain Endoscopic |
| A42.2 | Biopsy Brain Meninges |
| A08.- | Biopsy Brain Tissue NEC |
| A04.- | Biopsy Brain Tissue Open |
| B32.- | Biopsy Breast |
| E49.- | Biopsy Bronchus Endoscopic NEC |
| E51.- | Biopsy Bronchus Endoscopic Rigid |
| | |
| E49.1 | Biopsy Bronchus NEC |
| E47.1 | Biopsy Bronchus Open NEC |
| T62.3 | Biopsy Bursa |
| H22.- | Biopsy Caecum Endoscopic Fibreoptic |
| H22.- | Biopsy Caecum Endoscopic NEC |
| H19.1 | Biopsy Caecum NEC |
| H19.1 | Biopsy Caecum Open |
| C11.7 | Biopsy Canthus Lesion |
| E49.1 | Biopsy Carina Endoscopic NEC |
| E51.1 | Biopsy Carina Endoscopic Rigid |
| | |
| E44.3 | Biopsy Carina Open |
| Q03.- | Biopsy Cervix Uteri |
| C84.3 | Biopsy Choroid |
| H22.- | Biopsy Colon Endoscopic Fibreoptic NEC |
| H22.- | Biopsy Colon Endoscopic NEC |
| H19.1 | Biopsy Colon NEC |
| H19.1 | Biopsy Colon Open |
| H25.- | Biopsy Colon Sigmoid Endoscopic NEC |
| H25.- | Biopsy Colon Sigmoid Sigmoidoscope Fibreoptic |
| H28.- | Biopsy Colon Sigmoid Sigmoidoscope Rigid |
| | |
| H25.- | Biopsy Colon Sigmoidoscope Fibreoptic |
| H68.1 | Biopsy Colonic Pouch Colonoscope |
| H69.1 | Biopsy Colonic Pouch Sigmoidoscope Flexible |
| H70.1 | Biopsy Colonic Pouch Sigmoidoscope Rigid |
| C43.2 | Biopsy Conjunctiva |
| C51.1 | Biopsy Cornea |
| V05.2 | Biopsy Cranium |
| V52.4 | Biopsy Disc Intervertebral NEC |
| G55.- | Biopsy Duodenum Endoscopic NEC |
| G55.- | Biopsy Duodenum NEC |

| | |
|---|---|
| G53.1 | Biopsy Duodenum Open |
| G45.- | Biopsy Duodenum Prox. & Examination G.I. Tract Upper Endo. Fibreoptic |
| G45.- | Biopsy Duodenum Prox. & Examination G.I. Tract Upper Endoscopic NEC |
| D06.1 | Biopsy Ear External |
| D06.1 | Biopsy Ear External Skin |
| D20.1 | Biopsy Ear Middle |
| D28.1 | Biopsy Ear NEC |
| N15.5 | Biopsy Epididymis |
| C37.3 | Biopsy Eye Muscle |
| C86.1 | Biopsy Eye NEC |
| | |
| C10.6 | Biopsy Eyebrow Lesion |
| C22.2 | Biopsy Eyelid |
| C22.2 | Biopsy Eyelid Skin |
| Q39.- | Biopsy Fallopian Tube Access Minimal |
| Q39.- | Biopsy Fallopian Tube Endoscopic |
| Q39.- | Biopsy Fallopian Tube NEC |
| Q34.2 | Biopsy Fallopian Tube Open |
| T57.2 | Biopsy Fascia |
| R02.- | Biopsy Fetus Fetoscopic |
| R05.1 | Biopsy Fetus Percutaneous |
| | |
| J09.- | Biopsy Gall Bladder Access Minimal |
| J09.- | Biopsy Gall Bladder Endoscopic |
| J09.- | Biopsy Gall Bladder Laparoscopic |
| J23.2 | Biopsy Gall Bladder NEC |
| J23.2 | Biopsy Gall Bladder Open |
| J25.1 | Biopsy Gall Bladder Percutaneous |
| J09.- | Biopsy Gall Bladder Peritoneoscope |
| G45.- | Biopsy Gastrointestinal Tract Upper Endoscopic Fibreoptic |
| G45.- | Biopsy Gastrointestinal Tract Upper Endoscopic NEC |
| G45.- | Biopsy Gastrointestinal Tract Upper NEC |
| | |
| F20.3 | Biopsy Gingiva |
| K23.2 | Biopsy Heart NEC |
| K23.2 | Biopsy Heart Wall |
| H68.3 | Biopsy Ileoanal Pouch Colonoscope |
| H69.3 | Biopsy Ileoanal Pouch Sigmoidoscope Flexible |
| H70.3 | Biopsy Ileoanal Pouch Sigmoidoscope Rigid |
| G80.- | Biopsy Ileum Endoscopic |
| G78.1 | Biopsy Ileum NEC |
| G78.1 | Biopsy Ileum Open |
| G80.- | Biopsy Intestine Small Endoscopic NEC |
| | |
| G78.1 | Biopsy Intestine Small NEC |
| G78.1 | Biopsy Intestine Small Open NEC |
| T43.- | Biopsy Intra-abdominal Organ Access Minimal |
| T43.- | Biopsy Intra-abdominal Organ Laparoscopic NEC |
| T11.- | Biopsy Intrathoracic Organ Access Minimal |
| T11.- | Biopsy Intrathoracic Organ Thoracoscopic |
| C64.4 | Biopsy Iris |
| V19.4 | Biopsy Jaw NEC |
| G65.1 | Biopsy Jejunum Endoscopic |
| G67.3 | Biopsy Jejunum Mucosa Crosby Capsule |

| | |
|---|---|
| G63.1 | Biopsy Jejunum NEC |
| G63.1 | Biopsy Jejunum Open |
| W88.- | Biopsy Joint Endoscopic NEC |
| W87.- | Biopsy Joint Knee Endoscopic |
| W92.1 | Biopsy Joint NEC |
| W69.- | Biopsy Joint Synovial Membrane |
| M11.1 | Biopsy Kidney Endoscopic NEC |
| M11.2 | Biopsy Kidney Endoscopic Retrograde |
| M13.1 | Biopsy Kidney NEC |
| M08.1 | Biopsy Kidney Open |
| | |
| C24.4 | Biopsy Lacrimal Gland |
| C26.3 | Biopsy Lacrimal Sac |
| E36.1 | Biopsy Larynx Endoscopic |
| E37.1 | Biopsy Larynx Lesion Microendoscopic Diagnostic |
| E36.1 | Biopsy Larynx NEC |
| E33.4 | Biopsy Larynx Open |
| C77.3 | Biopsy Lens |
| | Biopsy Lesion – see also Biopsy site |
| | Biopsy Lesion Excision – see Excision Lesion |
| Y20.- | Biopsy Lesion NOC |
| | |
| W76.3 | Biopsy Ligament |
| F06.2 | Biopsy Lip |
| F06.2 | Biopsy Lip Skin |
| J09.- | Biopsy Liver Access Minimal |
| J09.- | Biopsy Liver Endoscopic |
| J09.- | Biopsy Liver Laparoscopic |
| J14.1 | Biopsy Liver NEC |
| J05.3 | Biopsy Liver Open |
| J13.2 | Biopsy Liver Percutaneous NEC *Needle* |
| J09.- | Biopsy Liver Peritoneoscope |
| | |
| J13.1 | Biopsy Liver Transjugular |
| J13.1 | Biopsy Liver Transluminal Percutaneous |
| J13.1 | Biopsy Liver Transvascular Percutaneous |
| J05.3 | Biopsy Liver Wedge Open |
| E49.- | Biopsy Lung Endoscopic NEC |
| E51.- | Biopsy Lung Endoscopic Rigid |
| E59.- | Biopsy Lung NEC |
| T87.- | Biopsy Lymph Node NEC |
| T91.1 | Biopsy Lymph Node Sentinel NEC |
| V19.4 | Biopsy Mandible |
| | |
| D12.3 | Biopsy Mastoid |
| E13.4 | Biopsy Maxillary Antrum |
| E12.8 | Biopsy Maxillary Antrum Approach Sublabial |
| E63.1 | Biopsy Mediastinum Endoscopic |
| E63.1 | Biopsy Mediastinum NEC |
| E61.2 | Biopsy Mediastinum Open |
| T38.3 | Biopsy Mesentery Colon NEC |
| T37.3 | Biopsy Mesentery NEC |
| F42.1 | Biopsy Mouth NEC |
| T81.- | Biopsy Muscle |

| | |
|---|---|
| C37.3 | Biopsy Muscle Eye |
| T81.- | Biopsy Muscle Study |
| S66.1 | Biopsy Nail Bed |
| E17.3 | Biopsy Nasal Sinus NEC |
| E25.- | Biopsy Nasopharynx |
| E25.- | Biopsy Nasopharynx Endoscopic |
| E27.1 | Biopsy Nasopharynx Open |
| A36.3 | Biopsy Nerve Cranial |
| A73.1 | Biopsy Nerve Peripheral |
| T81.- | Biopsy Neuromuscular Junction |
| | |
| B35.5 | Biopsy Nipple |
| B35.5 | Biopsy Nipple Skin |
| Y20.- | Biopsy NOC |
| E09.5 | Biopsy Nose External |
| E09.5 | Biopsy Nose External Skin |
| E10.1 | Biopsy Nose NEC |
| E03.3 | Biopsy Nose Septum |
| E04.5 | Biopsy Nose Turbinate |
| G45.- | Biopsy Oesophagus & Examination U.G.I. Tract Endoscopic Fibreoptic |
| G45.- | Biopsy Oesophagus & Examination U.G.I. Tract Endoscopic NEC |
| | |
| G16.- | Biopsy Oesophagus Endoscopic Fibreoptic |
| G16.- | Biopsy Oesophagus Endoscopic NEC |
| G16.- | Biopsy Oesophagus NEC |
| G13.1 | Biopsy Oesophagus Open |
| T36.4 | Biopsy Omentum |
| C06.1 | Biopsy Orbit |
| X55.1 | Biopsy Organ Unspecified |
| Q50.- | Biopsy Ovary Access Minimal |
| Q50.- | Biopsy Ovary Endoscopic |
| Q50.- | Biopsy Ovary NEC |
| | |
| Q47.3 | Biopsy Ovary Open |
| F32.1 | Biopsy Palate |
| J45.1 | Biopsy Pancreas Endoscopic Retrograde |
| J74.1 | Biopsy Pancreas Endoscopic Ultrasonic |
| J73.1 | Biopsy Pancreas Laparoscopic Ultrasonic |
| J65.1 | Biopsy Pancreas NEC |
| J65.1 | Biopsy Pancreas Open |
| J67.3 | Biopsy Pancreas Percutaneous |
| J45.1 | Biopsy Pancreatic Duct Endoscopic Retrograde |
| J43.- | Biopsy Pancreatic System Endoscopic Retrograde NEC |
| | |
| J36.2 | Biopsy Papilla Vater |
| B16.2 | Biopsy Parathyroid |
| N32.1 | Biopsy Penis |
| Y20.5 | Biopsy Percutaneous NOC |
| K71.1 | Biopsy Pericardium |
| T43.1 | Biopsy Peritoneal Cavity Access Minimal |
| T43.1 | Biopsy Peritoneal Cavity Endoscopic |
| T43.1 | Biopsy Peritoneum Endoscopic |
| T41.1 | Biopsy Peritoneum NEC |
| T39.3 | Biopsy Peritoneum Posterior |

| | |
|---|---|
| F36.2 | Biopsy Peritonsillar Region |
| E25.- | Biopsy Pharynx Endoscopic |
| E25.- | Biopsy Pharynx NEC |
| E27.1 | Biopsy Pharynx Open |
| B04.2 | Biopsy Pituitary |
| R10.5 | Biopsy Placenta NEC |
| R05.1 | Biopsy Placenta Percutaneous |
| T11.- | Biopsy Pleura Access Minimal |
| T11.- | Biopsy Pleura Endoscopic |
| T14.- | Biopsy Pleura NEC |
| | |
| T09.2 | Biopsy Pleura Open |
| T11.- | Biopsy Pleural Cavity Access Minimal |
| T11.- | Biopsy Pleural Cavity Endoscopic |
| Y20.6 | Biopsy Plugged NOC |
| H68.- | Biopsy Pouch Colonoscope |
| H69.- | Biopsy Pouch Sigmoidoscope Flexible |
| H70.- | Biopsy Pouch Sigmoidoscope Rigid |
| M45.2 | Biopsy Prostate Endoscopic |
| M70.- | Biopsy Prostate NEC |
| M70.- | Biopsy Prostate Needle |
| | |
| M62.2 | Biopsy Prostate Open |
| G45.1 | Biopsy Pylorus NEC |
| G41.1 | Biopsy Pylorus Open |
| H25.- | Biopsy Rectum Endoscopic NEC |
| H41.2 | Biopsy Rectum Peranal |
| H25.- | Biopsy Rectum Sigmoidoscope Fibreoptic |
| H28.- | Biopsy Rectum Sigmoidoscope Rigid |
| H40.2 | Biopsy Rectum Trans-sphincteric |
| E49.- | Biopsy Respiratory Tract Lower Endoscopic NEC |
| E51.1 | Biopsy Respiratory Tract Lower Endoscopic Rigid |
| | |
| E49.- | Biopsy Respiratory Tract Lower NEC |
| C84.3 | Biopsy Retina |
| F48.1 | Biopsy Salivary Gland |
| C57.1 | Biopsy Sclera |
| N03.1 | Biopsy Scrotum |
| N03.1 | Biopsy Scrotum Skin |
| N22.4 | Biopsy Seminal Vesicle Transrectal Needle |
| S15.- | Biopsy Skin NEC |
| S13.- | Biopsy Skin Punch |
| S14.- | Biopsy Skin Shave |
| | |
| N20.2 | Biopsy Spermatic Cord |
| J36.2 | Biopsy Sphincter Oddi |
| J43.- | Biopsy Sphincter Oddi Endoscopic Retrograde |
| A51.3 | Biopsy Spinal Cord Meninges |
| A48.1 | Biopsy Spinal Cord NEC |
| A45.4 | Biopsy Spinal Cord Open |
| A45.4 | Biopsy Spinal Tract Open |
| V47.- | Biopsy Spine |
| J72.3 | Biopsy Spleen |
| Y20.- | Biopsy Stereotactic NOC |

| | |
|---|---|
| G45.1 | Biopsy Stomach Endoscopic |
| G19.- | Biopsy Stomach Gastroscope Rigid |
| G45.1 | Biopsy Stomach NEC |
| G38.1 | Biopsy Stomach Open |
| S15.- | Biopsy Subcutaneous Tissue |
| T74.1 | Biopsy Tendon NEC |
| T72.2 | Biopsy Tendon Sheath |
| N13.4 | Biopsy Testis |
| B20.1 | Biopsy Thymus |
| B10.3 | Biopsy Thyroglossal Tract |
| | |
| B12.2 | Biopsy Thyroid |
| F24.1 | Biopsy Tongue |
| F36.2 | Biopsy Tonsil |
| E49.- | Biopsy Trachea Endoscopic NEC |
| E51.- | Biopsy Trachea Endoscopic Rigid |
| E49.1 | Biopsy Trachea NEC |
| E43.4 | Biopsy Trachea Open |
| T29.4 | Biopsy Umbilicus |
| M30.5 | Biopsy Ureter Endoscopic NEC |
| M25.4 | Biopsy Ureter Open |
| | |
| M30.6 | Biopsy Ureter Ureteroscope Rigid |
| M77.- | Biopsy Urethra Endoscopic |
| M77.- | Biopsy Urethra NEC |
| M75.1 | Biopsy Urethra Open |
| Q18.1 | Biopsy Uterus Endoscopic |
| Q20.2 | Biopsy Uterus NEC |
| Q09.4 | Biopsy Uterus Open |
| P29.3 | Biopsy Vagina |
| L93.1 | Biopsy Vein |
| K58.4 | Biopsy Ventricular Left Transluminal Percutaneous |
| | |
| K58.3 | Biopsy Ventricular Right Transluminal Percutaneous |
| V47.- | Biopsy Vertebra |
| P09.1 | Biopsy Vulva |
| P09.1 | Biopsy Vulva Skin |
| M39.- | Bladder Contents Operations Open NEC |
| M44.- | Bladder Operations Endoscopic Therapeutic NEC |
| M43.- | Bladder Operations Increase Capacity Endoscopic |
| M49.- | Bladder Operations NEC |
| M41.- | Bladder Operations Open NEC |
| M48.- | Bladder Operations Other NEC |
| | |
| M56.- | Bladder Outlet Female Operations Endoscopic Therapeutic |
| M58.- | Bladder Outlet Female Operations NEC |
| M54.- | Bladder Outlet Female Operations Open NEC |
| M55.- | Bladder Outlet Female Operations Open Other NEC |
| M66.- | Bladder Outlet Male Operations Endoscopic Therapeutic NEC |
| M70.- | Bladder Outlet Male Operations NEC |
| M64.- | Bladder Outlet Male Operations Open NEC |
| Z42.- | Bladder site |
| F13.6 | Bleaching Teeth |
| C65.- | Bleb Operations |

| | |
|---|---|
| C13.- | Blepharoplasty |
| | Block Nerve – see Nerve Block |
| W77.- | Blocking Joint |
| X36.1 | Blood Donation |
| E92.4 | Blood Gas Analysis |
| X32.- | Blood Transfusion Exchange |
| X32.1 | Blood Transfusion Exchange Neonatal |
| X33.1 | Blood Transfusion Intra-arterial |
| X33.- | Blood Transfusion Intravenous |
| X33.- | Blood Transfusion NEC |
| | |
| O15.- | Blood Vessel Operations NEC (L) |
| L97.- | Blood Vessel Operations Other NEC |
| X36.- | Blood Withdrawal |
| Z92.- | Body Region site NEC |
| Z72.- | Bone Arm site NEC |
| | Bone Autograft – see Autograft Bone |
| Z63.- | Bone Cranium site |
| V13.- | Bone Face Operations NEC |
| Z64.- | Bone Face site NEC |
| | Bone Flap – see Flap site |
| | |
| Z80.- | Bone Foot site NEC |
| | Bone Graft – see Graft Bone |
| Z73.- | Bone Hand site NEC |
| Z78.- | Bone Leg Lower site NEC |
| W33.- | Bone Operations Open NEC |
| Z68.- | Bone Shoulder Girdle site |
| | Bone site – see also Named Bone site |
| Z87.1 | Bone site NEC |
| Z72.- | Bone Wrist site NEC |
| | Bouginage – see also Dilation |
| | |
| M79.1 | Bouginage Urethra |
| H24.- | Bowel Lower Operations Therapeutic Sigmoidoscope Fibreoptic NEC |
| H62.- | Bowel Operations NEC |
| Z29.- | Bowel site NEC |
| Z08.- | Brachial Plexus site |
| J48.7 | Brachytherapy Bile Duct Lesion Percutaneous |
| A42.- | Brain Meninges Operations NEC |
| Z05.- | Brain Meninges site |
| A07.- | Brain Tissue Operations Open |
| A10.- | Brain Tissue Operations Other |
| | |
| Z01.- | Brain Tissue site |
| A20.- | Brain Ventricle Operations |
| A17.- | Brain Ventricle Operations Endoscopic Therapeutic |
| A16.- | Brain Ventricle Operations Open |
| Z02.- | Brain Ventricle site |
| T94.- | Branchial Cleft Operations |
| | Bravo Ph Capsule – see Insertion Bravo Ph Capsule |
| B34.- | Breast Duct Operations |
| B37.- | Breast Operations NEC |
| B31.- | Breast Operations Plastic NEC |

| | |
|---|---|
| Z15.- | Breast site |
| R19.- | Breech Delivery Extraction |
| R20.- | Breech Delivery NEC |
| E49.- | Bronchoscopy NEC |
| E51.- | Bronchoscopy Rigid |
| E48.- | Bronchus Operations Endoscopic NEC |
| E50.- | Bronchus Operations Endoscopic Rigid |
| E52.- | Bronchus Operations NEC |
| E47.- | Bronchus Operations Open NEC |
| Z24.5 | Bronchus site |
| | |
| S01.- | Browlift |
| Y21.1 | Brush Cytology NEC |
| G45.8 | Brushing Gastric NEC |
| C54.- | Buckling Sclera |
| W79.2 | Bunionectomy |
| Y47.- | Burr Hole Cranium Contents Approach |
| V03.6 | Burr Hole Cranium Exploratory |
| T62.- | Bursa Operations |
| Q32.2 | Burying Fimbria Uterus Wall |
| S03.1 | Buttock Lift |
| | |
| M53.1 | Buttressing Urethra Vaginal |
| | Bypass – see also Anastomosis |
| | Bypass Aorta – see also Replacement Aorta |
| L16.- | Bypass Aorta |
| L16.3 | Bypass Aorta Anastomosis Artery Axillary Femoral Bilateral |
| L16.- | Bypass Aorta Emergency |
| L16.- | Bypass Aorta Extra-anatomic |
| L20.- | Bypass Aorta Segment Emergency NEC |
| L21.- | Bypass Aorta Segment NEC |
| L20.- | Bypass Aorta Segment Prosthesis Emergency NEC |
| | |
| L21.- | Bypass Aorta Segment Prosthesis NEC |
| | Bypass Artery – see also Replacement Artery |
| L37.1 | Bypass Artery Axillary NEC |
| L37.1 | Bypass Artery Brachial NEC |
| L29.2 | Bypass Artery Carotid Intracranial NEC |
| L29.3 | Bypass Artery Carotid NEC |
| L45.1 | Bypass Artery Coeliac |
| K46.- | Bypass Artery Coronary |
| K44.- | Bypass Artery Coronary Graft NEC |
| L58.- | Bypass Artery Femoral Emergency NEC |
| | |
| L59.- | Bypass Artery Femoral NEC |
| L50.- | Bypass Artery Iliac Emergency NEC |
| L50.- | Bypass Artery Iliac Emergency Prosthesis NEC |
| L51.- | Bypass Artery Iliac NEC |
| L51.- | Bypass Artery Iliac Prosthesis NEC |
| L45.1 | Bypass Artery Mesenteric |
| L68.- | Bypass Artery NEC |
| L58.- | Bypass Artery Popliteal Emergency NEC |
| L59.- | Bypass Artery Popliteal NEC |
| L41.2 | Bypass Artery Renal |

| | |
|---|---|
| L37.1 | Bypass Artery Subclavian NEC |
| L45.1 | Bypass Artery Suprarenal |
| L37.1 | Bypass Artery Vertebral NEC |
| H13.- | Bypass Caecum |
| Y73.1 | Bypass Cardiopulmonary |
| H13.- | Bypass Colon |
| G51.- | Bypass Duodenum |
| G71.- | Bypass Ileum |
| G73.- | Bypass Ileum Attention |
| G73.- | Bypass Intestine Small Attention |
| | |
| G71.- | Bypass Intestine Small NEC |
| G61.- | Bypass Jejunum |
| M19.6 | Bypass Kidney to Bladder Tunnelled Percutaneous |
| T89.2 | Bypass Lymphatic Duct Obstruction |
| Y16.3 | Bypass NOC |
| G06.- | Bypass Oesophagus Attention |
| G05.- | Bypass Oesophagus NEC |
| L81.2 | Bypass Priapism |
| G31.- | Bypass Stomach Anastomosis Duodenum |
| G33.- | Bypass Stomach Jejunum NEC |
| | |
| G32.- | Bypass Stomach Jejunum Transposed |
| L81.- | Bypass Vein NEC |

# C

| | |
|---|---|
| M36.1 | Caecocystoplasty |
| H18.- | Caecoscopy Open |
| H14.- | Caecostomy |
| H16.2 | Caecotomy |
| H18.- | Caecum Operations Endoscopic Open |
| H19.- | Caecum Operations Open NEC |
| Z28.2 | Caecum site |
| R17.- | Caesarean Delivery Elective |
| R18.- | Caesarean Delivery Emergency |
| R18.- | Caesarean Delivery NEC |
| | |
| R25.1 | Caesarean Hysterectomy |
| M79.3 | Calibration Urethra |
| A07.6 | Callosotomy Complete |
| A07.7 | Callosotomy Partial |
| C25.1 | Canaliculodacryocystorhinostomy |
| C29.5 | Canaliculotomy |
| | Canalisation – see Recanalisation |
| L70.4 | Cannulation Artery Open |
| L71.4 | Cannulation Artery Transluminal Percutaneous |
| J08.- | Cannulation Gall Bladder |
| | |
| J08.2 | Cannulation Gall Bladder Access Minimal |
| J08.2 | Cannulation Gall Bladder Endoscopic |
| J07.- | Cannulation Liver |
| J08.2 | Cannulation Liver Access Minimal |
| J08.2 | Cannulation Liver Endoscopic |
| T89.4 | Cannulation Lymphatic Duct |
| L91.6 | Cannulation Vein NEC |
| L93.4 | Cannulation Vein Open |
| L94.2 | Cannulation Vein Transluminal Percutaneous |
| C15.1 | Canthoplasty Medial Ectropion Correction |
| | |
| C11.6 | Canthotomy |
| C11.- | Canthus Operations |
| Z16.3 | Canthus site |
| Z87.3 | Capsule Joint site |
| Z19.1 | Capsule Lens site |
| C77.1 | Capsulectomy |
| B37.4 | Capsulectomy Breast |
| W81.6 | Capsulorrhaphy Joint |
| B33.2 | Capsulotomy Breast |
| C73.- | Capsulotomy Lens |

| | |
|---|---|
| K76.- | Cardiac Conduit Operations Transluminal |
| K59.- | Cardiac Defibrillator NEC |
| K59.- | Cardiac Defibrillator Transvenous |
| K61.- | Cardiac Pacemaker System NEC |
| K60.- | Cardiac Pacemaker System Transvenous |
| K23.6 | Cardiomyoplasty |
| G09.1 | Cardiomyotomy |
| K66.1 | Cardiotachygraphy |
| K53.- | Cardiotomy |
| K62.4 | Cardioversion Internal Transluminal Percutaneous NEC |
| | |
| X50.- | Cardioversion NEC |
| K59.- | Cardioverter NEC |
| K59.- | Cardioverter Transvenous |
| E48.- | Carina Operations Endoscopic NEC |
| E50.- | Carina Operations Endoscopic Rigid |
| E44.- | Carina Operations NEC |
| E44.- | Carina Operations Open |
| Z24.4 | Carina site |
| L30.5 | Carotid Body Operations |
| Z40.3 | Carotid Body site |
| | |
| W02.1 | Carpectomy Proximal Row |
| W02.2 | Carpus Operations Metacarpal Support |
| Z72.- | Carpus site |
| W83.- | Cartilage Articular Operations Endoscopic Therapeutic NEC |
| W89.- | Cartilage Articular Operations Endoscopic Therapeutic Other NEC |
| W82.- | Cartilage Articular Semilunar Operations Endoscopic Therapeutic |
| W70.- | Cartilage Articular Semilunar Operations NEC |
| W70.- | Cartilage Articular Semilunar Operations Open |
| N05.- | Castration Male NEC |
| A13.- | Catheter Cerebroventricular Shunt Maintenance |
| | |
| A13.- | Catheter Ventricle Brain Shunt Maintenance |
| A13.- | Catheter Ventriculoperitoneal Shunt Maintenance |
| A13.- | Catheter Ventriculopleural Shunt Maintenance |
| A13.- | Catheter Ventriculovascular Shunt Maintenance |
| O15.3 | Catheterisation Arterial Umbilical (L) |
| M47.- | Catheterisation Bladder Urethral |
| K65.- | Catheterisation Heart |
| X41.- | Catheterisation Peritoneal Ambulatory Dialysis |
| X42.- | Catheterisation Peritoneal Temporary Dialysis |
| M30.2 | Catheterisation Ureter Endoscopic |
| | |
| L91.- | Catheterisation Venous Central |
| L99.7 | Catheterisation Venous Central Peripheral Insertion Transluminal Percutaneous |
| L94.3 | Catheterisation Venous Central Port Subcutaneous Transluminal Percutaneous |
| O15.2 | Catheterisation Venous Umbilical (L) |
| | Cauterisation – see also Destruction |
| C66.2 | Cauterisation Ciliary Body |
| Q35.1 | Cauterisation Fallopian Tube Bilateral Access Minimal |
| Q35.1 | Cauterisation Fallopian Tube Bilateral Endoscopic |
| Y13.1 | Cauterisation Lesion NOC |
| Y11.1 | Cauterisation NOC |

| | |
|---|---|
| E05.1 | Cauterisation Nose Internal |
| E04.6 | Cauterisation Nose Turbinate |
| S08.- | Cauterisation Skin Lesion & Curettage |
| S08.- | Cauterisation Subcutaneous Tissue Lesion & Curettage |
| X20.3 | Centralisation Carpus Correction Forearm Deformity Congenital |
| X23.5 | Centralisation Tarsus Correction Leg Deformity Congenital |
| R21.- | Cephalic Delivery Forceps |
| R24.- | Cephalic Delivery Normal |
| R23.- | Cephalic Delivery Vaginal NEC |
| | Cerclage – see also Wiring |
| | |
| R12.- | Cerclage Uterus Gravid Cervix |
| R12.2 | Cerclage Uterus Gravid Cervix Removal |
| Z06.5 | Cerebrospinal Fluid site |
| Q55.- | Cervical Smear |
| Q05.- | Cervix Uteri Operations NEC |
| Z45.1 | Cervix Uteri site |
| E94.4 | Challenge Bronchial |
| | Change – see also Renewal |
| X51.- | Change Body Temperature |
| | Change Pack – see Packing |
| | |
| X48.2 | Change Plaster Cast |
| | Change Tube – see Drainage |
| | Change Tube – see Tube |
| C51.2 | Chelation Cornea |
| L71.3 | Chemoembolisation Artery Transluminal Percutaneous |
| X72.- | Chemotherapy Delivery Neoplasm |
| X73.- | Chemotherapy Delivery Neoplasm Oral |
| X70.- | Chemotherapy Drugs Neoplasm Procurement Bands 1-5 |
| X71.- | Chemotherapy Drugs Neoplasm Procurement Bands 6-10 |
| X37.3 | Chemotherapy Intramuscular |
| | |
| X35.2 | Chemotherapy Intravenous |
| X38.4 | Chemotherapy Subcutaneous |
| T05.- | Chest Wall Operations NEC |
| Z52.- | Chest Wall site |
| J37.- | Cholangiography Access Minimal |
| J44.- | Cholangiography Endoscopic Retrograde |
| J37.- | Cholangiography Operative |
| J50.2 | Cholangiography Percutaneous NEC |
| J50.1 | Cholangiography T Tube |
| J50.5 | Cholangiography Transhepatic Percutaneous |
| | |
| J50.4 | Cholangiography Transjejunal Percutaneous |
| J43.- | Cholangiopancreatography Endoscopic Retrograde |
| U16.2 | Cholangiopancreatography Magnetic Resonance |
| J50.7 | Cholangioscopy Transhepatic Percutaneous |
| J19.1 | Cholecystantrostomy |
| J18.- | Cholecystectomy NEC |
| J18.- | Cholecystectomy Partial |
| J18.- | Cholecystectomy Total |
| X31.1 | Cholecystography Intravenous |
| J19.3 | Cholecystojejunostomy |

| | |
|---|---|
| J21.2 | Cholecystostomy NEC |
| J20.2 | Cholecystotomy Closure |
| J21.- | Cholecystotomy NEC |
| J30.1 | Choledochoduodenostomy |
| J37.4 | Choledochoscopy Operative NEC |
| O19.1 | Chondrogenesis Joint Matrix Induced Autologous Endoscopic (W) |
| W83.4 | Chondroplasty Articular Abrasion Endoscopic |
| W83.5 | Chondroplasty Articular Thermal Endoscopic |
| W89.1 | Chondroplasty Endoscopic NEC |
| E33.3 | Chondroplasty Larynx |
| | |
| K38.2 | Chordae Tendineae Operations |
| A44.1 | Chordectomy Spinal Cord |
| E29.5 | Chordectomy Vocal Chord & Excision Larynx |
| E33.2 | Chordopexy Vocal Chord |
| A45.2 | Chordotomy Spinal Cord Open NEC |
| A47.3 | Chordotomy Spinal Cord Percutaneous |
| A45.1 | Chordotomy Spinal Cord Stereotactic |
| A45.2 | Chordotomy Spinal Tract Open NEC |
| A45.1 | Chordotomy Spinal Tract Stereotactic |
| C84.- | Choroid Operations NEC |
| | |
| Z19.4 | Choroid site |
| C67.- | Ciliary Body Operations NEC |
| | Circle Willis – see Artery Circle Willis |
| Y73.2 | Circulation Extracorporeal NEC |
| N30.3 | Circumcision |
| A22.3 | Cisternography Isotopic |
| S54.6 | Cleansing & Sterilisation Skin Burnt Head |
| S55.6 | Cleansing & Sterilisation Skin Burnt NEC |
| S54.6 | Cleansing & Sterilisation Skin Burnt Neck |
| S56.6 | Cleansing & Sterilisation Skin Head |
| | |
| S57.6 | Cleansing & Sterilisation Skin NEC |
| S56.6 | Cleansing & Sterilisation Skin Neck |
| | Clearance – see also Dissection site Block |
| E52.2 | Clearance Airway |
| D07.- | Clearance Auditory Canal External |
| F10.- | Clearance Dental |
| D15.2 | Clearance Ear Middle Suction |
| E08.8 | Clearance Nasal Cavity Suction |
| X14.- | Clearance Pelvis |
| E89.1 | Clearance Respiratory Tract Secretions |
| | |
| E42.8 | Clearance Tracheostomy Suction |
| | Clip – see also Clipping |
| S41.- | Clip Skin Head Insertion |
| S42.- | Clip Skin Insertion NEC |
| S41.- | Clip Skin Neck Insertion |
| S43.- | Clip Skin Removal |
| S41.- | Clip Subcutaneous Tissue Head Insertion |
| S42.- | Clip Subcutaneous Tissue Insertion NEC |
| S41.- | Clip Subcutaneous Tissue Neck Insertion |
| S43.- | Clip Subcutaneous Tissue Removal |

| | |
|---|---|
| | Clip Wound – see Clip Skin |
| | Clipping – see also Clip |
| L33.2 | Clipping Artery Cerebral Aneurysmal |
| L33.2 | Clipping Artery Circle Willis Aneurysmal |
| Q36.- | Clipping Fallopian Tube Access Minimal NEC |
| Q35.2 | Clipping Fallopian Tube Bilateral Access Minimal |
| Q35.2 | Clipping Fallopian Tube Bilateral Endoscopic |
| Q27.2 | Clipping Fallopian Tube Bilateral Open |
| Q36.- | Clipping Fallopian Tube Endoscopic NEC |
| Q28.- | Clipping Fallopian Tube Open NEC |
| | |
| Y07.2 | Clipping NOC |
| P01.1 | Clitoridectomy |
| P01.- | Clitoris Operations |
| Z44.1 | Clitoris site |
| | Closure – see also Operation site |
| | Closure – see also Repair |
| T28.- | Closure Abdomen |
| T28.8 | Closure Abdominal Wall Fistula |
| L01.4 | Closure Aortopulmonary Window |
| L07.3 | Closure Artery Shunt Prosthetic Subclavian Pulmonary |
| | |
| D08.6 | Closure Auditory Canal External Blind Sac |
| T94.2 | Closure Branchial Fistula |
| E47.2 | Closure Bronchus Fistula |
| | Closure Bypass – see Bypass site |
| C47.- | Closure Cornea |
| T16.3 | Closure Diaphragm Fistula |
| L02.3 | Closure Ductus Arteriosus Patent NEC |
| G53.2 | Closure Duodenum Perforation NEC |
| G52.- | Closure Duodenum Ulcer NEC |
| T28.8 | Closure Enterocutaneous Fistula |
| | |
| T28.1 | Closure Exomphalos |
| M37.4 | Closure Exstrophy |
| | Closure Fistula – see Closure site Fistula |
| Y07.3 | Closure Fistula NOC |
| J20.1 | Closure Gall Bladder Fistula |
| G31.5 | Closure Gastroduodenostomy |
| G33.5 | Closure Gastroenterostomy NEC |
| T28.1 | Closure Gastroschisis |
| G78.4 | Closure Ileum Perforation |
| G78.4 | Closure Intestine Small Perforation NEC |
| | |
| G63.3 | Closure Jejunum Perforation |
| F03.1 | Closure Lip Cleft Primary |
| F03.2 | Closure Lip Cleft Primary Revision |
| E13.5 | Closure Maxillary Antrum Mouth Fistula |
| E08.6 | Closure Nares Anterior Surgical |
| E03.4 | Closure Nose Septum Perforation NEC |
| G07.- | Closure Oesophagus Fistula |
| K16.5 | Closure Oval Foramen Patent Prosthesis Transluminal Percutaneous |
| | Closure Perforation – see Closure site Perforation |
| P13.4 | Closure Perineum Female Fistula |

| T08.4 | Closure Pleura Fenestration |
| T08.2 | Closure Pleural Cavity Drainage Open |
| K34.6 | Closure Pulmonary Valve |
| H33.5 | Closure Rectal Stump & Exteriorisation Bowel & Rectosigmoidectomy |
| H33.5 | Closure Rectal Stump & Rectosigmoidectomy & Exteriorisation Bowel |
| F48.2 | Closure Salivary Gland Fistula |
| Y07.3 | Closure Sinus Track NOC |
| S40.- | Closure Skin NEC |
| A49.3 | Closure Spinal Meningocele |
| A49.2 | Closure Spinal Myelomeningocele |
| | |
| G31.5 | Closure Stomach Duodenum Connection |
| G33.5 | Closure Stomach Jejunum Connection |
| G32.4 | Closure Stomach Jejunum Transposed Connection |
| G36.3 | Closure Stomach Opening Abnormal NEC |
| G36.2 | Closure Stomach Perforation NEC |
| G35.- | Closure Stomach Ulcer NEC |
| E43.5 | Closure Tracheocutaneous Fistula |
| K34.5 | Closure Tricuspid Valve |
| K38.4 | Closure Tunnel Ventricular Aorto-Left |
| G52.- | Closure Ulcer Duodenal Blood Vessel |
| | |
| M22.3 | Closure Ureteric Fistula |
| M73.3 | Closure Urethra Fistula |
| K38.5 | Closure Valsalva Fistula Aortic Sinus |
| K34.6 | Closure Valve Pulmonary |
| K34.5 | Closure Valve Tricuspid |
| | Coagulation Blood Vessel – see Haemostasis |
| Y10.1 | Coblation NOC |
| Z75.7 | Coccyx site |
| D24.- | Cochlea Operations |
| Z21.4 | Cochlea site |
| | |
| H11.- | Colectomy NEC |
| H10.- | Colectomy Sigmoid NEC |
| H05.- | Colectomy Total NEC |
| H08.- | Colectomy Transverse NEC |
| | Collar – see Prosthesis |
| J43.3 | Collection Bile Endoscopic Retrograde |
| J45.- | Collection Pancreatic Juice Endoscopic Retrograde |
| N34.- | Collection Sperm |
| M36.3 | Colocystoplasty |
| H21.- | Colon Operations Endoscopic Fibreoptic Therapeutic NEC |
| | |
| H18.- | Colon Operations Endoscopic Open |
| H21.- | Colon Operations Endoscopic Therapeutic NEC |
| | Colon Operations NEC – see also Bowel Operations NEC |
| H30.- | Colon Operations NEC |
| H19.- | Colon Operations Open NEC |
| H24.- | Colon Operations Therapeutic Sigmoidoscope Fibreoptic NEC |
| H24.- | Colon Sigmoid Operations Endoscopic NEC |
| H62.- | Colon Sigmoid Operations NEC |
| H27.- | Colon Sigmoid Operations Sigmoidoscope Rigid NEC |
| H24.- | Colon Sigmoid Operations Therapeutic Sigmoidoscope Fibreoptic NEC |

| | |
|---|---|
| Z28.- | Colon site |
| H22.- | Colonoscopy NEC |
| H18.- | Colonoscopy Open |
| Z29.4 | Colorectal site |
| Y51.4 | Colostomy Approach |
| H33.1 | Colostomy End & Excision Rectum Abdominoperineal |
| H15.- | Colostomy NEC |
| H15.7 | Colostomy Sigmoid Endoscopic Percutaneous |
| H16.3 | Colotomy |
| P17.- | Colpectomy |
| | |
| P18.- | Colpocleisis |
| P25.5 | Colpoperineorrhaphy |
| P22.- | Colporrhaphy & Amputation Cervix Uteri |
| P23.- | Colporrhaphy NEC |
| Q55.4 | Colposcopy Cervix |
| N34.3 | Colposcopy Male |
| Q55.4 | Colposcopy NEC |
| P27.3 | Colposcopy Vagina |
| M52.3 | Colposuspension Bladder Neck NEC |
| P29.2 | Colpotomy NEC |
| | |
| F26.1 | Commissurectomy Tongue |
| X43.- | Compensation Liver Failure |
| X40.- | Compensation Renal Failure |
| O15.1 | Compression Pseudoaneurysm Duplex Ultrasound Guided (L) |
| M75.2 | Compression Urethra Bulb Male Prosthesis Insertion |
| Y53.3 | Computed Tomography Scan Control Approach |
| K18.- | Conduit Cardiac Valved |
| M19.- | Conduit Ileal |
| C43.- | Conjunctiva Operations NEC |
| Z18.1 | Conjunctiva site |
| | |
| C25.2 | Conjunctivodacryocystorhinostomy |
| | Connection – see also Anastomosis |
| | Connection – see also Shunt |
| L06.- | Connection Aortopulmonary NEC |
| L05.- | Connection Aortopulmonary Prosthesis Interposition Tube Creation |
| K45.- | Connection Artery Mammary Coronary |
| L09.- | Connection Artery Pulmonary NEC |
| L08.- | Connection Artery Subclavian Pulmonary NEC |
| L07.- | Connection Artery Subclavian Pulmonary Prosthesis Tube Creation |
| K45.- | Connection Artery Thoracic Coronary |
| | |
| J30.- | Connection Bile Duct Common |
| A13.- | Connection Brain Ventricle Component Attention |
| A12.- | Connection Brain Ventricle Creation |
| A14.- | Connection Brain Ventricle NEC |
| K17.- | Connection Cavopulmonary Total |
| J19.- | Connection Gall Bladder |
| J29.- | Connection Hepatic Duct |
| G73.- | Connection Ileum Attention |
| G72.- | Connection Ileum NEC |
| G73.- | Connection Intestine Small Attention |

| | |
|---|---|
| G72.- | Connection Intestine Small NEC |
| C25.- | Connection Lacrimal Apparatus Nose |
| Y16.- | Connection NOC |
| G06.- | Connection Oesophagus Attention |
| G05.- | Connection Oesophagus NEC |
| J59.- | Connection Pancreatic Duct |
| G31.- | Connection Stomach Duodenum |
| G33.- | Connection Stomach Jejunum NEC |
| G32.- | Connection Stomach Jejunum Transposed |
| M21.- | Connection Ureter NEC |
| | |
| Q19.1 | Connection Uterus Vagina |
| L77.- | Connection Vena Cava |
| L77.- | Connection Vena Cava Branch |
| T96.- | Connective Tissue Operations NEC |
| | Construction – see also Reconstruction |
| M19.1 | Construction Bladder Artificial Ileal |
| | Construction Conduit – see Conduit site |
| N28.1 | Construction Penis |
| X15.4 | Construction Scrotum |
| P21.1 | Construction Vagina |
| | |
| | Contraceptive Device – see also Operation site |
| Q12.- | Contraceptive Device Intrauterine |
| Y97.- | Contrast Radiology |
| | Control Bleeding – see Arrest Bleeding |
| | Control Bleeding – see Haemostasis |
| E89.4 | Control Respiration |
| | Conversion – see Primary Operation site |
| | Conversion Prosthesis – see Prosthesis site |
| | Conversion Shunt – see Shunt site |
| Y15.5 | Conversion Stent NOC |
| | |
| X51.2 | Cooling Active |
| C51.- | Cornea Operations NEC |
| C46.- | Cornea Operations Plastic |
| C44.- | Cornea Operations Plastic Other |
| Z18.2 | Cornea site |
| V22.4 | Corpectomy Spine Cervical Reconstruction Anterior NEC |
| V22.4 | Corpectomy Spine Cervical Reconstruction Anterior Primary |
| V23.4 | Corpectomy Spine Cervical Reconstruction Anterior Revisional |
| V25.7 | Corpectomy Spine Lumbar Reconstruction Anterior NEC |
| V25.7 | Corpectomy Spine Lumbar Reconstruction Anterior Primary |
| | |
| V26.7 | Corpectomy Spine Lumbar Reconstruction Anterior Revisional |
| V24.4 | Corpectomy Spine Thoracic Reconstruction Anterior NEC |
| V24.4 | Corpectomy Spine Thoracic Reconstruction Anterior Primary |
| V24.5 | Corpectomy Spine Thoracic Reconstruction Anterior Revisional |
| | Correction – see also Repair |
| X19.- | Correction Arm Upper Deformity Congenital |
| K05.- | Correction Arteries Great Transposition Atrial Inversion |
| T02.1 | Correction Chest Wall Deformity Pectus |
| E08.3 | Correction Choana Atresia Congenital |
| W03.3 | Correction Claw Toe Total |

|  | Correction Deformity – see also Correction site Deformity |
|---|---|
| L02.- | Correction Ductus Arteriosus Patent Open |
| G53.6 | Correction Duodenum Malrotation |
| D03.3 | Correction Ear Prominent |
| C15.4 | Correction Ectropion Cicatricial |
| C15.1 | Correction Ectropion NEC |
| C15.5 | Correction Entropion Cicatricial |
| C15.2 | Correction Entropion NEC |
| C11.3 | Correction Epicanthus |
| C15.- | Correction Eyelid Deformity |
| | |
| C18.- | Correction Eyelid Ptosis |
| X21.- | Correction Finger Syndactyly |
| X27.- | Correction Foot Deformity Congenital Minor |
| X25.- | Correction Foot Deformity Congenital NEC |
| X24.- | Correction Foot Deformity Congenital Primary |
| X24.- | Correction Foot Deformity Congenital Release Foot Joint |
| X25.2 | Correction Foot Deformity Congenital Tarsectomy Wedge |
| X20.- | Correction Forearm Deformity Congenital |
| W79.- | Correction Hallux Valgus |
| W59.5 | Correction Hammer Toe |
| | |
| X21.- | Correction Hand Deformity Congenital |
| X21.2 | Correction Hand Mirror |
| X22.- | Correction Hip Deformity Congenital |
| T19.3 | Correction Hydrocele Infancy |
| C62.- | Correction Iridodialysis NEC |
| X23.- | Correction Leg Deformity Congenital |
| F03.- | Correction Lip Deformity |
| F03.- | Correction Lip Skin Deformity |
| E07.1 | Correction Nasal Pyriform Aperture Stenosis |
| X19.2 | Correction Obstetric Palsy |
| | |
| G07.3 | Correction Oesophagus Atresia Congenital |
| F29.- | Correction Palate Deformity |
| T02.- | Correction Pectus Deformity |
| N28.5 | Correction Penis Chordee |
| K07.- | Correction Pulmonary Venous Connection Anomalous Total |
| K20.2 | Correction Pulmonary Venous Drainage Anomalous Partial |
| H50.4 | Correction Rectum Atresia Congenital Reanastomosis Anal Canal |
| X19.- | Correction Shoulder Deformity Congenital |
| K20.1 | Correction Sinus Venosus Persistent |
| V41.- | Correction Spine Deformity Instrumental |
| | |
| V42.- | Correction Spine Deformity NEC |
| Y15.3 | Correction Stent Displacement NOC |
| C11.4 | Correction Telecanthus |
| X23.2 | Correction Tibia Pseudoarthrosis |
| W03.3 | Correction Toe Claw Total |
| X27.5 | Correction Toe Crossed Congenital |
| X27.4 | Correction Toe Fifth Curly |
| W59.5 | Correction Toe Hammer |
| C15.3 | Correction Trichiasis |
| L01.1 | Correction Truncus Arteriosus Persistent |

| | |
|---|---|
| V31.3 | Costotransversectomy Disc Intervertebral Thoracic NEC |
| V32.3 | Costotransversectomy Disc Intervertebral Thoracic Revisional |
| C77.2 | Couching Lens |
| V01.- | Cranioplasty |
| V01.5 | Cranioplasty Revision NEC |
| V03.- | Craniotomy |
| Z63.- | Cranium Bone site |
| Y47.- | Cranium Contents Approach Burr Hole |
| Y46.- | Cranium Contents Approach Open |
| V05.- | Cranium Operations NEC |
| | |
| | Creation – see also Operation site |
| | Creation Anastomosis – see Anastomosis site |
| K19.- | Creation Conduit Cardiac Other |
| K18.- | Creation Conduit Cardiac Valved |
| C43.6 | Creation Conjunctiva Hood |
| | Creation Connection – see Connection site |
| | Creation Fistula – see Fistulisation |
| H57.4 | Creation Graciloplasty Sphincter |
| F63.1 | Creation Impression Denture Obturator |
| F15.1 | Creation Impression Orthodontic |
| | |
| F17.2 | Creation Impression Tooth Crown Dental |
| T36.5 | Creation Omental Flap |
| | Creation Reservoir – see Reservoir site |
| | Creation Shunt – see Shunt site |
| E42.2 | Cricothyroidostomy |
| M10.4 | Cryoablation Kidney Lesion Endoscopic |
| C72.3 | Cryoextraction Lens |
| | Cryotherapy – see also Destruction |
| C66.3 | Cryotherapy Ciliary Body |
| Y13.2 | Cryotherapy Lesion NOC |
| | |
| A77.- | Cryotherapy Nerve Sympathetic |
| Y11.2 | Cryotherapy NOC |
| Z79.4 | Cuboid site |
| P31.1 | Culdoplasty |
| P31.4 | Culdotomy NEC |
| Z79.5 | Cuneiform site |
| | Curettage – see also Destruction |
| S08.- | Curettage & Cauterisation Skin Lesion |
| S08.- | Curettage & Cauterisation Subcutaneous Tissue Lesion |
| W09.- | Curettage Bone Lesion |
| | |
| C74.1 | Curettage Lens |
| Y13.3 | Curettage Lesion NOC |
| Y11.3 | Curettage NOC |
| S08.- | Curettage Skin Lesion NEC |
| S08.- | Curettage Subcutaneous Tissue Lesion NEC |
| R28.1 | Curettage Uterus Delivered |
| Q10.- | Curettage Uterus NEC |
| Q10.- | Curettage Uterus Products Conception |
| H50.3 | Cutback Anus Covered |
| C67.1 | Cyclodialysis |

| | |
|---|---|
| F18.1 | Cystectomy Dental |
| M34.- | Cystectomy NEC |
| M35.- | Cystectomy Partial |
| J61.1 | Cystogastrotomy Pancreas Open |
| M49.6 | Cystography Micturating |
| U12.7 | Cystography Nuclear |
| M47.8 | Cystometry |
| M34.1 | Cystoprostatectomy |
| M45.- | Cystoscopy |
| M45.5 | Cystoscopy Rigid NEC |
| | |
| | Cystostomy – see also Drainage Bladder |
| Y52.3 | Cystostomy Approach |
| M49.1 | Cystostomy Closure |
| M38.3 | Cystostomy NEC |
| M34.2 | Cystourethrectomy |
| U12.1 | Cystourethrogram Voiding |
| M37.1 | Cystourethroplasty |
| M45.- | Cystourethroscopy |
| Y21.1 | Cytology Brush NOC |
| Y21.- | Cytology NOC |
| | |
| E49.- | Cytology Respiratory Tract Lower Brush Endoscopic |
| E49.- | Cytology Respiratory Tract Lower Brush NEC |

# D

| | |
|---|---|
| C25.- | Dacryocystorhinostomy |
| U06.2 | Dacryoscintigraphy |
| F15.7 | Debonding Bracket Orthodontic |
| W33.2 | Debridement Bone Fracture |
| W33.6 | Debridement Bone NEC |
| C45.7 | Debridement Cornea Lesion |
| W80.- | Debridement Joint |
| T77.4 | Debridement Muscle NEC |
| Y05.5 | Debridement Organ NOC |
| S54.1 | Debridement Skin Burnt Head |
| | |
| S55.1 | Debridement Skin Burnt NEC |
| S54.1 | Debridement Skin Burnt Neck |
| S58.1 | Debridement Skin Head Larvae Therapy |
| S56.1 | Debridement Skin Head NEC |
| S58.2 | Debridement Skin Larvae Therapy |
| S57.1 | Debridement Skin NEC |
| S58.1 | Debridement Skin Neck Larvae Therapy |
| S56.1 | Debridement Skin Neck NEC |
| T96.3 | Debridement Soft Tissue NEC |
| S54.1 | Debridement Subcutaneous Tissue Burnt Head |
| | |
| S55.1 | Debridement Subcutaneous Tissue Burnt NEC |
| S54.1 | Debridement Subcutaneous Tissue Burnt Neck |
| S56.1 | Debridement Subcutaneous Tissue Head NEC |
| S57.1 | Debridement Subcutaneous Tissue NEC |
| S56.1 | Debridement Subcutaneous Tissue Neck NEC |
| E42.7 | Decannulation Tracheostomy |
| W18.4 | Decompression Bone Fourage |
| K68.1 | Decompression Cardiac Tamponade |
| V60.- | Decompression Disc Intervertebral Coblation Percutaneous NEC |
| V60.- | Decompression Disc Intervertebral Coblation Percutaneous Primary |
| | |
| V61.- | Decompression Disc Intervertebral Coblation Percutaneous Revisional |
| W84.4 | Decompression Joint Endoscopic |
| A32.- | Decompression Nerve Cranial NEC |
| A73.3 | Decompression Nerve Peripheral NEC |
| C06.3 | Decompression Orbit |
| B04.3 | Decompression Pituitary |
| V22.- | Decompression Posterior Fossa & Spine Cervical Primary |
| V23.- | Decompression Posterior Fossa & Spine Cervical Revisional |
| V22.- | Decompression Spine Cervical NEC |
| V23.- | Decompression Spine Cervical Revisional |

| | |
|---|---|
| V44.- | Decompression Spine Fracture |
| V25.- | Decompression Spine Lumbar NEC |
| V26.- | Decompression Spine Lumbar Revisional |
| V27.- | Decompression Spine NEC |
| V27.3 | Decompression Spine Revisional NEC |
| V24.- | Decompression Spine Thoracic |
| V24.3 | Decompression Spine Thoracic Revisional |
| O29.1 | Decompression Subacromial (W) |
| E55.1 | Decortication Lung Lesion Open |
| T07.1 | Decortication Pleura |
| | |
| X50.4 | Defibrillation Cardiac NEC |
| X50.4 | Defibrillation Ventricular External |
| E57.3 | Deflation Lung Bulla |
| C80.3 | Delamination Epiretinal Fibrovascular Membrane |
| R19.- | Delivery Breech Extraction |
| R20.- | Delivery Breech NEC |
| R17.- | Delivery Caesarean Elective |
| R18.- | Delivery Caesarean Emergency |
| R18.- | Delivery Caesarean NEC |
| R21.- | Delivery Cephalic Forceps |
| | |
| R24.- | Delivery Cephalic Normal |
| R23.- | Delivery Cephalic Vaginal NEC |
| X72.- | Delivery Chemotherapy Neoplasm |
| X73.- | Delivery Chemotherapy Neoplasm Oral |
| R27.- | Delivery Facilitated NEC |
| R25.2 | Delivery Facilitated Operations Destructive |
| R25.- | Delivery NEC |
| R24.- | Delivery Normal |
| X65.- | Delivery Radiotherapy |
| | Delivery Rehabilitation – see Rehabilitation |
| | |
| R22.- | Delivery Vacuum |
| | Demonstration – see Education |
| C22.7 | Denervation Eyelid Nerve |
| M08.2 | Denervation Kidney Open |
| M08.2 | Denervation Kidney Pelvis Open |
| A60.6 | Denervation Nerve Peripheral |
| A36.5 | Denervation Nerve Trigeminal (v) |
| V48.- | Denervation Vertebra Spinal Facet Joint |
| V48.- | Denervation Vertebra Spinal Facet Joint Radiofrequency Controlled |
| F10.- | Dental Clearance |
| | |
| S60.- | Dermabrasion Skin |
| S60.5 | Dermatoscopy Skin |
| T56.- | Dermofasciectomy |
| | Deroofing – see also Marsupialisation |
| Y06.2 | Deroofing Cyst NOC |
| M04.1 | Deroofing Kidney Cyst |
| M10.3 | Deroofing Kidney Cyst Multiple Endoscopic |
| | Deslough – see Escharotomy |
| | Deslough – see Removal from Skin Slough |
| | Destruction – see also Avulsion |

| | |
|---|---|
| | Destruction – see also Extirpation |
| | Destruction – see also Photodestruction |
| T31.4 | Destruction Abdominal Wall Anterior Lesion |
| T31.4 | Destruction Abdominal Wall Lesion NEC |
| T39.2 | Destruction Abdominal Wall Posterior Lesion |
| H49.- | Destruction Anus Lesion |
| D08.1 | Destruction Auditory Canal External Lesion |
| J28.2 | Destruction Bile Duct Lesion |
| M42.- | Destruction Bladder Lesion Endoscopic |
| M41.1 | Destruction Bladder Lesion Open |
| | |
| W09.- | Destruction Bone Lesion |
| H23.- | Destruction Bowel Lower Lesion Sigmoidoscope Fibreoptic |
| A38.- | Destruction Brain Meninges Lesion |
| A17.1 | Destruction Brain Ventricle Lesion Endoscopic |
| B40.- | Destruction Breast Lesion |
| B40.1 | Destruction Breast Lesion Laser Interstitial |
| E48.- | Destruction Bronchus Lesion Endoscopic NEC |
| E50.- | Destruction Bronchus Lesion Endoscopic Rigid |
| E46.4 | Destruction Bronchus Lesion Open |
| E46.- | Destruction Bronchus Partial |
| | |
| H20.- | Destruction Caecum Lesion Endoscopic Fibreoptic |
| H20.- | Destruction Caecum Lesion Endoscopic NEC |
| H12.3 | Destruction Caecum Lesion NEC |
| | Destruction Calculus – see Fragmentation |
| C11.2 | Destruction Canthus Lesion |
| E48.- | Destruction Carina Lesion Endoscopic NEC |
| E50.- | Destruction Carina Lesion Endoscopic Rigid |
| Q02.- | Destruction Cervix Uteri Lesion |
| Y09.- | Destruction Chemical NOC |
| C66.- | Destruction Ciliary Body |
| | |
| H20.- | Destruction Colon Lesion Endoscopic Fibreoptic |
| H20.- | Destruction Colon Lesion Endoscopic NEC |
| H12.3 | Destruction Colon Lesion NEC |
| H23.- | Destruction Colon Lesion Sigmoidoscope Fibreoptic |
| H23.- | Destruction Colon Sigmoid Lesion Endoscopic NEC |
| H23.- | Destruction Colon Sigmoid Lesion Sigmoidoscope Fibreoptic |
| H26.- | Destruction Colon Sigmoid Lesion Sigmoidoscope Rigid |
| C39.- | Destruction Conjunctiva Lesion |
| C45.- | Destruction Cornea Lesion |
| V05.1 | Destruction Cranium Lesion |
| | |
| T17.2 | Destruction Diaphragm Lesion |
| V52.- | Destruction Disc Intervertebral |
| G54.1 | Destruction Duodenum Lesion Endoscopic NEC |
| G50.2 | Destruction Duodenum Lesion Open |
| G43.- | Destruction Duodenum Proximal Lesion & Exam. U.G.I. Tract Endo. Fibreop. |
| G43.- | Destruction Duodenum Proximal Lesion & Exam. U.G.I. Tract Endo. NEC |
| D02.2 | Destruction Ear External Lesion |
| D02.2 | Destruction Ear External Skin Lesion |
| D19.2 | Destruction Ear Middle Lesion |
| C12.- | Destruction Eyelid Lesion |

| | |
|---|---|
| C12.- | Destruction Eyelid Skin Lesion |
| A38.5 | Destruction Falx Cerebri Lesion |
| T53.2 | Destruction Fascia Lesion |
| R25.2 | Destruction Fetus Facilitate Delivery |
| R03.- | Destruction Fetus Selective |
| Y11.7 | Destruction Gamma Wave NOC |
| A26.3 | Destruction Ganglion Trigeminal |
| G43.- | Destruction Gastrointestinal Tract Upper Lesion Endoscopic Fibreoptic |
| G42.- | Destruction Gastrointestinal Tract Upper Lesion Endoscopic Fibreoptic Other |
| G43.- | Destruction Gastrointestinal Tract Upper Lesion Endoscopic NEC |
| | |
| G42.- | Destruction Gastrointestinal Tract Upper Lesion Endoscopic Other NEC |
| H52.- | Destruction Haemorrhoid |
| G79.1 | Destruction Ileum Lesion Endoscopic |
| G70.3 | Destruction Ileum Lesion Open |
| G79.1 | Destruction Intestine Small Lesion Endoscopic NEC |
| G70.3 | Destruction Intestine Small Lesion Open NEC |
| C64.3 | Destruction Iris Lesion |
| G64.1 | Destruction Jejunum Lesion Endoscopic |
| G59.2 | Destruction Jejunum Lesion Open |
| M10.1 | Destruction Kidney Lesion Endoscopic |
| | |
| M04.3 | Destruction Kidney Lesion Open |
| C24.- | Destruction Lacrimal Gland |
| C26.2 | Destruction Lacrimal Sac Lesion |
| E35.3 | Destruction Larynx Lesion Endoscopic |
| E34.- | Destruction Larynx Lesion Endoscopic Microtherapeutic |
| E30.3 | Destruction Larynx Lesion Open |
| Y08.- | Destruction Laser NOC |
| | Destruction Lesion – see also Destruction site |
| Y12.- | Destruction Lesion Chemical NOC |
| Y13.7 | Destruction Lesion Microwave NOC |
| | |
| Y13.- | Destruction Lesion NOC |
| Y13.4 | Destruction Lesion Thermal Radiofrequency Controlled NOC |
| Y13.5 | Destruction Lesion Ultrasonic NOC |
| F02.2 | Destruction Lip Lesion |
| F02.2 | Destruction Lip Mucosa Lesion |
| F02.2 | Destruction Lip Skin Lesion |
| J03.2 | Destruction Liver Lesion Open |
| E48.- | Destruction Lung Lesion Endoscopic NEC |
| E50.- | Destruction Lung Lesion Endoscopic Rigid |
| E55.- | Destruction Lung Lesion Open |
| | |
| E62.1 | Destruction Mediastinum Lesion Endoscopic |
| A43.1 | Destruction Meninges Skull Base Lesion |
| A43.2 | Destruction Meninges Skull Clivus Lesion |
| T38.2 | Destruction Mesentery Colon Lesion |
| T37.2 | Destruction Mesentery Intestine Small Lesion |
| Y11.6 | Destruction Microwave NOC |
| F38.- | Destruction Mouth Lesion NEC |
| T83.1 | Destruction Muscle Lesion |
| S64.- | Destruction Nail Bed |
| E24.1 | Destruction Nasopharynx Lesion Endoscopic |

| | |
|---|---|
| | Destruction Nerve – see also Denervation |
| A28.8 | Destruction Nerve Abducens (vi) Extracranial |
| A26.2 | Destruction Nerve Abducens (vi) NEC |
| A26.8 | Destruction Nerve Accessory (xi) Intracranial |
| A28.8 | Destruction Nerve Accessory (xi) NEC |
| A28.8 | Destruction Nerve Acoustic (viii) Extracranial |
| A26.5 | Destruction Nerve Acoustic (viii) NEC |
| A28.- | Destruction Nerve Cranial Extracranial |
| A26.- | Destruction Nerve Cranial Intracranial |
| A26.4 | Destruction Nerve Facial (vii) Intracranial |
| | |
| A28.8 | Destruction Nerve Facial (vii) NEC |
| A28.8 | Destruction Nerve Glossopharyngeal (ix) Extracranial |
| A26.6 | Destruction Nerve Glossopharyngeal (ix) NEC |
| A28.8 | Destruction Nerve Hypoglossal (xii) Extracranial |
| A26.8 | Destruction Nerve Hypoglossal (xii) NEC |
| A28.8 | Destruction Nerve Oculomotor (iii) Extracranial |
| A26.2 | Destruction Nerve Oculomotor (iii) NEC |
| A28.8 | Destruction Nerve Optic (ii) Extracranial |
| A26.1 | Destruction Nerve Optic (ii) NEC |
| A60.- | Destruction Nerve Peripheral |
| | |
| A61.- | Destruction Nerve Peripheral Lesion |
| A60.4 | Destruction Nerve Peripheral Thermal Radiofrequency Controlled |
| A57.1 | Destruction Nerve Root Spinal Lesion |
| A57.5 | Destruction Nerve Root Spinal NEC |
| A57.3 | Destruction Nerve Root Spinal Thermal Radiofrequency Controlled |
| A76.- | Destruction Nerve Sympathetic Chemical |
| A79.- | Destruction Nerve Sympathetic NEC |
| A78.- | Destruction Nerve Sympathetic Thermal Radiofrequency Controlled |
| A26.3 | Destruction Nerve Trigeminal (v) Intracranial |
| A28.8 | Destruction Nerve Trigeminal (v) NEC |
| | |
| A28.8 | Destruction Nerve Trochlear (iv) Extracranial |
| A26.2 | Destruction Nerve Trochlear (iv) NEC |
| A26.7 | Destruction Nerve Vagus (x) Intracranial |
| A27.- | Destruction Nerve Vagus (x) NEC |
| B35.3 | Destruction Nipple Lesion |
| B35.3 | Destruction Nipple Skin Lesion |
| Y11.- | Destruction NOC |
| E09.- | Destruction Nose External Lesion |
| E09.- | Destruction Nose External Skin Lesion |
| E08.2 | Destruction Nose Internal Lesion NEC |
| | |
| G43.- | Destruction Oesophagus Lesion & Exam. U.G.I. Tract Endo. Fibreoptic |
| G43.- | Destruction Oesophagus Lesion & Exam. U.G.I. Tract Endoscopic NEC |
| G14.- | Destruction Oesophagus Lesion Endoscopic Fibreoptic |
| G14.- | Destruction Oesophagus Lesion Endoscopic NEC |
| G17.- | Destruction Oesophagus Lesion Oesophagoscope Rigid |
| G04.- | Destruction Oesophagus Lesion Open |
| T36.3 | Destruction Omentum Lesion |
| C02.2 | Destruction Orbit Lesion |
| X53.- | Destruction Organ Unspecified |
| Q49.- | Destruction Ovary Lesion Endoscopic |

| | |
|---|---|
| Q44.- | Destruction Ovary Lesion Open |
| F28.2 | Destruction Palate Lesion |
| J58.3 | Destruction Pancreas Lesion |
| N27.- | Destruction Penis Lesion |
| N27.- | Destruction Penis Skin Lesion |
| H49.- | Destruction Perianal Region Lesion |
| P11.- | Destruction Perineum Female Lesion |
| N24.8 | Destruction Perineum Male Lesion |
| P11.- | Destruction Perineum Skin Female Lesion |
| N24.8 | Destruction Perineum Skin Male Lesion |
| T42.2 | Destruction Peritoneum Lesion Access Minimal |
| T42.2 | Destruction Peritoneum Lesion Endoscopic |
| T33.2 | Destruction Peritoneum Lesion Open |
| T39.2 | Destruction Peritoneum Posterior Lesion |
| E24.2 | Destruction Pharynx Lesion Endoscopic |
| H60.1 | Destruction Pilonidal Sinus |
| B02.- | Destruction Pituitary |
| T10.1 | Destruction Pleura Lesion Endoscopic |
| T09.1 | Destruction Pleura Lesion Open |
| M67.1 | Destruction Prostate Endoscopic Cryotherapy |
| M67.5 | Destruction Prostate Endoscopic Microwave |
| M67.2 | Destruction Prostate Endoscopic NEC |
| M67.2 | Destruction Prostate Endoscopic Ultrasound |
| M67.- | Destruction Prostate Lesion Endoscopic |
| M62.1 | Destruction Prostate Lesion Open |
| G43.- | Destruction Pylorus Lesion Endoscopic Fibreoptic |
| G43.- | Destruction Pylorus Lesion Endoscopic NEC |
| H23.- | Destruction Rectum Lesion Endoscopic NEC |
| H34.- | Destruction Rectum Lesion Open |
| H41.3 | Destruction Rectum Lesion Peranal |
| H23.- | Destruction Rectum Lesion Sigmoidoscope Fibreoptic |
| H26.- | Destruction Rectum Lesion Sigmoidoscope Rigid |
| H40.3 | Destruction Rectum Lesion Trans-sphincteric |
| E48.- | Destruction Respiratory Tract Lower Lesion Endoscopic NEC |
| E50.- | Destruction Respiratory Tract Lower Lesion Endoscopic Rigid |
| C82.- | Destruction Retina |
| F45.5 | Destruction Salivary Gland Lesion |
| C53.- | Destruction Sclera Lesion |
| N01.- | Destruction Scrotum |
| N01.- | Destruction Scrotum Skin |
| S10.- | Destruction Skin Lesion Head NEC |
| S09.- | Destruction Skin Lesion Laser |
| S11.- | Destruction Skin Lesion NEC |
| S10.- | Destruction Skin Lesion Neck NEC |
| A47.1 | Destruction Spinal Cord Cervical Substantia Gelatinosa Needle |
| A44.2 | Destruction Spinal Cord Lesion NEC |
| A51.1 | Destruction Spinal Cord Meninges Lesion |
| A47.- | Destruction Spinal Cord NEC |
| A44.- | Destruction Spinal Cord Partial |
| V43.- | Destruction Spine Lesion |

| | |
|---|---|
| A47.2 | Destruction Spinothalamic Tract Thermal Radiofrequency Controlled |
| G43.- | Destruction Stomach Lesion Endoscopic Fibreoptic |
| G43.- | Destruction Stomach Lesion Endoscopic NEC |
| G17.- | Destruction Stomach Lesion Gastroscope Rigid |
| G29.- | Destruction Stomach Lesion Open |
| S10.- | Destruction Subcutaneous Tissue Lesion Head NEC |
| S09.- | Destruction Subcutaneous Tissue Lesion Laser |
| S11.- | Destruction Subcutaneous Tissue Lesion NEC |
| S10.- | Destruction Subcutaneous Tissue Lesion Neck NEC |
| C88.- | Destruction Subretinal Lesion |
| | |
| A38.6 | Destruction Tentorium Cerebelli Lesion |
| N07.2 | Destruction Testis Lesion |
| Y11.4 | Destruction Thermal Radiofrequency Controlled NOC |
| F23.2 | Destruction Tongue Lesion |
| F36.1 | Destruction Tonsil |
| E48.- | Destruction Trachea Lesion Endoscopic NEC |
| E50.- | Destruction Trachea Lesion Endoscopic Rigid |
| E43.1 | Destruction Trachea Lesion Open |
| A26.3 | Destruction Trigeminal Ganglion |
| Y13.5 | Destruction Ultrasonic NOC |
| | |
| T29.3 | Destruction Umbilicus Lesion |
| M29.1 | Destruction Ureter Lesion Endoscopic |
| M32.1 | Destruction Ureteric Orifice Lesion Endoscopic |
| M76.1 | Destruction Urethra Lesion Endoscopic |
| M81.1 | Destruction Urethra Meatus Lesion |
| M76.5 | Destruction Urethral Valves Endoscopic |
| Q17.- | Destruction Uterus Endoscopic |
| Q52.2 | Destruction Uterus Ligament Broad Lesion |
| P20.- | Destruction Vagina Lesion |
| C79.- | Destruction Vitreous Body |
| | |
| P06.- | Destruction Vulva Lesion |
| P06.- | Destruction Vulva Skin Lesion |
| J07.1 | Devascularisation Liver Open |
| | Device Intrauterine – see Contraceptive Device |
| X41.- | Dialysis Catheter Ambulatory |
| X40.- | Dialysis NEC |
| X40.6 | Dialysis Peritoneal Ambulatory Continuous |
| X40.5 | Dialysis Peritoneal Automated |
| X40.2 | Dialysis Peritoneal NEC |
| X42.1 | Dialysis Peritoneal Temporary Catheter Insertion |
| | |
| X40.1 | Dialysis Renal |
| T17.- | Diaphragm Operations NEC |
| Z53.1 | Diaphragm site |
| | Diathermy – see also Cauterisation |
| E04.1 | Diathermy Nose Turbinate Submucous |
| O11.- | Digestive Tract Upper Other site (Z) |
| Z27.- | Digestive Tract Upper site |
| | Dilatation – see Dilation |
| H54.- | Dilation Anal Sphincter |
| H53.2 | Dilation Anus Haemorrhoid Forced Manual |

| | |
|---|---|
| L08.6 | Dilation Artery Anast. Subclavian Pulmonary Balloon Trans. Percut |
| L05.4 | Dilation Artery Shunt Pulmonary Aorta Balloon Transluminal Percutaneous |
| L07.4 | Dilation Artery Shunt Subclavian Pulmonary Balloon Transluminal Percutaneous |
| L71.5 | Dilation Artery Transluminal Percutaneous |
| J30.5 | Dilation Bile Duct Anastomosis Open |
| J46.- | Dilation Bile Duct Anastomosis Percutaneous |
| J76.2 | Dilation Bile Duct Balloon Percutaneous |
| J41.- | Dilation Bile Duct Endoscopic NEC |
| M58.2 | Dilation Bladder Outlet Female |
| H24.1 | Dilation Bowel Lower Sigmoidoscope Fibreoptic |
| | |
| H62.3 | Dilation Bowel NEC |
| H21.1 | Dilation Caecum Endoscopic Fibreoptic NEC |
| H21.1 | Dilation Caecum Endoscopic NEC |
| K76.1 | Dilation Cardiac Conduit Balloon Percutaneous Transluminal |
| Q10.- | Dilation Cervix Uteri & Curettage Uterus NEC |
| Q11.- | Dilation Cervix Uteri & Evacuation Uterus Products Conception NEC |
| Q05.2 | Dilation Cervix Uteri NEC |
| H21.1 | Dilation Colon Endoscopic Fibreoptic NEC |
| H21.1 | Dilation Colon Endoscopic NEC |
| H24.1 | Dilation Colon Sigmoid Endoscopic NEC |
| | |
| H24.1 | Dilation Colon Sigmoid Sigmoidoscope Fibreoptic |
| H27.1 | Dilation Colon Sigmoid Sigmoidoscope Rigid |
| H24.1 | Dilation Colon Sigmoidoscope Fibreoptic |
| H31.3 | Dilation Colorectal Stricture Balloon Image Guided |
| G54.2 | Dilation Duodenum Endoscopic NEC |
| G44.3 | Dilation Duodenum Prox. & Examination U.G.I. Tract Endoscopic Fibreop. |
| G44.3 | Dilation Duodenum Prox. & Examination U.G.I. Tract Endoscopic NEC |
| Q41.5 | Dilation Fallopian Tube NEC |
| Q34.3 | Dilation Fallopian Tube Open |
| G44.3 | Dilation Gastrointestinal Tract Upper Endoscopic Fibreoptic NEC |
| | |
| G44.3 | Dilation Gastrointestinal Tract Upper Endoscopic NEC |
| J29.4 | Dilation Hepatic Duct Anastomosis Open |
| G75.4 | Dilation Ileostomy |
| G79.2 | Dilation Ileum Endoscopic |
| G79.2 | Dilation Intestine Small Endoscopic NEC |
| G64.2 | Dilation Jejunum Endoscopic |
| C27.2 | Dilation Lacrimal Duct |
| C27.2 | Dilation Nasolacrimal Duct |
| E27.5 | Dilation Nasopharynx |
| Y40.- | Dilation NOC |
| | |
| G44.3 | Dilation Oesophagus & Examination U.G.I. Tract Endoscopic Fibreoptic |
| G44.3 | Dilation Oesophagus & Examination U.G.I. Tract Endoscopic NEC |
| G15.- | Dilation Oesophagus Endoscopic Fibreoptic |
| G18.- | Dilation Oesophagus Endoscopic NEC |
| G44.6 | Dilation Oesophagus Sphincter Endoscopic Pressure Controlled |
| G15.5 | Dilation Oesophagus Web Endoscopic Fibreoptic |
| G18.5 | Dilation Oesophagus Web Oesophagoscope Rigid |
| J60.- | Dilation Pancreatic Duct |
| J42.5 | Dilation Pancreatic Duct Endoscopic Retrograde |
| F55.1 | Dilation Parotid Duct |

| | |
|---|---|
| E27.5 | Dilation Pharynx |
| M70.4 | Dilation Prostate Balloon |
| G44.3 | Dilation Pylorus Endoscopic Fibreoptic |
| G44.3 | Dilation Pylorus Endoscopic NEC |
| G40.6 | Dilation Pylorus Open |
| H24.1 | Dilation Rectum Endoscopic NEC |
| H24.1 | Dilation Rectum Sigmoidoscope Fibreoptic |
| H27.1 | Dilation Rectum Sigmoidoscope Rigid |
| F55.- | Dilation Salivary Duct |
| G44.3 | Dilation Stomach Endoscopic Fibreoptic |
| | |
| G44.3 | Dilation Stomach Endoscopic NEC |
| G18.- | Dilation Stomach Gastroscope Rigid |
| Y40.1 | Dilation Stricture NOC |
| F55.2 | Dilation Submandibular Duct |
| M29.4 | Dilation Ureter Endoscopic |
| M27.7 | Dilation Ureter Ureteroscopic |
| M32.4 | Dilation Ureteric Orifice Endoscopic |
| M76.4 | Dilation Urethra Endoscopic |
| M81.4 | Dilation Urethra Meatus |
| M79.2 | Dilation Urethra NEC |
| | |
| P29.5 | Dilation Vagina |
| K35.6 | Dilation Valve Pulmonary Transluminal Percutaneous & Perforation |
| W08.6 | Disarticulation Bone NEC |
| X10.- | Disarticulation Foot |
| X09.2 | Disarticulation Hip |
| X11.- | Disarticulation Toe |
| V52.- | Disc Intervertebral Operations NEC |
| Z99.- | Disc Intervertebral site |
| C74.2 | Discission Cataract |
| V52.3 | Discography Disc Intervertebral |
| | |
| G10.1 | Disconnection Vein Azygos |
| T96.8 | Disruption Ganglion Compression |
| C84.1 | Dissection Epiretinal |
| T85.- | Dissection Lymph Nodes Block, Neck - celvical |
| J24.3 | Dissolution Call Bladder Calculus Percutaneous |
| M43.2 | Distension Bladder Hydrostatic Endoscopic |
| W92.2 | Distension Joint |
| M19.- | Diversion Urinary |
| M35.1 | Diverticulectomy Bladder |
| | Division – see also Ligation |
| | |
| | Division – see also Transection |
| | Division Adhesions – see Freeing site Adhesions |
| W14.- | Division Bone Diaphyseal |
| V10.- | Division Bone Face |
| W15.- | Division Bone Foot |
| W16.- | Division Bone NEC |
| W12.- | Division Bone Periarticular Angulation |
| W13.- | Division Bone Periarticular NEC |
| A07.1 | Division Brain Tissue Open |
| N06.5 | Division Cremaster |

| | |
|---|---|
| L02.1 | Division Ductus Arteriosus Patent |
| A51.4 | Division Epidural Adhesions Endoscopic |
| C34.- | Division Eye Tendon Partial |
| T54.- | Division Fascia |
| K52.4 | Division Heart Accessory Pathway Open |
| K52.5 | Division Heart Conducting System Open NEC |
| V16.- | Division Jaw NEC |
| M03.2 | Division Kidney Horseshoe Isthmus |
| E31.3 | Division Larynx Stenosis & Insertion Prosthesis |
| V16.- | Division Mandible |
| | |
| P14.1 | Division Muscle Levator Ani & Episiotomy Posterior |
| T83.2 | Division Muscle NEC |
| G09.3 | Division Oesophagus Web |
| J62.1 | Division Pancreas Annular |
| T41.2 | Division Peritoneum Band |
| A49.1 | Division Spinal Filum Terminale Tether |
| W84.3 | Division Synovial Plica Endoscopic |
| W84.3 | Division Synovial Plica Knee Endoscopic |
| W69.5 | Division Synovial Plica Open |
| C34.- | Division Tendon Eye Partial |
| | |
| Q54.3 | Division Uteropelvic Ligament |
| X36.1 | Donation Blood |
| X46.1 | Donation Bone Marrow |
| X45.2 | Donation Heart |
| X45.1 | Donation Kidney |
| X45.3 | Donation Lung Lobe |
| X45.- | Donation Organ |
| X46.2 | Donation Skin |
| X46.- | Donation Tissue NEC |
| Y99.- | Donor Status |
| | |
| | Doppler – see Ultrasound site Doppler |
| K06.4 | Double Switch Procedure |
| | Drainage – see also Aspiration |
| | Drainage – see also Evacuation |
| | Drainage – see also Puncture |
| T34.3 | Drainage Abdominal Abscess Open NEC |
| T45.3 | Drainage Abdominal Abscess Percutaneous Image Controlled NEC |
| T45.4 | Drainage Abdominal Cavity Lesion Percutaneous Image Controlled NEC |
| T31.5 | Drainage Abdominal Wall Anterior |
| T31.5 | Drainage Abdominal Wall NEC |
| | |
| T39.8 | Drainage Abdominal Wall Posterior |
| | Drainage Abscess – see Drainage site Lesion |
| | Drainage Abscess – see Incision site Lesion |
| R10.1 | Drainage Amniotic Cavity |
| R07.2 | Drainage Amniotic Fluid Twin to Twin Serial Endoscopic |
| R08.2 | Drainage Amniotic Fluid Twin to Twin Serial Percutaneous |
| X12.5 | Drainage Amputation Stump |
| H03.- | Drainage Appendix |
| C60.5 | Drainage Aqueous Humour |
| T46.- | Drainage Ascites |

| | |
|---|---|
| D08.3 | Drainage Auditory Canal External |
| P03.4 | Drainage Bartholin Gland |
| J33.- | Drainage Bile Duct NEC |
| J48.- | Drainage Bile Duct Transhepatic Percutaneous |
| | Drainage Bladder – see also Catheterisation |
| M38.1 | Drainage Bladder & Urethrostomy Perineal |
| M38.- | Drainage Bladder Open |
| M38.2 | Drainage Bladder Suprapubic Tube |
| W18.- | Drainage Bone |
| A40.- | Drainage Brain Extradural Space |
| | |
| A22.1 | Drainage Brain Subarachnoid Space NEC |
| A41.- | Drainage Brain Subdural Space |
| A41.2 | Drainage Brain Subdural Space Abscess |
| A05.- | Drainage Brain Tissue Lesion |
| A20.1 | Drainage Brain Ventricle NEC |
| A16.1 | Drainage Brain Ventricle Open NEC |
| B33.1 | Drainage Breast Lesion |
| H16.1 | Drainage Caecum |
| A53.5 | Drainage Cerebrospinal Fluid NEC |
| T12.4 | Drainage Chest Underwater Insertion |
| | |
| H16.1 | Drainage Colon |
| D04.- | Drainage Ear External Lesion |
| D04.- | Drainage Ear External Skin Lesion |
| N15.4 | Drainage Epididymis |
| C60.- | Drainage Eye Anterior Chamber Tube |
| C19.1 | Drainage Eyelid Lesion |
| C19.1 | Drainage Eyelid Skin Lesion |
| Q31.2 | Drainage Fallopian Tube |
| J21.- | Drainage Gall Bladder |
| J24.1 | Drainage Gall Bladder Percutaneous |
| | |
| N11.4 | Drainage Hydrocele Sac |
| H58.1 | Drainage Ischiorectal Abscess |
| W81.3 | Drainage Joint |
| M06.2 | Drainage Kidney NEC |
| M13.2 | Drainage Kidney Percutaneous |
| M16.- | Drainage Kidney Tube |
| M13.6 | Drainage Kidney Tube Insertion Percutaneous |
| C27.- | Drainage Lacrimal Duct |
| | Drainage Lesion – see Drainage site Lesion |
| J05.1 | Drainage Liver Open |
| | |
| J12.1 | Drainage Liver Percutaneous |
| E59.4 | Drainage Lung |
| T88.- | Drainage Lymph Node Lesion |
| E12.2 | Drainage Maxillary Antrum Approach Sublabial |
| E13.1 | Drainage Maxillary Antrum NEC |
| E61.3 | Drainage Mediastinum Open |
| C27.- | Drainage Nasolacrimal Duct |
| Y22.- | Drainage NOC |
| G09.4 | Drainage Oesophagus |
| C06.2 | Drainage Orbit |

| | |
|---|---|
| Q49.3 | Drainage Ovary Cyst Access Minimal |
| Q49.3 | Drainage Ovary Cyst Endoscopic |
| Q47.4 | Drainage Ovary Cyst Open |
| J42.4 | Drainage Pancreas Lesion Endoscopic Retrograde |
| J61.- | Drainage Pancreas Lesion Open |
| J66.- | Drainage Pancreas Lesion Percutaneous |
| J60.- | Drainage Pancreatic Duct |
| M83.1 | Drainage Paravesical Abscess |
| T34.2 | Drainage Pelvic Abscess Open |
| T45.2 | Drainage Pelvic Abscess Percutaneous Image Controlled |
| | |
| N32.2 | Drainage Penis |
| H58.2 | Drainage Perianal Abscess |
| K68.- | Drainage Pericardium |
| K77.- | Drainage Pericardium Transluminal |
| H16.1 | Drainage Pericolonic Tissue |
| H58.- | Drainage Perineal Region Through |
| P13.1 | Drainage Perineum Female |
| P13.1 | Drainage Perineum Skin Female |
| G09.4 | Drainage Perioesophageal Tissue |
| H58.3 | Drainage Perirectal Abscess |
| | |
| T46.- | Drainage Peritoneal Cavity NEC |
| T34.- | Drainage Peritoneum Open |
| F36.3 | Drainage Peritonsillar Region Abscess |
| H60.3 | Drainage Pilonidal Sinus |
| T12.1 | Drainage Pleura Lesion NEC |
| T12.- | Drainage Pleural Cavity NEC |
| T08.- | Drainage Pleural Cavity Open |
| T12.4 | Drainage Pleural Cavity Tube Insertion |
| P31.2 | Drainage Pouch Douglas |
| M67.3 | Drainage Prostate Endoscopic |
| | |
| | Drainage Removal – see also Removal from site |
| E27.2 | Drainage Retropharyngeal Abscess |
| C55.1 | Drainage Sclera Lesion |
| N03.2 | Drainage Scrotum |
| S47.- | Drainage Skin Lesion |
| N20.3 | Drainage Spermatic Cord |
| E15.1 | Drainage Sphenoid Sinus |
| A53.- | Drainage Spinal Canal |
| S47.- | Drainage Subcutaneous Tissue Lesion |
| T34.1 | Drainage Subphrenic Abscess Open |
| | |
| T45.1 | Drainage Subphrenic Abscess Percutaneous Image Controlled |
| C84.5 | Drainage Subretinal Fluid Through Retina |
| C55.3 | Drainage Subretinal Fluid Through Sclera |
| N13.1 | Drainage Testis |
| F16.1 | Drainage Tooth Alveolus Abscess |
| M28.- | Drainage Ureter Calculus Endoscopic |
| P09.2 | Drainage Vulva Lesion |
| S54.- | Dressing Skin Burnt Head |
| S55.- | Dressing Skin Burnt NEC |
| S54.- | Dressing Skin Burnt Neck |

| | |
|---|---|
| S56.- | Dressing Skin Head NEC |
| S57.- | Dressing Skin NEC |
| S56.- | Dressing Skin Neck NEC |
| S54.- | Dressing Subcutaneous Tissue Burnt Head |
| S55.- | Dressing Subcutaneous Tissue Burnt NEC |
| S54.- | Dressing Subcutaneous Tissue Burnt Neck |
| S56.- | Dressing Subcutaneous Tissue Head NEC |
| S57.- | Dressing Subcutaneous Tissue NEC |
| S56.- | Dressing Subcutaneous Tissue Neck NEC |
| W36.3 | Drilling Bone Diagnostic |
| | |
| W35.4 | Drilling Bone Therapeutic NEC |
| W71.1 | Drilling Cartilage Articular |
| W83.1 | Drilling Cartilage Articular Lesion Endoscopic |
| W84.5 | Drilling Epiphysis Cartilage Articular Repair Endoscopic |
| Y33.2 | Drilling NOC |
| Q49.4 | Drilling Ovary Endoscopic |
| L03.- | Ductus Arteriosus Patent Operations Transluminal |
| G49.- | Duodenectomy |
| G51.4 | Duodeno-colostomy |
| G51.2 | Duodeno-duodenostomy |
| | |
| G51.3 | Duodeno-jejunostomy |
| G55.- | Duodenoscopy |
| G53.5 | Duodenotomy NEC |
| G54.- | Duodenum Operations Endoscopic Therapeutic NEC |
| G57.- | Duodenum Operations NEC |
| G53.- | Duodenum Operations Open NEC |
| Z27.4 | Duodenum site |
| G52.- | Duodenum Ulcer Operations |
| Q41.3 | Dye Test Fallopian Tube |

# E

| | |
|---|---|
| D06.- | Ear External Operations NEC |
| D03.- | Ear External Operations Plastic |
| Z20.1 | Ear External site |
| D06.- | Ear External Skin Operations NEC |
| D03.- | Ear External Skin Operations Plastic |
| Z20.1 | Ear External Skin site |
| D23.- | Ear Inner Operations NEC |
| Z21.6 | Ear Inner site |
| D20.- | Ear Middle Operations NEC |
| Z21.2 | Ear Middle site |
| | |
| D28.- | Ear Operations NEC |
| D17.- | Ear Ossicle Operations NEC |
| Z21.1 | Ear Ossicle site |
| Z20.- | Ear Outer site |
| Z21.- | Ear site NEC |
| Z20.4 | Eardrum site |
| Y70.- | Early Operations NOC |
| U20.- | Echocardiography Diagnostic |
| U20.3 | Echocardiography Intravascular |
| K58.5 | Echocardiography Transluminal |
| | |
| U20.2 | Echocardiography Transoesophageal |
| U20.1 | Echocardiography Transthoracic |
| E97.1 | Education Inhaler |
| E97.1 | Education Nebuliser |
| E97.2 | Education Peak Flow Technique |
| E97.- | Education Respiratory |
| E97.3 | Education Respiratory Health Self-management |
| E97.1 | Education Therapy Inhaled |
| U36.4 | Elastography Ultrasound |
| A70.5 | Electroacupuncture |
| | |
| U19.- | Electrocardiography Diagnostic |
| D24.5 | Electrocochleography Transtympanic |
| A83.- | Electroconvulsive Therapy |
| S10.5 | Electrodessication Skin Lesion Head |
| S11.5 | Electrodessication Skin Lesion NEC |
| S10.5 | Electrodessication Skin Lesion Neck |
| A11.1 | Electroencephalography Depth Electrodes Placement |
| A84.1 | Electroencephalography NEC |
| A11.2 | Electroencephalography Surface Electrodes Placement |
| | Electrofulguration – see Cauterisation |

|           |                                                                                              |
|-----------|----------------------------------------------------------------------------------------------|
|           | Electrolysis – see also Epilation                                                            |
| S60.6     | Electrolysis Hair                                                                            |
| S60.6     | Electrolysis NEC                                                                             |
| S10.4     | Electrolysis Skin Lesion Head                                                                |
| S11.4     | Electrolysis Skin Lesion NEC                                                                 |
| S10.4     | Electrolysis Skin Lesion Neck                                                                |
| A84.2     | Electromyography                                                                             |
| A84.-     | Electroretinography                                                                          |
| V05.3     | Elevation Cranium Fracture Depressed                                                         |
| L25.3     | Embolectomy Aorta Bifurcation NEC                                                            |
|           |                                                                                              |
| L26.3     | Embolectomy Aorta Bifurcation Transluminal Percutaneous                                      |
| L38.3     | Embolectomy Artery Axillary NEC                                                              |
| L39.2     | Embolectomy Artery Axillary Transluminal Percutaneous                                        |
| L38.3     | Embolectomy Artery Brachial NEC                                                              |
| L39.2     | Embolectomy Artery Brachial Transluminal Percutaneous                                        |
| L30.3     | Embolectomy Artery Carotid NEC                                                               |
| L34.3     | Embolectomy Artery Cerebral NEC                                                              |
| L34.3     | Embolectomy Artery Circle Willis NEC                                                         |
| L46.1     | Embolectomy Artery Coeliac NEC                                                               |
| L62.2     | Embolectomy Artery Femoral NEC                                                               |
|           |                                                                                              |
| L63.2     | Embolectomy Artery Femoral Transluminal Percutaneous                                         |
| L53.2     | Embolectomy Artery Iliac NEC                                                                 |
| L54.2     | Embolectomy Artery Iliac Transluminal Percutaneous                                           |
| L46.1     | Embolectomy Artery Mesenteric NEC                                                            |
| L70.1     | Embolectomy Artery NEC                                                                       |
| L62.2     | Embolectomy Artery Popliteal NEC                                                             |
| L63.2     | Embolectomy Artery Popliteal Transluminal Percutaneous                                       |
| L12.4     | Embolectomy Artery Pulmonary NEC                                                             |
| L13.1     | Embolectomy Artery Pulmonary Transluminal Percutaneous                                       |
| L42.1     | Embolectomy Artery Renal NEC                                                                 |
|           |                                                                                              |
| L43.2     | Embolectomy Artery Renal Transluminal Percutaneous                                           |
| L38.3     | Embolectomy Artery Subclavian NEC                                                            |
| L39.2     | Embolectomy Artery Subclavian Transluminal Percutaneous                                      |
| L46.1     | Embolectomy Artery Suprarenal NEC                                                            |
| L71.2     | Embolectomy Artery Transluminal Percutaneous                                                 |
| L38.3     | Embolectomy Artery Vertebral NEC                                                             |
| L39.2     | Embolectomy Artery Vertebral Transluminal Percutaneous                                       |
| B25.3     | Embolisation Adrenal                                                                         |
| L75.-     | Embolisation Arteriovenous Abnormality                                                       |
| O05.-     | Embolisation Arteriovenous Dural Fistula Transluminal Percutaneous (L)                       |
|           |                                                                                              |
| O02.-     | Embolisation Artery Aneurysmal Coil Balloon Assisted Transluminal Percutaneous (L)           |
| O03.-     | Embolisation Artery Aneurysmal Coil Stent Assisted Transluminal Percutaneous (L)             |
| O01.-     | Embolisation Artery Aneurysmal Coil Transluminal Percutaneous NEC (L)                        |
| O04.-     | Embolisation Artery Aneurysmal Transluminal Percutaneous NEC (L)                             |
| L39.3     | Embolisation Artery Axillary NEC                                                             |
| L38.8     | Embolisation Artery Axillary Open                                                            |
| L39.3     | Embolisation Artery Brachial NEC                                                             |
| L38.8     | Embolisation Artery Brachial Open                                                            |
| L35.1     | Embolisation Artery Cerebral NEC                                                             |
| L34.4     | Embolisation Artery Cerebral Open                                                            |

| | |
|---|---|
| L35.1 | Embolisation Artery Circle Willis NEC |
| L34.4 | Embolisation Artery Circle Willis Open |
| L47.2 | Embolisation Artery Coeliac NEC |
| L46.2 | Embolisation Artery Coeliac Open |
| L69.3 | Embolisation Artery Collateral Systemic to Pulmonary Transluminal Percutaneous |
| L63.3 | Embolisation Artery Femoral NEC |
| L62.8 | Embolisation Artery Femoral Open |
| J10.1 | Embolisation Artery Hepatic Transluminal Percutaneous |
| L47.2 | Embolisation Artery Mesenteric NEC |
| L46.2 | Embolisation Artery Mesenteric Open |
| | |
| L71.3 | Embolisation Artery NEC |
| E05.3 | Embolisation Artery Nose Internal |
| L70.2 | Embolisation Artery Open NEC |
| L63.3 | Embolisation Artery Popliteal NEC |
| L62.8 | Embolisation Artery Popliteal Open |
| L13.2 | Embolisation Artery Pulmonary NEC |
| L12.5 | Embolisation Artery Pulmonary Open |
| L43.3 | Embolisation Artery Renal NEC |
| L42.2 | Embolisation Artery Renal Open |
| J72.2 | Embolisation Artery Splenic |
| | |
| L39.3 | Embolisation Artery Subclavian NEC |
| L38.8 | Embolisation Artery Subclavian Open |
| L47.2 | Embolisation Artery Suprarenal NEC |
| L46.2 | Embolisation Artery Suprarenal Open |
| L71.3 | Embolisation Artery Transluminal Percutaneous |
| L39.3 | Embolisation Artery Vertebral NEC |
| L38.8 | Embolisation Artery Vertebral Open |
| E05.3 | Embolisation Nose Internal Artery |
| J72.2 | Embolisation Spleen |
| N19.2 | Embolisation Varicocele |
| | |
| L94.1 | Embolisation Vein NEC |
| J10.2 | Embolisation Vein Portal Transluminal Percutaneous |
| Y70.1 | Emergency Operations NOC |
| | Encirclement – see Cerclage |
| | Encirclement – see Wiring |
| L25.- | Endarterectomy Aorta |
| L37.- | Endarterectomy Artery Axillary |
| L37.- | Endarterectomy Artery Brachial |
| L29.- | Endarterectomy Artery Carotid |
| L45.- | Endarterectomy Artery Coeliac |
| | |
| K47.1 | Endarterectomy Artery Coronary |
| L60.- | Endarterectomy Artery Femoral |
| L52.- | Endarterectomy Artery Iliac |
| L45.- | Endarterectomy Artery Mesenteric |
| L68.- | Endarterectomy Artery NEC |
| L60.- | Endarterectomy Artery Popliteal |
| L41.4 | Endarterectomy Artery Renal |
| L37.- | Endarterectomy Artery Subclavian |
| L45.- | Endarterectomy Artery Suprarenal |
| L37.- | Endarterectomy Artery Vertebral |

| | |
|---|---|
| Z13.- | Endocrine Gland Neck site |
| Z14.- | Endocrine Gland site NEC |
| U29.- | Endocrinology Diagnostic |
| D26.1 | Endolymphatic Sac Operations |
| | Endoscopic – refer to Index Introduction |
| | Endoscopic – see Operation site |
| G80.2 | Endoscopy Capsule |
| G80.2 | Endoscopy Wireless Capsule |
| M36.- | Enlargement Bladder |
| C29.2 | Enlargement Lacrimal Punctum |
| | |
| C05.3 | Enlargement Orbit Cavity |
| K15.1 | Enlargement Septum Atrial Defect Closed |
| K14.1 | Enlargement Septum Atrial Defect Open |
| K14.5 | Enlargement Septum Ventricular Defect Open |
| H19.3 | Enterorrhaphy Caecum |
| H19.3 | Enterorrhaphy Colon |
| G80.- | Enteroscopy NEC |
| C01.2 | Enucleation Eye |
| C01.2 | Enucleation Eyeball |
| F18.1 | Enucleation Jaw Cyst Dental |
| | |
| Y06.3 | Enucleation Lesion NOC |
| A60.1 | Enucleation Nerve Peripheral |
| N15.- | Epididymectomy |
| N15.- | Epididymis Operations |
| Z43.3 | Epididymis site |
| N15.7 | Epididymovasostomy |
| Y81.- | Epidural Injection Anaesthetic |
| A52.- | Epidural Injection Therapeutic |
| A52.3 | Epidural Patch Blood |
| C22.6 | Epilation Eyelash |
| | |
| S60.7 | Epilation NEC |
| V42.2 | Epiphysiodesis Joint Spinal Apophyseal |
| W27.- | Epiphysiodesis NEC |
| V42.4 | Epiphysiodesis Spine Anterior & Posterior |
| V42.5 | Epiphysiodesis Spine Anterior NEC |
| V42.6 | Epiphysiodesis Spine Posterior NEC |
| W27.2 | Epiphysioplasty |
| R27.1 | Episiotomy Delivery |
| P14.- | Episiotomy Nondelivery |
| S54.2 | Escharotomy Skin Burnt Head |
| | |
| S55.2 | Escharotomy Skin Burnt NEC |
| S54.2 | Escharotomy Skin Burnt Neck |
| S56.2 | Escharotomy Skin Head NEC |
| S57.2 | Escharotomy Skin NEC |
| S56.2 | Escharotomy Skin Neck NEC |
| S54.2 | Escharotomy Subcutaneous Tissue Burnt Head |
| S55.2 | Escharotomy Subcutaneous Tissue Burnt NEC |
| S54.2 | Escharotomy Subcutaneous Tissue Burnt Neck |
| S56.2 | Escharotomy Subcutaneous Tissue Head NEC |
| S57.2 | Escharotomy Subcutaneous Tissue NEC |

| | |
|---|---|
| S56.2 | Escharotomy Subcutaneous Tissue Neck NEC |
| E85.2 | Establishing Pressure Airway Continuous Positive |
| E85.2 | Establishing Pressure Chest-wall Continuous Negative |
| E14.- | Ethmoid Operations |
| E14.- | Ethmoid Sinus Operations |
| Z23.3 | Ethmoid Sinus site |
| E14.- | Ethmoidectomy NEC |
| D22.- | Eustachian Canal Operations |
| Z21.3 | Eustachian Canal site |
| | Evacuation – see also Aspiration |
| | |
| | Evacuation – see also Drainage |
| Y44.1 | Evacuation Contents NOC |
| A40.1 | Evacuation Extradural Haematoma |
| H53.1 | Evacuation Haemorrhoid Thrombosed |
| H53.1 | Evacuation Perianal Haematoma |
| H44.3 | Evacuation Rectum Faeces Impacted Manual |
| T96.4 | Evacuation Soft Tissue Seroma |
| A41.1 | Evacuation Subdural Haematoma |
| Q11.- | Evacuation Uterus Contents NEC |
| Q11.- | Evacuation Uterus Products Conception |
| | |
| P27.1 | Evacuation Vagina Haematoma |
| P09.3 | Evacuation Vulva Haematoma |
| C87.- | Evaluation Retina |
| C87.1 | Evaluation Retina Electrodiagnostic |
| C87.2 | Evaluation Retina Indocyanine Angiography |
| C87.5 | Evaluation Retina Scanning Laser Ophthalmoscopy |
| C87.3 | Evaluation Retina Tomography |
| C87.4 | Evaluation Retina Ultrasound |
| N11.3 | Eversion Hydrocele Sac |
| B35.6 | Eversion Nipple |
| | |
| C01.3 | Evisceration Eye |
| C01.3 | Evisceration Eyeball Contents |
| A84.4 | Evoked Potential Recording |
| Y41.- | Examination Anaesthetic NOC |
| J43.- | Examination Bile Duct & Pancreatic Duct Endoscopic Retrograde |
| J44.- | Examination Bile Duct Endoscopic Retrograde |
| J53.- | Examination Bile Duct Endoscopic Ultrasonic |
| J51.- | Examination Bile Duct Laparoscopic Ultrasound |
| J50.- | Examination Bile Duct Percutaneous |
| J50.6 | Examination Bile Duct Percutaneous Transjejunal NEC |
| | |
| M45.- | Examination Bladder Endoscopic |
| H25.- | Examination Bowel Lower Sigmoidoscope Fibreoptic |
| A18.- | Examination Brain Ventricle Endoscopic Diagnostic |
| E49.- | Examination Bronchus Endoscopic NEC |
| E51.- | Examination Bronchus Endoscopic Rigid |
| H22.- | Examination Caecum Endoscopic Fibreoptic |
| H22.- | Examination Caecum Endoscopic NEC |
| U17.6 | Examination Capsule Patency |
| E49.- | Examination Carina Endoscopic NEC |
| E51.- | Examination Carina Endoscopic Rigid |

| Q55.- | Examination Cervix Uteri NEC |
| H22.- | Examination Colon Endoscopic Fibreoptic NEC |
| H22.- | Examination Colon Endoscopic NEC |
| H25.- | Examination Colon Sigmoid Endoscopic NEC |
| H25.- | Examination Colon Sigmoid Sigmoidoscope Fibreoptic |
| H28.- | Examination Colon Sigmoid Sigmoidoscope Rigid |
| H25.- | Examination Colon Sigmoidoscope Fibreoptic |
| H68.2 | Examination Colonic Pouch Colonoscope |
| H69.2 | Examination Colonic Pouch Sigmoidoscope Flexible |
| H70.2 | Examination Colonic Pouch Sigmoidoscope Rigid |
| | |
| G55.- | Examination Duodenum Endoscopic NEC |
| D28.2 | Examination Ear Anaesthetic |
| C86.6 | Examination Eye Anaesthetic |
| Q39.- | Examination Fallopian Tube Endoscopic |
| R02.- | Examination Fetus Endoscopic |
| R05.- | Examination Fetus Percutaneous |
| J09.- | Examination Gall Bladder Endoscopic |
| G45.- | Examination Gastrointestinal Tract Upper Endoscopic Fibreoptic |
| G45.- | Examination Gastrointestinal Tract Upper Endoscopic NEC |
| G45.2 | Examination Gastrointestinal Tract Upper Ultrasound Endoscopic |
| | |
| Q55.- | Examination Genital Tract Female Anaesthetic |
| Q55.- | Examination Genital Tract Female NEC |
| Q55.5 | Examination Genital Tract Female Ultrasound Transvaginal |
| Q55.- | Examination Gynaecological Anaesthetic |
| H68.4 | Examination Ileoanal Pouch Colonoscope |
| H69.4 | Examination Ileoanal Pouch Sigmoidoscope Flexible |
| H70.4 | Examination Ileoanal Pouch Sigmoidoscope Rigid |
| G80.- | Examination Ileum Endoscopic |
| G80.3 | Examination Ileum Endoscopic Balloon Diagnostic |
| G80.- | Examination Intestine Small Endoscopic NEC |
| | |
| G65.- | Examination Jejunum Endoscopic |
| W88.- | Examination Joint Endoscopic NEC |
| W87.- | Examination Joint Knee Endoscopic |
| W92.- | Examination Joint NEC |
| M11.- | Examination Kidney Endoscopic |
| M11.3 | Examination Kidney Endoscopic Retrograde NEC |
| M17.5 | Examination Kidney Post-transplantation Live Donor |
| M17.4 | Examination Kidney Post-transplantation Recipient |
| E36.- | Examination Larynx Endoscopic |
| E37.- | Examination Larynx Microendoscopic Diagnostic |
| | |
| J09.- | Examination Liver Endoscopic NEC |
| J17.- | Examination Liver Endoscopic Ultrasonic |
| J09.- | Examination Liver Laparoscopic Ultrasonic |
| E49.- | Examination Lung Endoscopic NEC |
| E51.- | Examination Lung Endoscopic Rigid |
| E63.- | Examination Mediastinum Endoscopic |
| E63.3 | Examination Mediastinum Ultrasound Endo-oesophageal |
| E63.2 | Examination Mediastinum Ultrasound Endobronchial |
| F43.- | Examination Mouth Other |
| E27.6 | Examination Nasopharynx Anaesthetic |

| | |
|---|---|
| E25.- | Examination Nasopharynx Endoscopic |
| Y41.- | Examination NOC |
| G16.- | Examination Oesophagus Endoscopic Fibreoptic NEC |
| G16.- | Examination Oesophagus Endoscopic NEC |
| G16.2 | Examination Oesophagus Ultrasound Endoscopic Fibreoptic |
| Q50.- | Examination Ovary Endoscopic |
| J74.- | Examination Pancreas Endoscopic Ultrasonic |
| J73.- | Examination Pancreas Laparoscopic Ultrasonic |
| J63.- | Examination Pancreas Open |
| J43.- | Examination Pancreatic Duct & Bile Duct Endoscopic Retrograde |
| | |
| J45.- | Examination Pancreatic Duct Endoscopic Retrograde |
| T43.- | Examination Peritoneal Cavity Endoscopic |
| T43.- | Examination Peritoneal Cavity Endoscopic Ultrasonic |
| T43.- | Examination Peritoneum Endoscopic |
| E27.6 | Examination Pharynx Anaesthetic |
| E25.- | Examination Pharynx Endoscopic |
| R05.- | Examination Placenta Percutaneous |
| T11.- | Examination Pleura Endoscopic |
| T11.- | Examination Pleural Cavity Endoscopic |
| H68.- | Examination Pouch Colonoscope |
| | |
| H69.- | Examination Pouch Sigmoidoscope Flexible |
| H70.- | Examination Pouch Sigmoidoscope Rigid |
| G45.- | Examination Pylorus Endoscopic Fibreoptic |
| G45.- | Examination Pylorus Endoscopic NEC |
| H44.4 | Examination Rectum Anaesthetic |
| H25.- | Examination Rectum Endoscopic NEC |
| H25.- | Examination Rectum Sigmoidoscope Fibreoptic |
| H28.- | Examination Rectum Sigmoidoscope Rigid |
| E49.- | Examination Respiratory Tract Lower Endoscopic NEC |
| E51.- | Examination Respiratory Tract Lower Endoscopic Rigid |
| | |
| G45.- | Examination Stomach Endoscopic Fibreoptic |
| G45.- | Examination Stomach Endoscopic NEC |
| G19.- | Examination Stomach Gastroscope Rigid |
| E49.- | Examination Trachea Endoscopic NEC |
| E51.- | Examination Trachea Endoscopic Rigid |
| | Examination Ultrasound Endoscopic – see Examination site |
| | Examination Under Anaesthetic – see Examination site |
| M30.5 | Examination Ureter & Biopsy Endoscopic NEC |
| M30.6 | Examination Ureter & Biopsy Ureteroscope Rigid |
| M30.- | Examination Ureter Endoscopic |
| | |
| M77.- | Examination Urethra Endoscopic |
| M85.- | Examination Urinary Diversion Endoscopic |
| Q18.- | Examination Uterus Endoscopic |
| Q55.- | Examination Uterus NEC |
| Q55.- | Examination Vagina NEC |
| Q55.5 | Examination Vagina Ultrasound |
| U11.- | Examination Vascular Ultrasound |
| | Exchange Fluid – see Transfusion |
| | Excision – see also Extirpation |
| | Excision – see also Resection |

| | |
|---|---|
| T31.- | Excision Abdominal Wall Anterior Lesion |
| T31.- | Excision Abdominal Wall Lesion NEC |
| T39.1 | Excision Abdominal Wall Posterior Lesion |
| E20.1 | Excision Adenoid |
| B22.- | Excision Adrenal |
| B25.1 | Excision Adrenal Lesion |
| B23.1 | Excision Adrenal Tissue Aberrant Lesion |
| J36.1 | Excision Ampulla Vater |
| J27.1 | Excision Ampulla Vater & Replantation Bile Duct Common |
| X12.2 | Excision Amputation Stump Lesion |
| | |
| H56.4 | Excision Anal Fissure |
| | Excision Aneurysm – see Operation site Aneurysmal |
| H47.- | Excision Anus |
| H48.- | Excision Anus Lesion |
| H01.- | Excision Appendix Emergency |
| H02.- | Excision Appendix NEC |
| S03.3 | Excision Arm Fat Redundant |
| L75.1 | Excision Arteriovenous Malformation Congenital |
| L33.1 | Excision Artery Cerebral Aneurysmal |
| L33.1 | Excision Artery Circle Willis Aneurysmal |
| | |
| L67.- | Excision Artery NEC |
| | Excision Arthroplasty – see Arthroplasty site |
| K22.1 | Excision Atrium Lesion |
| D08.1 | Excision Auditory Canal External Lesion |
| V54.1 | Excision Axis Odontoid Process Transoral |
| P03.- | Excision Bartholin Gland |
| J27.- | Excision Bile Duct |
| J27.5 | Excision Bile Duct Extrahepatic |
| J28.1 | Excision Bile Duct Lesion |
| J27.5 | Excision Biliary Tree Extrahepatic |
| | |
| | Excision Biopsy Lesion – see Excision Lesion |
| M41.1 | Excision Bladder Lesion Open |
| M35.- | Excision Bladder Partial |
| M34.- | Excision Bladder Total |
| W08.3 | Excision Bone Calcium Deposit |
| W07.1 | Excision Bone Cross Union |
| W07.- | Excision Bone Ectopic |
| W08.3 | Excision Bone Excrescence |
| V07.- | Excision Bone Face |
| W06.5 | Excision Bone Foot Total NEC |
| | |
| W08.4 | Excision Bone Fragment |
| W21.2 | Excision Bone Fragment Intra-articular Fracture Primary |
| W09.- | Excision Bone Lesion |
| W03.1 | Excision Bone Metatarsal Lesser Multiple Head |
| W08.- | Excision Bone NEC |
| W08.2 | Excision Bone Overgrowth |
| W06.7 | Excision Bone Pelvis Total |
| W06.4 | Excision Bone Sesamoid Total NEC |
| W06.- | Excision Bone Total |
| W08.1 | Excision Bone Tuberosity |

| | |
|---|---|
| A38.- | Excision Brain Meninges Lesion |
| A02.6 | Excision Brain Stem Tissue Lesion |
| A07.4 | Excision Brain Tissue Abscess |
| A02.- | Excision Brain Tissue Lesion |
| A01.- | Excision Brain Tissue Major |
| T94.1 | Excision Branchial Cyst |
| B28.6 | Excision Breast Accessory Tissue |
| B28.3 | Excision Breast Lesion NEC |
| B28.7 | Excision Breast Lesion Wire Guided |
| B28.- | Excision Breast NEC |
| | |
| B28.- | Excision Breast Partial |
| B28.1 | Excision Breast Quadrant |
| B27.- | Excision Breast Total |
| B28.- | Excision Breast Wedge |
| B28.- | Excision Breast Wide |
| B28.- | Excision Breast Wire Guided |
| E46.- | Excision Bronchus Lesion |
| E46.- | Excision Bronchus Partial |
| W79.2 | Excision Bunion NEC |
| W79.2 | Excision Bunionette |
| | |
| T62.- | Excision Bursa |
| H06.- | Excision Caecum Extended |
| H12.- | Excision Caecum Lesion |
| H07.- | Excision Caecum NEC |
| C11.1 | Excision Canthus Lesion |
| E44.- | Excision Carina |
| W83.6 | Excision Cartilage Articular Endoscopic NEC |
| W82.- | Excision Cartilage Semilunar Endoscopic |
| W70.- | Excision Cartilage Semilunar NEC |
| Q01.- | Excision Cervix Uteri |
| | |
| T01.3 | Excision Chest Wall Lesion |
| T01.- | Excision Chest Wall Partial |
| C84.2 | Excision Choroid Lesion |
| C66.- | Excision Ciliary Body |
| W06.6 | Excision Coccyx Total |
| H29.- | Excision Colon & Rectum Subtotal |
| H04.- | Excision Colon & Rectum Total |
| H09.- | Excision Colon Left |
| H20.6 | Excision Colon Lesion Endoscopic Fibreoptic NEC |
| H12.- | Excision Colon Lesion NEC |
| | |
| H11.- | Excision Colon NEC |
| H06.- | Excision Colon Right Extended |
| H07.- | Excision Colon Right NEC |
| H10.- | Excision Colon Sigmoid NEC |
| H33.- | Excision Colon Sigmoid Part & Rectum |
| H29.- | Excision Colon Subtotal |
| H05.- | Excision Colon Total NEC |
| H08.- | Excision Colon Transverse NEC |
| C39.1 | Excision Conjunctiva Lesion |
| C45.2 | Excision Cornea Lesion NEC |

| | |
|---|---|
| V05.1 | Excision Cranium Lesion |
| T96.1 | Excision Cystic Hygroma |
| T17.1 | Excision Diaphragm Lesion |
| V58.- | Excision Disc Intervertebral Automated Mechanical Percutaneous NEC |
| V58.- | Excision Disc Intervertebral Automated Mechanical Percutaneous Primary |
| V59.- | Excision Disc Intervertebral Automated Mechanical Percutaneous Revisional |
| V29.- | Excision Disc Intervertebral Cervical NEC |
| V30.- | Excision Disc Intervertebral Cervical Revisional |
| V58.3 | Excision Disc Intervertebral Lumbar Automated Mechanical Percutaneous NEC |
| V59.3 | Excision Disc Intervertebral Lumbar Automated Mechanical Percutaneous Revisional |
| | |
| V33.- | Excision Disc Intervertebral Lumbar NEC |
| V34.- | Excision Disc Intervertebral Lumbar Revisional |
| V35.- | Excision Disc Intervertebral NEC |
| V35.2 | Excision Disc Intervertebral Revisional NEC |
| V31.- | Excision Disc Intervertebral Thoracic NEC |
| V32.- | Excision Disc Intervertebral Thoracic Revisional |
| G70.1 | Excision Diverticulum Meckel's |
| G49.- | Excision Duodenum |
| G50.1 | Excision Duodenum Lesion NEC |
| D01.- | Excision Ear External |
| | |
| D02.1 | Excision Ear External Lesion |
| D02.1 | Excision Ear External Skin Lesion |
| D19.1 | Excision Ear Middle Lesion |
| N15.3 | Excision Epididymis Hydatid Morgagni |
| N15.3 | Excision Epididymis Lesion |
| C01.- | Excision Eye |
| C37.1 | Excision Eye Muscle Lesion |
| C10.1 | Excision Eyebrow Lesion |
| C10.1 | Excision Eyebrow Skin Lesion |
| C12.1 | Excision Eyelid Lesion NEC |
| | |
| C12.6 | Excision Eyelid Lesion Wedge |
| C12.1 | Excision Eyelid Skin Lesion |
| C13.- | Excision Eyelid Skin Redundant |
| Q25.- | Excision Fallopian Tube Partial |
| A38.5 | Excision Falx Cerebri Lesion |
| T51.- | Excision Fascia Abdomen |
| T53.1 | Excision Fascia Lesion |
| T52.- | Excision Fascia NEC |
| T56.- | Excision Fascia Other NEC |
| T51.2 | Excision Fascia Pelvis |
| | |
| X23.3 | Excision Fibula Anlage |
| Q32.1 | Excision Fimbria |
| Q32.3 | Excision Fimbria Hydatid Morgagni |
| Y05.3 | Excision Fistula NOC |
| J23.1 | Excision Gall Bladder Lesion NEC |
| J18.- | Excision Gall Bladder NEC |
| T59.- | Excision Ganglion |
| F20.- | Excision Gingiva |
| F20.2 | Excision Gingiva Lesion |
| H51.- | Excision Haemorrhoid |

| | |
|---|---|
| K52.- | Excision Heart Rhythmogenic Focus |
| K36.- | Excision Heart Valve NEC |
| K34.4 | Excision Heart Valve Vegetations |
| K23.1 | Excision Heart Ventricle Lesion |
| K23.1 | Excision Heart Wall Lesion NEC |
| T19.- | Excision Hernial Sac Inguinal Simple |
| Q32.3 | Excision Hydatid Morgagni Female |
| N11.1 | Excision Hydrocele Sac |
| P15.2 | Excision Hymenal Tag |
| H66.1 | Excision Ileoanal Pouch |
| | |
| G69.- | Excision Ileum |
| G79.1 | Excision Ileum Lesion Endoscopic |
| G70.2 | Excision Ileum Lesion NEC |
| V07.4 | Excision Infratemporal Fossa Lesion |
| G79.1 | Excision Intestine Small Lesion Endoscopic NEC |
| G70.2 | Excision Intestine Small Lesion NEC |
| G69.- | Excision Intestine Small NEC |
| C59.- | Excision Iris |
| C64.2 | Excision Iris Lesion |
| C64.1 | Excision Iris Prolapsed |
| | |
| J58.1 | Excision Islet Langerhans Lesion |
| F18.- | Excision Jaw Lesion Dental |
| V14.- | Excision Jaw NEC |
| G58.- | Excision Jejunum |
| G59.1 | Excision Jejunum Lesion |
| G64.1 | Excision Jejunum Lesion Endoscopic |
| | Excision Joint – see Decompression |
| O19.2 | Excision Joint Knee Infrapatellar Fat Pad Endoscopic (W) |
| W81.1 | Excision Joint Lesion NEC |
| W71.2 | Excision Joint Osteophyte |
| | |
| M04.2 | Excision Kidney Lesion Open NEC |
| M02.- | Excision Kidney NEC |
| M03.- | Excision Kidney Partial |
| P05.5 | Excision Labial Tissue Excess |
| C24.1 | Excision Lacrimal Gland |
| C26.1 | Excision Lacrimal Sac |
| E29.- | Excision Larynx |
| E35.2 | Excision Larynx Lesion Endoscopic NEC |
| E30.- | Excision Larynx Lesion Open |
| Y08.- | Excision Laser NOC |
| | |
| L87.5 | Excision Leg Vein Varicose Local |
| | Excision Lesion – see also Excision site |
| | Excision Lesion – see also Excision site Partial |
| | Excision Lesion – see also Resection site |
| Y06.- | Excision Lesion NOC |
| W76.- | Excision Ligament |
| F02.1 | Excision Lip Lesion |
| F05.1 | Excision Lip Mucosa Excess |
| F02.1 | Excision Lip Mucosa Lesion |
| F01.- | Excision Lip Partial |

| | |
|---|---|
| F02.1 | Excision Lip Skin Lesion |
| F01.- | Excision Lip Skin Partial |
| F01.1 | Excision Lip Vermilion Border & Advancement Mucosa |
| J03.1 | Excision Liver Lesion |
| J03.5 | Excision Liver Lesion Multiple |
| J02.- | Excision Liver Partial |
| E55.2 | Excision Lung Lesion NEC |
| E54.- | Excision Lung NEC |
| T87.- | Excision Lymph Node NEC |
| T92.1 | Excision Lymphocele |
| | |
| T92.- | Excision Lymphoedematous Tissue |
| B34.- | Excision Mammary Duct |
| V14.- | Excision Mandible |
| D10.- | Excision Mastoid |
| V06.- | Excision Maxilla |
| E13.2 | Excision Maxillary Antrum Lesion |
| E62.1 | Excision Mediastinum Lesion Endoscopic |
| E61.1 | Excision Mediastinum Lesion Open |
| A43.1 | Excision Meninges Skull Base Lesion |
| A43.2 | Excision Meninges Skull Clivus Lesion |
| | |
| T38.1 | Excision Mesentery Colon Lesion |
| T37.1 | Excision Mesentery Intestine Small Lesion |
| W03.- | Excision Metatarsal Head Multiple |
| F38.- | Excision Mouth Lesion NEC |
| F42.3 | Excision Mouth Mucosa Excess NEC |
| T77.- | Excision Muscle |
| C37.1 | Excision Muscle Eye Lesion |
| S68.- | Excision Nail |
| S64.1 | Excision Nail Bed |
| E17.2 | Excision Nasal Sinus Lesion NEC |
| | |
| E17.1 | Excision Nasal Sinus NEC |
| E19.- | Excision Nasopharynx |
| E24.1 | Excision Nasopharynx Lesion Endoscopic |
| E23.1 | Excision Nasopharynx Lesion Open |
| | Excision Nerve – see also Avulsion Nerve |
| | Excision Nerve – see also Denervation |
| | Excision Nerve – see also Sacrifice Nerve |
| | Excision Nerve – see also Transection Nerve |
| A29.- | Excision Nerve Cranial Lesion |
| A59.- | Excision Nerve Peripheral |
| | |
| A61.1 | Excision Nerve Peripheral Lesion |
| A59.- | Excision Nerve Peripheral Sacrifice |
| A57.1 | Excision Nerve Root Spinal Lesion |
| A75.- | Excision Nerve Sympathetic |
| A27.- | Excision Nerve Vagus (x) NEC |
| B35.- | Excision Nipple |
| B35.- | Excision Nipple Skin |
| Y05.- | Excision NOC |
| E01.- | Excision Nose |
| E09.1 | Excision Nose External Lesion |

| | |
|---|---|
| E09.1 | Excision Nose External Skin Lesion |
| E08.2 | Excision Nose Internal Lesion NEC |
| E03.2 | Excision Nose Septum Lesion |
| E03.1 | Excision Nose Septum Submucous |
| E04.- | Excision Nose Turbinate |
| G01.- | Excision Oesophagus & Stomach |
| G07.- | Excision Oesophagus Fistula |
| G04.1 | Excision Oesophagus Lesion |
| G03.- | Excision Oesophagus NEC |
| G02.- | Excision Oesophagus Total |
| | |
| T36.2 | Excision Omentum Lesion |
| C13.- | Excision Orbit Fat |
| C02.1 | Excision Orbit Lesion |
| Y06.7 | Excision Organ Lesion Radiofrequency |
| Y06.6 | Excision Organ Lesion Vacuum |
| X53.- | Excision Organ Unspecified |
| W08.7 | Excision Ossicle Accessory |
| W71.2 | Excision Osteophyte Intra-articular |
| Q43.2 | Excision Ovary Lesion |
| Q49.1 | Excision Ovary Lesion Endoscopic |
| | |
| Q43.- | Excision Ovary Partial |
| Q43.1 | Excision Ovary Wedge |
| X15.3 | Excision Ovotestis |
| F28.1 | Excision Palate Lesion |
| J56.- | Excision Pancreas Head |
| J58.2 | Excision Pancreas Lesion NEC |
| J57.- | Excision Pancreas Partial NEC |
| J57.- | Excision Pancreas Tail |
| J55.- | Excision Pancreas Total |
| J55.3 | Excision Pancreas Transplanted |
| | |
| J36.1 | Excision Papilla Vater |
| B14.- | Excision Parathyroid |
| W06.3 | Excision Patella Total |
| N27.1 | Excision Penis Lesion |
| N27.1 | Excision Penis Skin Lesion |
| H48.- | Excision Perianal Region Lesion |
| K67.- | Excision Pericardium |
| K67.1 | Excision Pericardium Lesion |
| P11.1 | Excision Perineum Female Lesion |
| P11.1 | Excision Perineum Skin Female Lesion |
| | |
| P13.7 | Excision Perineum Skin Sweat Gland Bearing Female |
| N24.1 | Excision Perineum Skin Sweat Gland Bearing Male |
| T33.1 | Excision Peritoneum Lesion Open |
| T39.1 | Excision Peritoneum Posterior Lesion |
| N24.3 | Excision Periurethral Tissue Male NEC |
| Q07.- | Excision Periuterine Tissue & Hysterectomy Abdominal NEC |
| Q08.- | Excision Periuterine Tissue & Hysterectomy Vaginal NEC |
| E19.- | Excision Pharynx |
| E24.2 | Excision Pharynx Lesion Endoscopic |
| E23.1 | Excision Pharynx Lesion Open |

| | |
|---|---|
| H59.- | Excision Pilonidal Sinus |
| B06.1 | Excision Pineal |
| B01.- | Excision Pituitary |
| B04.1 | Excision Pituitary Lesion |
| T10.1 | Excision Pleura Lesion Endoscopic |
| T07.- | Excision Pleura Open |
| D01.3 | Excision Preauricular Abnormality |
| M61.1 | Excision Prostate & Capsule Total |
| M62.1 | Excision Prostate Lesion Open |
| M61.- | Excision Prostate Open |
| | |
| X20.1 | Excision Radius Anlage |
| H33.- | Excision Rectum |
| H33.- | Excision Rectum & Colon Sigmoid Part |
| H29.- | Excision Rectum & Colon Subtotal |
| H04.- | Excision Rectum & Colon Total |
| H33.1 | Excision Rectum Abdominoperineal & Colostomy End |
| H34.1 | Excision Rectum Lesion Open |
| H41.2 | Excision Rectum Lesion Peranal |
| H40.2 | Excision Rectum Lesion Trans-sphincteric |
| H40.1 | Excision Rectum Mucosa Trans-sphincteric |
| | |
| H42.5 | Excision Rectum Prolapse Mucosal NEC |
| C84.2 | Excision Retina Lesion |
| T08.1 | Excision Rib & Drainage Pleural Cavity Open |
| V42.1 | Excision Rib Hump |
| W06.- | Excision Rib Total |
| F44.- | Excision Salivary Gland |
| F45.- | Excision Salivary Gland Lesion |
| | Excision Scar – see Excision Skin Lesion |
| Y06.4 | Excision Scar Tissue NOC |
| C52.- | Excision Sclera |
| | |
| C53.2 | Excision Sclera Lesion NEC |
| N01.- | Excision Scrotum |
| N01.- | Excision Scrotum Skin |
| N22.1 | Excision Seminal Vesicle |
| Y05.3 | Excision Sinus Track NOC |
| S02.- | Excision Skin Abdominal Wall Plastic |
| S54.2 | Excision Skin Burnt Head |
| S55.2 | Excision Skin Burnt NEC |
| S54.2 | Excision Skin Burnt Neck |
| S56.1 | Excision Skin Devitalised Head NEC |
| | |
| S57.1 | Excision Skin Devitalised NEC |
| S56.1 | Excision Skin Devitalised Neck NEC |
| S01.- | Excision Skin Head Plastic |
| S05.- | Excision Skin Lesion Microscopically Controlled |
| S06.- | Excision Skin Lesion NEC |
| S04.- | Excision Skin NEC |
| S01.- | Excision Skin Neck Plastic |
| S03.- | Excision Skin Plastic NEC |
| S03.3 | Excision Skin Redundant Arm |
| S04.- | Excision Skin Sweat Gland Bearing |

| | |
|---|---|
| T96.2 | Excision Soft Tissue Lesion NEC |
| N20.1 | Excision Spermatic Cord Hydatid Morgagni |
| N20.1 | Excision Spermatic Cord Lesion |
| J36.1 | Excision Sphincter Oddi |
| A44.4 | Excision Spinal Cord Extradural Lesion |
| A44.5 | Excision Spinal Cord Intradural Extramedullary Lesion |
| A44.3 | Excision Spinal Cord Intradural Intramedullary Lesion |
| A44.2 | Excision Spinal Cord Lesion NEC |
| A51.1 | Excision Spinal Cord Meninges Lesion |
| A44.- | Excision Spinal Cord Partial |
| | |
| V43.- | Excision Spine Lesion |
| J69.3 | Excision Spleen Accessory |
| J70.- | Excision Spleen NEC |
| J69.- | Excision Spleen Total |
| J69.1 | Excision Spleen Total & Replantation Spleen Fragments |
| G01.- | Excision Stomach & Oesophagus |
| G29.- | Excision Stomach Lesion Open |
| G28.- | Excision Stomach Partial |
| G28.5 | Excision Stomach Partial Sleeve |
| G28.4 | Excision Stomach Partial Sleeve & Duodenal Switch |
| | |
| G28.- | Excision Stomach Sleeve |
| G27.- | Excision Stomach Total |
| S02.- | Excision Subcutaneous Tissue Abdominal Wall Plastic |
| S54.2 | Excision Subcutaneous Tissue Burnt Head |
| S55.2 | Excision Subcutaneous Tissue Burnt NEC |
| S54.2 | Excision Subcutaneous Tissue Burnt Neck |
| S56.1 | Excision Subcutaneous Tissue Devitalised Head NEC |
| S57.1 | Excision Subcutaneous Tissue Devitalised NEC |
| S56.1 | Excision Subcutaneous Tissue Devitalised Neck NEC |
| S01.- | Excision Subcutaneous Tissue Head Plastic |
| | |
| S05.- | Excision Subcutaneous Tissue Lesion Microscopically Controlled |
| S06.- | Excision Subcutaneous Tissue Lesion NEC |
| S01.- | Excision Subcutaneous Tissue Neck Plastic |
| S03.- | Excision Subcutaneous Tissue Plastic NEC |
| K37.5 | Excision Supramitral Ring |
| W84.6 | Excision Synovial Plica Endoscopic |
| T65.2 | Excision Tendon Lesion |
| T65.- | Excision Tendon NEC |
| T65.1 | Excision Tendon Sacrifice |
| T71.- | Excision Tendon Sheath |
| | |
| A38.6 | Excision Tentorium Cerebelli Lesion |
| N06.4 | Excision Testicular Appendage |
| N06.2 | Excision Testis Aberrant |
| N05.- | Excision Testis Bilateral |
| N07.1 | Excision Testis Hydatid Morgagni |
| N07.1 | Excision Testis Lesion |
| N06.- | Excision Testis NEC |
| B18.- | Excision Thymus |
| B10.1 | Excision Thyroglossal Cyst |
| B10.2 | Excision Thyroglossal Tract |

| | |
|---|---|
| B08.- | Excision Thyroid |
| B12.1 | Excision Thyroid Lesion |
| B09.2 | Excision Thyroid Tissue Sublingual |
| B09.1 | Excision Thyroid Tissue Substernal |
| X23.4 | Excision Tibia Anlage |
| F22.- | Excision Tongue |
| F26.2 | Excision Tongue Frenulum |
| F23.1 | Excision Tongue Lesion |
| F34.- | Excision Tonsil |
| E39.1 | Excision Trachea Lesion NEC |
| | |
| E39.- | Excision Trachea Partial |
| Q01.4 | Excision Transformation Zone Large Loop |
| V05.6 | Excision Transpetrous Lesion Jugular Foramen |
| X20.2 | Excision Ulna Anlage |
| T29.1 | Excision Umbilicus |
| T29.5 | Excision Umbilicus Fistula |
| T29.3 | Excision Umbilicus Lesion |
| T29.5 | Excision Umbilicus Sinus |
| T29.2 | Excision Urachus |
| M18.- | Excision Ureter |
| | |
| M18.4 | Excision Ureter Duplex |
| M25.2 | Excision Ureter Lesion Open |
| M32.1 | Excision Ureteric Orifice Lesion Endoscopic |
| M25.1 | Excision Ureterocele |
| M72.- | Excision Urethra |
| M76.1 | Excision Urethra Lesion Endoscopic |
| M81.1 | Excision Urethra Meatus Lesion |
| Q07.- | Excision Uterus Abdominal |
| Q07.6 | Excision Uterus Accessory |
| Q22.- | Excision Uterus Adnexa Bilateral |
| | |
| Q24.- | Excision Uterus Adnexa NEC |
| Q23.- | Excision Uterus Adnexa Unilateral |
| Q09.3 | Excision Uterus Lesion NEC |
| Q16.1 | Excision Uterus Lesion Vaginal |
| Q52.1 | Excision Uterus Ligament Broad Lesion |
| Q07.4 | Excision Uterus NEC |
| Q08.- | Excision Uterus Vaginal |
| P17.- | Excision Vagina |
| P19.- | Excision Vagina Band |
| P20.1 | Excision Vagina Lesion |
| | |
| P19.- | Excision Vagina Septum |
| N17.- | Excision Vas Deferens |
| L93.6 | Excision Vein Lesion NEC |
| L93.1 | Excision Vein NEC |
| L79.7 | Excision Vena Cava Lesion |
| V43.- | Excision Vertebra Lesion |
| C79.- | Excision Vitreous Body |
| C79.1 | Excision Vitreous Body Anterior Approach |
| C79.2 | Excision Vitreous Body NEC |
| C79.2 | Excision Vitreous Body Pars Plana Approach |

| | |
|---|---|
| P05.- | Excision Vulva |
| P05.- | Excision Vulva Lesion |
| P05.- | Excision Vulva Skin |
| P06.- | Excision Vulva Skin Lesion |
| G78.5 | Exclusion Ileum Segment |
| G78.5 | Exclusion Intestine Small Segment NEC |
| D10.- | Exenteration Mastoid Air Cells |
| C01.1 | Exenteration Orbit |
| X14.- | Exenteration Pelvis |
| S49.- | Expander Skin Attention |
| | |
| S48.- | Expander Skin Insertion |
| C55.4 | Expansion Sclera |
| E89.2 | Expectoration Respiratory Tract Sputum Induced |
| C54.6 | Explant Sclera Removal |
| | Exploration – see also Examination |
| | Exploration – see also Operation site |
| | Exploration – see also Re-exploration |
| B25.4 | Exploration Adrenal |
| B23.2 | Exploration Adrenal Tissue Aberrant |
| K48.4 | Exploration Artery Coronary |
| | |
| J33.- | Exploration Bile Duct NEC |
| M41.5 | Exploration Bladder |
| A07.3 | Exploration Brain Tissue |
| B33.3 | Exploration Breast |
| T62.6 | Exploration Bursa |
| C43.5 | Exploration Conjunctiva |
| C51.3 | Exploration Cornea |
| D15.3 | Exploration Ear Middle |
| C22.5 | Exploration Eyelid |
| Q34.4 | Exploration Fallopian Tube |
| | |
| Y31.1 | Exploration Fistula NOC |
| J23.3 | Exploration Gall Bladder |
| T30.4 | Exploration Groin & Opening Abdomen |
| T31.7 | Exploration Groin NEC |
| K53.2 | Exploration Heart NEC |
| W81.5 | Exploration Joint NEC |
| M08.- | Exploration Kidney |
| J07.3 | Exploration Liver |
| B34.5 | Exploration Mammary Duct |
| D12.4 | Exploration Mastoid |
| | |
| E61.5 | Exploration Mediastinum |
| T83.4 | Exploration Muscle |
| A34.- | Exploration Nerve Cranial |
| A73.4 | Exploration Nerve Peripheral |
| Y31.- | Exploration NOC |
| C06.5 | Exploration Orbit |
| B16.3 | Exploration Parathyroid |
| K71.4 | Exploration Pericardium |
| B04.4 | Exploration Pituitary |
| M83.2 | Exploration Retropubic Space |

|          | Exploration Scar – see Exploration Skin |
|----------|------------------------------------------|
| N03.4    | Exploration Scrotum |
| Y31.1    | Exploration Sinus Track NOC |
| S54.-    | Exploration Skin Burnt Head |
| S55.-    | Exploration Skin Burnt NEC |
| S54.-    | Exploration Skin Burnt Neck |
| S56.-    | Exploration Skin Head NEC |
| S57.-    | Exploration Skin NEC |
| S56.-    | Exploration Skin Neck NEC |
| V49.-    | Exploration Spine |
|          | |
| S54.-    | Exploration Subcutaneous Tissue Burnt Head |
| S55.-    | Exploration Subcutaneous Tissue Burnt NEC |
| S54.-    | Exploration Subcutaneous Tissue Burnt Neck |
| S56.-    | Exploration Subcutaneous Tissue Head NEC |
| S57.-    | Exploration Subcutaneous Tissue NEC |
| S56.-    | Exploration Subcutaneous Tissue Neck NEC |
| T74.3    | Exploration Tendon NEC |
| T72.4    | Exploration Tendon Sheath |
| N13.5    | Exploration Testis |
| B20.2    | Exploration Thymus |
|          | |
| B12.4    | Exploration Thyroid |
| M25.5    | Exploration Ureter Open |
| R30.-    | Exploration Uterus Delivered |
| Q20.5    | Exploration Uterus NEC |
| P27.-    | Exploration Vagina |
| F14.5    | Exposure Tooth Surgical |
| R30.2    | Expression Placenta |
|          | Exteriorisation – see also Opening |
| H03.3    | Exteriorisation Appendix |
| H09.5    | Exteriorisation Bowel & Excision Colon Left |
|          | |
| H11.5    | Exteriorisation Bowel & Excision Colon NEC |
| H10.5    | Exteriorisation Bowel & Excision Colon Sigmoid NEC |
| H08.5    | Exteriorisation Bowel & Excision Colon Transverse NEC |
| H33.-    | Exteriorisation Bowel & Excision Rectum |
| H14.-    | Exteriorisation Caccum |
| H15.-    | Exteriorisation Colon NEC |
| Y16.1    | Exteriorisation NOC |
| G08.1    | Exteriorisation Oesophagus Pouch |
| E42.-    | Exteriorisation Trachea |
|          | Extirpation – see also Avulsion |
|          | |
|          | Extirpation – see also Destruction |
|          | Extirpation – see also Excision |
| D08.1    | Extirpation Auditory Canal External Lesion |
| J28.-    | Extirpation Bile Duct Lesion |
| M42.-    | Extirpation Bladder Lesion Endoscopic |
| M41.1    | Extirpation Bladder Lesion Open |
| W09.-    | Extirpation Bone Lesion |
| H23.-    | Extirpation Bowel Lower Lesion Sigmoidoscope Fibreoptic |
| A38.-    | Extirpation Brain Meninges Lesion |
| A17.1    | Extirpation Brain Ventricle Lesion Endoscopic |

| | |
|---|---|
| E46.- | Extirpation Bronchus Partial |
| H20.- | Extirpation Caecum Lesion Endoscopic Fibreoptic |
| H20.- | Extirpation Caecum Lesion Endoscopic NEC |
| H12.- | Extirpation Caecum Lesion NEC |
| C66.- | Extirpation Ciliary Body |
| H20.- | Extirpation Colon Lesion Endoscopic Fibreoptic |
| H20.- | Extirpation Colon Lesion Endoscopic NEC |
| H12.- | Extirpation Colon Lesion NEC |
| H23.- | Extirpation Colon Lesion Sigmoidoscope Fibreoptic |
| H23.- | Extirpation Colon Sigmoid Lesion Endoscopic NEC |
| | |
| H23.- | Extirpation Colon Sigmoid Lesion Sigmoidoscope Fibreoptic |
| H26.- | Extirpation Colon Sigmoid Lesion Sigmoidoscope Rigid |
| C39.- | Extirpation Conjunctiva Lesion |
| C45.- | Extirpation Cornea Lesion |
| V05.1 | Extirpation Cranium Lesion |
| G54.1 | Extirpation Duodenum Lesion Endoscopic NEC |
| G50.- | Extirpation Duodenum Lesion Open |
| G43.- | Extirpation Duodenum Proximal Lesion & Exam. U.G.I. Tract Endoscopic Fibreoptic |
| G43.- | Extirpation Duodenum Proximal Lesion & Exam. U.G.I. Tract Endoscopic NEC |
| D02.- | Extirpation Ear External Lesion |
| | |
| D02.- | Extirpation Ear External Skin Lesion |
| D19.- | Extirpation Ear Middle Lesion |
| Q17.- | Extirpation Endometrium Endoscopic |
| C12.- | Extirpation Eyelid Lesion |
| C12.- | Extirpation Eyelid Skin Lesion |
| A38.5 | Extirpation Falx Cerebri Lesion |
| T53.- | Extirpation Fascia Lesion |
| G43.- | Extirpation Gastrointestinal Tract Upper Lesion Endoscopic Fibreoptic |
| G42.- | Extirpation Gastrointestinal Tract Upper Lesion Endoscopic Fibreoptic Other |
| G43.- | Extirpation Gastrointestinal Tract Upper Lesion Endoscopic NEC |
| | |
| G42.- | Extirpation Gastrointestinal Tract Upper Lesion Endoscopic Other NEC |
| G79.1 | Extirpation Ileum Lesion Endoscopic |
| G70.- | Extirpation Ileum Lesion Open |
| G79.1 | Extirpation Intestine Small Lesion Endoscopic NEC |
| G70.- | Extirpation Intestine Small Lesion Open NEC |
| G64.1 | Extirpation Jejunum Lesion Endoscopic |
| G59.- | Extirpation Jejunum Lesion Open |
| M10.1 | Extirpation Kidney Lesion Endoscopic |
| M04.- | Extirpation Kidney Lesion Open |
| E30.- | Extirpation Larynx Lesion Open |
| | |
| | Extirpation Lesion – see Extirpation site Lesion |
| F02.- | Extirpation Lip Lesion |
| F02.- | Extirpation Lip Mucosa Lesion |
| F02.- | Extirpation Lip Skin Lesion |
| J03.- | Extirpation Liver Lesion |
| E55.- | Extirpation Lung Lesion Open |
| E62.1 | Extirpation Mediastinum Lesion Endoscopic |
| A43.1 | Extirpation Meninges Skull Base Lesion |
| A43.2 | Extirpation Meninges Skull Clivus Lesion |
| F38.- | Extirpation Mouth Lesion NEC |

| | |
|---|---|
| S64.- | Extirpation Nail Bed |
| E24.1 | Extirpation Nasopharynx Lesion Endoscopic |
| | Extirpation Nerve – see also Destruction Nerve |
| | Extirpation Nerve – see also Transection Nerve |
| A28.- | Extirpation Nerve Cranial Extracranial NEC |
| A61.- | Extirpation Nerve Peripheral Lesion |
| A57.1 | Extirpation Nerve Root Spinal Lesion |
| A27.- | Extirpation Nerve Vagus (x) |
| B35.3 | Extirpation Nipple Lesion |
| B35.3 | Extirpation Nipple Skin Lesion |
| | |
| E08.2 | Extirpation Nose Internal Lesion NEC |
| G43.- | Extirpation Oesophagus Lesion & Exam. U.G.I. Tract Endoscopic Fibreoptic |
| G43.- | Extirpation Oesophagus Lesion & Exam. U.G.I. Tract Endoscopic NEC |
| G14.- | Extirpation Oesophagus Lesion Endoscopic Fibreoptic |
| G14.- | Extirpation Oesophagus Lesion Endoscopic NEC |
| G17.- | Extirpation Oesophagus Lesion Endoscopic Rigid |
| G04.- | Extirpation Oesophagus Lesion Open |
| C02.- | Extirpation Orbit Lesion |
| X53.- | Extirpation Organ Unspecified |
| Q49.1 | Extirpation Ovary Lesion Access Minimal |
| | |
| Q49.1 | Extirpation Ovary Lesion Endoscopic |
| F28.- | Extirpation Palate Lesion |
| J58.- | Extirpation Pancreas Lesion |
| N27.- | Extirpation Penis Lesion |
| N27.- | Extirpation Penis Skin Lesion |
| P11.- | Extirpation Perineum Female Lesion |
| P11.- | Extirpation Perineum Skin Female Lesion |
| T33.- | Extirpation Peritoneum Lesion Open |
| E24.2 | Extirpation Pharynx Lesion Endoscopic |
| T10.1 | Extirpation Pleura Lesion Access Minimal |
| | |
| T10.1 | Extirpation Pleura Lesion Endoscopic |
| M62.1 | Extirpation Prostate Lesion Open |
| G43.- | Extirpation Pylorus Lesion Endoscopic Fibreoptic |
| G43.- | Extirpation Pylorus Lesion Endoscopic NEC |
| H23.- | Extirpation Rectum Lesion Endoscopic NEC |
| H34.- | Extirpation Rectum Lesion Open |
| H23.- | Extirpation Rectum Lesion Sigmoidoscope Fibreoptic |
| H26.- | Extirpation Rectum Lesion Sigmoidoscope Rigid |
| F45.- | Extirpation Salivary Gland Lesion |
| C53.- | Extirpation Sclera Lesion |
| | |
| N01.- | Extirpation Scrotum |
| N01.- | Extirpation Scrotum Skin |
| A44.2 | Extirpation Spinal Cord Lesion NEC |
| A51.1 | Extirpation Spinal Cord Meninges Lesion |
| A44.- | Extirpation Spinal Cord Partial |
| V43.- | Extirpation Spine Lesion |
| G43.- | Extirpation Stomach Lesion Endoscopic Fibreoptic |
| G43.- | Extirpation Stomach Lesion Endoscopic NEC |
| G17.- | Extirpation Stomach Lesion Gastroscope Rigid |
| G29.- | Extirpation Stomach Lesion Open |

| | |
|---|---|
| A38.6 | Extirpation Tentorium Cerebelli Lesion |
| N07.- | Extirpation Testis Lesion |
| F23.- | Extirpation Tongue Lesion |
| T29.3 | Extirpation Umbilicus Lesion |
| M29.1 | Extirpation Ureter Lesion Endoscopic |
| M32.1 | Extirpation Ureteric Orifice Lesion Endoscopic |
| M76.1 | Extirpation Urethra Lesion Endoscopic |
| M81.1 | Extirpation Urethra Meatus Lesion |
| P20.- | Extirpation Vagina Lesion |
| P06.- | Extirpation Vulva Lesion |
| | |
| P06.- | Extirpation Vulva Skin Lesion |
| X58.1 | Extracorporeal Membrane Oxygenation |
| | Extraction – see also Delivery |
| | Extraction – see also Removal from site |
| W36.5 | Extraction Bone Marrow Diagnostic NEC |
| B37.3 | Extraction Breast Milk |
| C71.- | Extraction Cataract Extracapsular |
| C72.- | Extraction Cataract Intracapsular |
| C74.- | Extraction Cataract NEC |
| C71.- | Extraction Lens Extracapsular |
| | |
| C72.1 | Extraction Lens Forceps |
| C72.- | Extraction Lens Intracapsular |
| C71.1 | Extraction Lens Linear Simple |
| C74.- | Extraction Lens NEC |
| C72.2 | Extraction Lens Suction |
| Q11.4 | Extraction Menses |
| N34.6 | Extraction Sperm Testicular |
| F51.2 | Extraction Submandibular Duct Calculus Open |
| F10.- | Extraction Tooth Multiple |
| F10.- | Extraction Tooth Simple |
| | |
| F10.- | Extraction Tooth Single |
| M75.4 | Extraction Urethral Calculus Open |
| C69.- | Eye Anterior Chamber Operations NEC |
| Z18.- | Eye Anterior Chamber site |
| Z16.- | Eye External Structure site |
| C31.- | Eye Muscle Operations Combined |
| C37.- | Eye Muscle Operations NEC |
| Z17.- | Eye Muscle site NEC |
| C86.- | Eye Operations NEC |
| Z19.- | Eye site NEC |
| | |
| Z17.- | Eye Tendon site NEC |
| C61.- | Eye Trabecular Meshwork Operations NEC |
| C10.- | Eyebrow Operations |
| Z16.2 | Eyebrow site |
| C10.- | Eyebrow Skin Operations |
| Z16.2 | Eyebrow Skin site |
| C22.- | Eyelid Operations NEC |
| Z16.4 | Eyelid site |
| C22.- | Eyelid Skin Operations NEC |
| Z16.4 | Eyelid Skin site |

# F

| | |
|---|---|
| S01.- | Facelift |
| V67.1 | Facetectomy Spine Lumbar Medial Posterior |
| V68.1 | Facetectomy Spine Lumbar Medial Posterior Revisional |
| Y73.- | Facilitating Operations NOC |
| Y71.4 | Failed Minimal Access Approach Converted to Open |
| | Failed Operations – refer to Tabular List Introduction |
| Y71.5 | Failed Percutaneous Approach Converted to Open |
| Q38.- | Fallopian Tube Operations Endoscopic Therapeutic NEC |
| Q41.- | Fallopian Tube Operations NEC |
| Q34.- | Fallopian Tube Operations Open NEC |
| | |
| Q41.5 | Fallopian Tube Operations Patency NEC |
| Z46.2 | Fallopian Tube site |
| Q39.9 | Falloposcopy NEC |
| T57.- | Fascia Operations NEC |
| Z62.1 | Fascia site |
| T52.- | Fasciectomy |
| T54.- | Fasciotomy |
| T55.- | Fasciotomy Release |
| Z76.- | Femur site |
| W18.1 | Fenestration Bone Cortex |
| | |
| | Fenestration Disc Intervertebral – see Excision Disc Intervertebral |
| E13.8 | Fenestration Maxillary |
| X55.3 | Fenestration Organ Unspecified |
| K69.2 | Fenestration Pericardium |
| T08.- | Fenestration Pleura |
| K14.2 | Fenestration Septum Atrial |
| K16.- | Fenestration Septum Atrial Transluminal Percutaneous |
| Y96.- | Fertilisation In Vitro |
| Q56.1 | Fertility Investigation Female NEC |
| Q41.- | Fertility Investigation Female Tubal Patency |
| | |
| N34.1 | Fertility Investigation Male NEC |
| Q56.2 | Fertiloscopy |
| R03.- | Feticide Selective |
| R02.- | Fetoscopy |
| R01.- | Fetus Operations Therapeutic Endoscopic |
| R04.- | Fetus Operations Therapeutic Percutaneous |
| Z45.3 | Fetus site |
| H25.- | Fibrosigmoidoscopy |
| Z78.1 | Fibula & Tibia Shaft Combination site |
| Z78.- | Fibula site NEC |

| L79.1 | Filter Vena Cava Insertion |
|---|---|
| C60.- | Filtering Iris |
| Q32.- | Fimbria Operations |
| Z46.1 | Fimbria site |
| H55.- | Fistula Anal Operations NEC |
| O05.- | Fistula Arteriovenous Dural Operations (L) |
| M37.5 | Fistula Bladder Repair NEC |
| M62.4 | Fistula Rectoprostatic Repair |
| L74.2 | Fistulisation Arteriovenous Dialysis |
| L74.2 | Fistulisation Arteriovenous NEC |
| | |
| L74.6 | Fistulisation Graft Dialysis |
| G08.2 | Fistulisation Oesophagus External NEC |
| M54.1 | Fistulisation Urethrovaginal |
| M41.2 | Fistulisation Vesicovaginal |
| Y39.1 | Fistulogram NOC |
| H55.5 | Fistulography Anal Fistula |
| F15.2 | Fitting Bracket Orthodontic |
| V04.1 | Fitting Cranioplasty Bands Dynamic |
| F63.2 | Fitting Denture or Obturator |
| F15.3 | Fitting Headgear Orthodontic |
| | |
| D13.6 | Fitting Hearing Prosthesis External to Bone Anchored Fixtures |
| F15.4 | Fitting Separators Orthodontic |
| F17.7 | Fitting Teeth Bridge |
| F17.3 | Fitting Tooth Crown Dental |
| W20.- | Fixation Bone & Reduction Fracture Open NEC |
| W19.- | Fixation Bone & Reduction Fragment Open |
| W30.- | Fixation Bone External |
| W25.- | Fixation Bone External & Reduction Fracture Closed |
| W25.3 | Fixation Bone External & Remanipulation Fracture |
| W25.- | Fixation Bone Fracture External NEC |
| | |
| W24.- | Fixation Bone Fracture Internal NEC |
| W21.- | Fixation Bone Fracture Intra-articular Primary |
| W28.- | Fixation Bone Internal |
| W24.- | Fixation Bone Internal & Reduction Fracture Closed |
| W19.- | Fixation Bone Intramedullary & Reduction Fracture Open |
| W30.- | Fixation Bone NEC |
| C08.3 | Fixation Bone Orbit Fracture Removal |
| W24.5 | Fixation Bone Screw & Reduction Fragment Closed |
| H19.2 | Fixation Caecum |
| W83.2 | Fixation Cartilage Articular Lesion Endoscopic |
| | |
| H19.2 | Fixation Colon |
| W27.- | Fixation Epiphysis |
| W27.5 | Fixation Epiphysis Temporary |
| V11.- | Fixation Face |
| C60.3 | Fixation Iris |
| V17.- | Fixation Jaw NEC |
| V17.- | Fixation Mandible |
| V11.- | Fixation Maxilla |
| C08.5 | Fixation Orbit Fracture |
| C08.3 | Fixation Orbit Removal |

| Q45.2 | Fixation Ovary NEC |
| H35.- | Fixation Rectum Prolapse NEC |
| C85.- | Fixation Retina |
| V46.- | Fixation Spine Fracture |
| N13.2 | Fixation Testis |
| P24.7 | Fixation Vagina Sacrospinous |
| | Fixator – see Fixation |
| E11.- | Fixture Nose Prosthesis Operations |
| | Flap Bone – see also Flap site |
| E14.5 | Flap Bone Ethmoid Sinus |
| | |
| E14.5 | Flap Bone Frontal Sinus |
| E14.5 | Flap Ethmoid Sinus Bone |
| C10.2 | Flap Eyebrow Hair Bearing |
| C14.1 | Flap Eyelid Skin |
| S18.- | Flap Fasciocutaneous Distant |
| S25.- | Flap Fasciocutaneous Local |
| E14.5 | Flap Frontal Sinus Bone |
| S28.- | Flap Mucosa |
| T76.1 | Flap Muscle Transfer Free Tissue Microvascular |
| S17.- | Flap Myocutaneous Distant |
| | |
| S24.- | Flap Myocutaneous Local |
| T36.5 | Flap Omental Creation |
| | Flap Skin – see also Flap site |
| S18.- | Flap Skin & Fascia Distant |
| S25.- | Flap Skin & Fascia Local |
| S17.- | Flap Skin & Muscle Distant |
| S24.- | Flap Skin & Muscle Local |
| S20.- | Flap Skin Distant NEC |
| S19.- | Flap Skin Distant Pedicle |
| S21.- | Flap Skin Hair Bearing |
| | |
| S30.- | Flap Skin Head Operations NEC |
| S27.- | Flap Skin Local NEC |
| S26.- | Flap Skin Local Subcutaneous Pedicle |
| S27.- | Flap Skin NEC |
| S30.- | Flap Skin Neck Operations NEC |
| S31.- | Flap Skin Operations NEC |
| S23.- | Flap Skin Operations Relax Contracture |
| S22.- | Flap Skin Sensory |
| S28.1 | Flap Tongue |
| Y53.4 | Fluoroscopic Control Approach |
| | |
| Y03.1 | Flushing Catheter NOC |
| W71.3 | Forage Joint |
| V56.- | Foraminoplasty Spine NEC |
| V56.- | Foraminoplasty Spine Primary |
| V57.- | Foraminoplasty Spine Revisional |
| V22.3 | Foraminotomy Spine Cervical NEC |
| V23.3 | Foraminotomy Spine Cervical Revisional |
| V25.6 | Foraminotomy Spine Lumbar Lateral NEC |
| V26.6 | Foraminotomy Spine Lumbar Lateral Revisional |
| W11.- | Fracture Bone Surgical NEC |

Adhesiolysis - Freeing Bowel

**F**

| | |
|---|---|
| W10.- | Fracture Bone Surgical Open |
| N28.6 | Fracture Penis Repair |
| | Fragmentation – see also Dissolution |
| | Fragmentation – see also Lithotripsy |
| J41.3 | Fragmentation Bile Duct Calculus Endoscopic Retrograde |
| J52.1 | Fragmentation Bile Duct Calculus Extracorporeal |
| J26.1 | Fragmentation Gall Bladder Calculus Extracorporeal |
| J24.2 | Fragmentation Gall Bladder Calculus Percutaneous |
| M09.- | Fragmentation Kidney Calculus Endoscopic NEC |
| M14.- | Fragmentation Kidney Calculus Extracorporeal |
| M09.- | Fragmentation Kidney Calculus Percutaneous NEC |
| M09.- | Fragmentation Kidney Calculus Percutaneous Nephroscopic |
| J68.1 | Fragmentation Pancreas Calculus Extracorporeal |
| M28.- | Fragmentation Ureter Calculus Endoscopic NEC |
| M31.- | Fragmentation Ureter Calculus Extracorporeal |
| M26.- | Fragmentation Ureter Calculus Nephroscopic |
| M27.- | Fragmentation Ureter Calculus Ureteroscopic |
| Y18.1 | Freeing Adhesions NOC |
| T42.3 | Freeing Bowel Adhesions Endoscopic |
| T41.5 | Freeing Bowel Adhesions Extensive |
| T41.3 | Freeing Bowel Adhesions Limited |
| C43.1 | Freeing Conjunctiva Adhesions |
| D17.3 | Freeing Ear Ossicle Adhesions |
| C37.2 | Freeing Eye Muscle Adhesions |
| Q38.1 | Freeing Fallopian Tube Adhesions Access Minimal |
| Q38.1 | Freeing Fallopian Tube Adhesions Endoscopic |
| Q34.1 | Freeing Fallopian Tube Adhesions Open |
| T57.1 | Freeing Fascia Adhesions |
| M08.8 | Freeing Kidney Adhesions |
| F06.1 | Freeing Lip Adhesions |
| T42.3 | Freeing Mesentery Adhesions Endoscopic |
| T41.3 | Freeing Mesentery Adhesions NEC |
| C37.2 | Freeing Muscle Eye Adhesions |
| A73.2 | Freeing Nerve Peripheral Adhesions NEC |
| E08.4 | Freeing Nose Internal Adhesions |
| E04.4 | Freeing Nose Turbinate Adhesions |
| Q49.2 | Freeing Ovary Adhesions Access Minimal |
| Q49.2 | Freeing Ovary Adhesions Endoscopic |
| Q47.2 | Freeing Ovary Adhesions Open |
| K69.1 | Freeing Pericardium Adhesions |
| T42.3 | Freeing Peritoneum Adhesions Access Minimal |
| T42.3 | Freeing Peritoneum Adhesions Endoscopic |
| T41.3 | Freeing Peritoneum Adhesions NEC |
| N30.2 | Freeing Prepuce Adhesions |
| A51.2 | Freeing Spinal Cord Meninges Adhesions |
| A49.4 | Freeing Spinal Tether Complex |
| A49.1 | Freeing Spinal Tether NEC |
| T69.- | Freeing Tendon |
| F26.4 | Freeing Tongue Adhesions |
| Q20.1 | Freeing Uterus Adhesions |

| | |
|---|---|
| P29.1 | Freeing Vagina Adhesions |
| F05.1 | Frenectomy Lip |
| F42.3 | Frenectomy NEC |
| F26.2 | Frenectomy Tongue |
| F26.3 | Frenotomy Tongue |
| N28.4 | Frenuloplasty Penis |
| E14.- | Frontal Sinus Operations Endoscopic Diagnostic |
| E14.- | Frontal Sinus Operations NEC |
| Z23.2 | Frontal Sinus site |
| E14.1 | Frontoethmoidectomy External |
| | |
| X61.1 | Functional Therapy Session |
| G24.- | Fundoplication Antireflux NEC |
| G25.1 | Fundoplication Stomach Revision |
| W61.- | Fusion Joint & Graft Bone Articular NEC |
| W60.- | Fusion Joint & Graft Bone NEC |
| V37.4 | Fusion Joint Atlanto-occipital |
| V66.1 | Fusion Joint Atlanto-occipital Revisional |
| V37.- | Fusion Joint Atlantoaxial NEC |
| V37.6 | Fusion Joint Atlantoaxial Posterior Pedicle Screw |
| V66.3 | Fusion Joint Atlantoaxial Posterior Pedicle Screw Revisional |
| | |
| V66.4 | Fusion Joint Atlantoaxial Posterior Revisional NEC |
| V37.5 | Fusion Joint Atlantoaxial Posterior Transarticular Screw |
| V66.2 | Fusion Joint Atlantoaxial Posterior Transarticular Screw Revisional |
| W64.- | Fusion Joint Conversion NEC |
| W04.- | Fusion Joint Hindfoot |
| W03.- | Fusion Joint Interphalangeal |
| W59.- | Fusion Joint Interphalangeal Toe |
| W59.- | Fusion Joint Metatarsophalangeal First |
| W03.5 | Fusion Joint Midfoot Forefoot Localised |
| W62.- | Fusion Joint NEC |
| | |
| W63.- | Fusion Joint Revisional NEC |
| V37.- | Fusion Joint Spine Cervical NEC |
| V39.1 | Fusion Joint Spine Cervical Revisional |
| V38.- | Fusion Joint Spine Lumbar NEC |
| V39.- | Fusion Joint Spine Lumbar Revisional |
| V38.- | Fusion Joint Spine NEC |
| V39.- | Fusion Joint Spine Revisional |
| V38.1 | Fusion Joint Spine Thoracic NEC |
| V39.2 | Fusion Joint Spine Thoracic Revisional |
| W59.- | Fusion Joint Toe |
| | |
| V37.7 | Fusion Junction Occipitocervical NEC |
| V66.1 | Fusion Junction Occipitocervical Revisional |
| V40.2 | Fusion Spine Cervical Instrumented Posterior NEC |
| V40.4 | Fusion Spine Lumbar Instrumented Posterior NEC |
| V40.3 | Fusion Spine Thoracic Instrumented Posterior NEC |

# G

| | |
|---|---|
| J08.- | Gall Bladder Operations Endoscopic Therapeutic |
| J08.- | Gall Bladder Operations Laparoscopic |
| J26.- | Gall Bladder Operations NEC |
| J23.- | Gall Bladder Operations Open NEC |
| J25.- | Gall Bladder Operations Percutaneous Diagnostic |
| J24.- | Gall Bladder Operations Percutaneous Therapeutic |
| J08.- | Gall Bladder Operations Peritoneoscope |
| Z30.2 | Gall Bladder site |
| Q38.3 | Gamete Intrafallopian Transfer Endoscopic |
| Q13.- | Gamete Uterine Cavity Introduction |
| | |
| G28.- | Gastrectomy NEC |
| G28.- | Gastrectomy Partial |
| G28.5 | Gastrectomy Sleeve |
| G27.- | Gastrectomy Total |
| G48.- | Gastric Bubble |
| O11.1 | Gastro-oesophageal Junction site (Z) |
| G49.1 | Gastroduodenectomy |
| G31.- | Gastroduodenostomy |
| G33.- | Gastroenterostomy |
| Y51.- | Gastrointestinal Tract Approach Opening Artificial |
| | |
| G46.- | Gastrointestinal Tract Upper Operations Endoscopic Therapeutic NEC |
| G44.- | Gastrointestinal Tract Upper Operations Endoscopic Therapeutic Other NEC |
| G46.- | Gastrointestinal Tract Upper Operations Therapeutic Fibreoptic NEC |
| G44.- | Gastrointestinal Tract Upper Operations Therapeutic Fibreoptic Other NEC |
| G33.1 | Gastrojejunostomy NEC |
| G24.4 | Gastropexy Antireflux |
| G36.1 | Gastropexy NEC |
| G24.5 | Gastroplasty & Antireflux Operations HFQ |
| G30.1 | Gastroplasty NEC |
| G45.- | Gastroscopy Fibreoptic |
| | |
| G45.- | Gastroscopy NEC |
| G19.- | Gastroscopy Rigid |
| Y51.2 | Gastrostomy Approach |
| G44.- | Gastrostomy Endoscopic Fibreoptic Percutaneous |
| G34.- | Gastrostomy NEC |
| G38.5 | Gastrotomy NEC |
| V19.2 | Genioplasty Jaw NEC |
| V19.2 | Genioplasty Mandible |
| Z43.- | Genital Organ Male site |
| Q56.- | Genital Tract Female Operations NEC |

| | |
|---|---|
| Z46.- | Genital Tract Female site NEC |
| N34.- | Genital Tract Male Operations NEC |
| N35.- | Genitalia Male Non-operative Interventions |
| Y95.- | Gestational Age |
| F20.- | Gingiva Operations |
| Z25.4 | Gingiva site |
| F20.- | Gingivectomy |
| F20.4 | Gingivoplasty |
| C65.- | Glaucoma Operations Following Surgery |
| U26.1 | Glomerular Filtration Rate Testing |
| | |
| F22.- | Glossectomy |
| F24.3 | Glossotomy |
| C47.4 | Gluing Cornea |
| C61.4 | Goniopuncture |
| C61.3 | Goniotomy |
| H57.- | Graciloplasty Dynamic Sphincter |
| H57.4 | Graciloplasty Sphincter |
| E02.7 | Graft Alar Reconstruction Cartilage |
| | Graft Artery – see Anastomosis Artery |
| | Graft Artery – see Bypass Artery |
| | |
| | Graft Artery – see Reconstruction Artery |
| | Graft Artery – see Repair Artery |
| | Graft Artery – see Replacement Artery |
| | Graft Bone – see also Autograft Bone |
| W60.- | Graft Bone & Fusion Joint NEC |
| W61.- | Graft Bone Articular & Fusion Joint NEC |
| V05.5 | Graft Bone Cranium |
| W34.- | Graft Bone Marrow |
| W32.- | Graft Bone NEC |
| V54.2 | Graft Bone Spine NEC |
| | |
| W32.4 | Graft Bone Synthetic |
| C11.5 | Graft Canthus Skin |
| C40.- | Graft Conjunctiva |
| C46.- | Graft Cornea |
| C46.6 | Graft Cornea Amniotic Membrane |
| C44.3 | Graft Cornea Endothelial |
| C46.5 | Graft Cornea Lamellar Deep |
| C46.2 | Graft Cornea Lamellar NEC |
| C46.3 | Graft Cornea Penetrating |
| C46.8 | Graft Cornea Revision |
| | |
| D22.1 | Graft Eustachian Canal |
| C10.3 | Graft Eyebrow Hair Bearing |
| C14.3 | Graft Eyelid Cartilage |
| C14.5 | Graft Eyelid Fascia |
| C14.2 | Graft Eyelid Skin |
| C14.4 | Graft Eyelid Skin & Fat |
| V19.3 | Graft Jaw Alveolar NEC |
| V19.3 | Graft Mandible Alveolar |
| V13.2 | Graft Maxilla Alveolar |
| F40.- | Graft Mouth NEC |

| | |
|---|---|
| S38.- | Graft Mucosa |
| A24.- | Graft Nerve Cranial Microsurgical |
| A24.- | Graft Nerve Cranial NEC |
| A62.- | Graft Nerve Peripheral Microsurgical |
| A62.6 | Graft Nerve Peripheral Multiple Microsurgical NEC |
| A63.- | Graft Nerve Peripheral NEC |
| Y27.- | Graft NOC |
| D16.2 | Graft Ossicular Chain |
| N28.7 | Graft Penis |
| Y27.6 | Graft Prosthetic NOC |
| | |
| C57.3 | Graft Sclera |
| E03.7 | Graft Septal Reconstruction |
| S34.- | Graft Skin Hair Bearing NEC |
| S33.- | Graft Skin Hair Bearing Scalp |
| S37.- | Graft Skin NEC |
| S36.- | Graft Skin Pinch |
| S35.- | Graft Skin Split |
| S39.- | Graft Skin Tissue NEC |
| V42.3 | Graft Spine & Release Anterolateral |
| W99.- | Graft Stem Cells Cord Blood to Bone Marrow |
| | |
| S39.- | Graft Subcutaneous Tissue NEC |
| L93.5 | Graft Vein |
| L83.1 | Graft Vein Saphenous Crossover |
| D20.- | Grommet Tympanic Membrane Attention |
| D15.1 | Grommet Tympanic Membrane Insertion |
| | Guidance – see Education |

# H

| | |
|---|---|
| X43.1 | Haemodialysis Albumin Extracorporeal |
| X40.3 | Haemodialysis NEC |
| X40.4 | Haemofiltration |
| X40.7 | Haemoperfusion |
| H53.- | Haemorrhoid Operations NEC |
| H51.- | Haemorrhoidectomy |
| H51.3 | Haemorrhoidectomy Stapled |
| | Haemostasis – see also Arrest Bleeding site Postoperative Surgical |
| | Haemostasis – see also Packing site |
| H21.- | Haemostasis Caecum Endoscopic Fibreoptic |
| H21.- | Haemostasis Caecum Endoscopic NEC |
| H21.- | Haemostasis Colon Endoscopic Fibreoptic NEC |
| H21.- | Haemostasis Colon Endoscopic NEC |
| H24.2 | Haemostasis Lower Bowel Sigmoidoscope Fibreoptic |
| E05.- | Haemostasis Nose Internal |
| Y66.- | Harvest Bone |
| Y66.7 | Harvest Bone Marrow |
| Y69.- | Harvest Cartilage |
| Y67.1 | Harvest Cartilage & Skin Composite Ear |
| W89.2 | Harvest Chondrocytes Autologous Endoscopic |
| Y67.2 | Harvest Dermis Fat |
| Y59.- | Harvest Fascia & Skin Flap |
| Y60.- | Harvest Fascia Lata |
| Y60.- | Harvest Fascia NEC |
| Y60.- | Harvest Fascia Sheet |
| Y62.- | Harvest Muscle & Skin Flap NEC |
| Y61.- | Harvest Muscle & Skin Flap Trunk |
| Y64.- | Harvest Muscle Flap NEC |
| Y63.- | Harvest Muscle Flap Trunk |
| Y54.- | Harvest Nerve |
| Y69.1 | Harvest Omentum |
| Y67.1 | Harvest Skin & Cartilage Composite Ear |
| Y59.- | Harvest Skin & Fascia Flap |
| Y67.2 | Harvest Skin & Fat Composite |
| Y62.- | Harvest Skin & Muscle Flap NEC |
| Y61.- | Harvest Skin & Muscle Flap Trunk |
| Y55.- | Harvest Skin Flap Limb Pattern Random |
| Y57.- | Harvest Skin Flap Pattern Axial |
| Y56.- | Harvest Skin Flap Pattern Random NEC |
| Y58.1 | Harvest Skin Flap Post Auricular |

| | |
|---|---|
| Y58.- | Harvest Skin Graft NEC |
| Y65.- | Harvest Tendon |
| Y67.- | Harvest Tissue Multiple NEC |
| Y69.- | Harvest Tissue NEC |
| Y69.3 | Harvest Vein |
| K54.- | Heart Assist Operations Open |
| K56.- | Heart Assist Operations Transluminal |
| K56.- | Heart Assist System Transluminal |
| K52.- | Heart Conducting System Operations Open |
| K58.- | Heart Conducting System Study |
| | |
| K66.- | Heart Operations NEC |
| K55.- | Heart Operations Open NEC |
| K58.- | Heart Operations Transluminal Diagnostic |
| K62.- | Heart Operations Transluminal Therapeutic NEC |
| K57.- | Heart Operations Transluminal Therapeutic Other NEC |
| K15.- | Heart Septum Operations Closed |
| K14.- | Heart Septum Operations Open NEC |
| K16.- | Heart Septum Operations Transluminal Therapeutic |
| Z33.- | Heart site NEC |
| K34.- | Heart Valve Operations Open NEC |
| | |
| K35.- | Heart Valve Operations Transluminal Therapeutic |
| Z32.- | Heart Valve site |
| K38.- | Heart Valve Structure Adjacent Operations NEC |
| Z33.2 | Heart Ventricle Septum site |
| K23.- | Heart Wall Operations NEC |
| Z33.3 | Heart Wall site |
| | Hemiarthroplasty – see also Arthroplasty |
| W52.- | Hemiarthroplasty Bone Articulation Prosthetic Cemented NEC |
| W54.- | Hemiarthroplasty Bone Articulation Prosthetic NEC |
| W53.- | Hemiarthroplasty Bone Articulation Prosthetic Uncemented NEC |
| | |
| W46.- | Hemiarthroplasty Femur Head Prosthetic Cemented |
| W48.- | Hemiarthroplasty Femur Head Prosthetic NEC |
| W47.- | Hemiarthroplasty Femur Head Prosthetic Uncemented |
| W49.- | Hemiarthroplasty Humerus Head Prosthetic Cemented |
| W51.- | Hemiarthroplasty Humerus Head Prosthetic NEC |
| W50.- | Hemiarthroplasty Humerus Head Prosthetic Uncemented |
| O24.- | Hemiarthroplasty Radius Head Prosthetic Cemented (W) |
| O26.- | Hemiarthroplasty Radius Head Prosthetic NEC (W) |
| O25.- | Hemiarthroplasty Radius Head Prosthetic Uncemented (W) |
| H09.- | Hemicolectomy Left |
| | |
| H11.- | Hemicolectomy NEC |
| H06.- | Hemicolectomy Right Extended |
| H07.- | Hemicolectomy Right NEC |
| V05.7 | Hemicraniotomy |
| J02.- | Hemihepatectomy |
| | Hemilaminectomy – see also Laminectomy |
| V67.2 | Hemilaminectomy Spine Lumbar |
| V68.2 | Hemilaminectomy Spine Lumbar Revisional |
| V14.1 | Hemimandibulectomy |
| M03.1 | Heminephrectomy Kidney Duplex |

| | |
|---|---|
| A01.1 | Hemispherectomy |
| B08.3 | Hemithyroidectomy |
| Z30.4 | Hepatic Duct site |
| O30.1 | Hepatic Flexure site (Z) |
| | Herniorrhaphy – see also Repair Hernia |
| T27.- | Herniorrhaphy Abdominal Wall NEC |
| T22.- | Herniorrhaphy Femoral NEC |
| T25.- | Herniorrhaphy Incisional NEC |
| T20.- | Herniorrhaphy Inguinal NEC |
| T24.- | Herniorrhaphy Umbilical |
| | |
| T27.- | Herniorrhaphy Ventral |
| T19.- | Herniotomy |
| X97.- | High Cost Anaesthesia Drugs |
| X86.- | High Cost Anti-infective Drugs |
| X83.- | High Cost Cardiovascular Drugs |
| X95.- | High Cost Dermatology Drugs |
| X94.- | High Cost Ear Nose & Throat Drugs |
| X87.- | High Cost Endocrinology Drugs |
| X81.- | High Cost Gastrointestinal Drugs |
| X90.- | High Cost Haematology & Nutrition Drugs |
| | |
| X82.- | High Cost Hypertensive Drugs |
| X96.- | High Cost Immunology Drugs |
| X89.- | High Cost Immunosuppressant Drugs |
| X91.- | High Cost Metabolic Drugs |
| X92.- | High Cost Musculoskeletal Drugs |
| X85.- | High Cost Neurology Drugs |
| X93.- | High Cost Ophthalmology Drugs |
| X88.- | High Cost Reproductive & Urinary Tract Drugs |
| X84.- | High Cost Respiratory Drugs |
| Z69.- | Humerus site |
| | |
| N11.- | Hydrocele Sac Operations |
| Q41.2 | Hydrotubation Fallopian Tube |
| P15.1 | Hymenectomy |
| P15.4 | Hymenotomy |
| X52.1 | Hyperbaric Therapy |
| B01.- | Hypophysectomy |
| X51.1 | Hypothermia Therapy |
| Q07.- | Hysterectomy Abdominal |
| R25.1 | Hysterectomy Caesarean |
| Q07.- | Hysterectomy NEC |
| | |
| Q08.- | Hysterectomy Vaginal |
| Q07.- | Hysterocolpectomy Abdominal |
| Q08.- | Hysterocolpectomy Vaginal |
| Q54.6 | Hysteropexy Infracoccygeal |
| Q41.1 | Hysterosalpingography |
| Q18.- | Hysteroscopy |
| U09.2 | Hysterosonography |
| Q09.- | Hysterotomy |
| Q09.6 | Hysterotomy NEC |

# I

| | |
|---|---|
| G69.- | Ileectomy |
| H68.- | Ileoanal Pouch Operations Diagnostic |
| H66.- | Ileoanal Pouch Operations Therapeutic |
| M36.2 | Ileocystoplasty |
| G80.- | Ileoscopy |
| H09.4 | Ileostomy & Excision Colon Left |
| H11.4 | Ileostomy & Excision Colon NEC |
| H07.4 | Ileostomy & Excision Colon Right |
| H06.4 | Ileostomy & Excision Colon Right Extended |
| H10.4 | Ileostomy & Excision Colon Sigmoid |
| | |
| H05.- | Ileostomy & Excision Colon Total |
| H08.4 | Ileostomy & Excision Colon Transverse |
| H04.1 | Ileostomy & Panproctocolectomy |
| Y51.3 | Ileostomy Approach |
| G75.3 | Ileostomy Closure |
| G74.- | Ileostomy Creation |
| G75.5 | Ileostomy Prolapse Reduction |
| G75.2 | Ileostomy Prolapse Repair |
| G75.1 | Ileostomy Refashioning |
| G79.- | Ileum Operations Endoscopic Therapeutic |
| | |
| G82.- | Ileum Operations NEC |
| G78.- | Ileum Operations Open NEC |
| Z27.6 | Ileum site |
| Z75.3 | Ilium Wing site |
| Y53.- | Image Control Approach |
| Y53.5 | Image Intensifier Control Approach NEC |
| | Imaging – see also Scan |
| U08.- | Imaging Abdomen Diagnostic |
| U08.5 | Imaging Abdomen Magnetic Resonance |
| U11.7 | Imaging Angiography Magnetic Resonance |
| | |
| U01.2 | Imaging Body Whole Magnetic Resonance |
| U01.- | Imaging Body Whole NEC |
| U13.3 | Imaging Bone Magnetic Resonance |
| U05.2 | Imaging Brain Magnetic Resonance |
| U05.3 | Imaging Brain Magnetic Resonance Functional |
| U18.- | Imaging Breast Diagnostic |
| U10.3 | Imaging Cardiac Magnetic Resonance |
| U05.- | Imaging Central Nervous Diagnostic |
| U07.- | Imaging Chest Diagnostic |
| U07.2 | Imaging Chest Magnetic Resonance |

| | |
|---|---|
| U04.- | Imaging Dental |
| U21.- | Imaging Diagnostic NEC |
| U36.- | Imaging Diagnostic Other NEC |
| Y94.4 | Imaging Diethylenetriamine Pentacetic Acid |
| U17.- | Imaging Digestive Tract |
| Y94.1 | Imaging Dopamine Transporter Scan |
| U06.- | Imaging Face Neck Diagnostic |
| Y93.- | Imaging Gallium-67 |
| U08.4 | Imaging Gastrointestinal Upper Series |
| U12.- | Imaging Genitourinary System Diagnostic |
| | |
| U37.- | Imaging Genitourinary System Diagnostic Other |
| U05.2 | Imaging Head Magnetic Resonance |
| U05.3 | Imaging Head Magnetic Resonance Functional |
| U10.- | Imaging Heart Diagnostic |
| U16.- | Imaging Hepatobiliary System |
| U13.3 | Imaging Joint Magnetic Resonance |
| U37.1 | Imaging Kidney Magnetic Resonance |
| Y94.3 | Imaging Metaiodobenzylguanidine |
| U13.- | Imaging Musculoskeletal System Diagnostic |
| Y94.2 | Imaging Octreotide |
| | |
| U09.- | Imaging Pelvis Diagnostic |
| U09.3 | Imaging Pelvis Magnetic Resonance |
| Y94.- | Imaging Radiopharmaceutical |
| U15.- | Imaging Respiratory System |
| C87.1 | Imaging Retina Digital |
| U05.5 | Imaging Spinal Cord Magnetic Resonance |
| U05.5 | Imaging Spine Magnetic Resonance |
| U11.- | Imaging Vascular System Diagnostic |
| U35.- | Imaging Vascular System Diagnostic Other |
| U11.7 | Imaging Venography Magnetic Resonance |
| | |
| C54.2 | Imbrication Sclera |
| Y70.2 | Immediate Operations NOC |
| | Immobilisation – see also Support |
| X48.- | Immobilisation Plaster Cast |
| X37.3 | Immunotherapy Intramuscular |
| X35.3 | Immunotherapy Intravenous |
| X38.4 | Immunotherapy Subcutaneous |
| | Implant – see also Implantation |
| C04.- | Implant Orbit Attention |
| C03.- | Implant Orbit Insertion |
| | |
| C54.6 | Implant Sclera Removal |
| | Implantation – see also Transfer |
| L03.2 | Implantation Arterial Duct Stent Transluminal Percutaneous |
| K46.- | Implantation Artery Mammary Heart |
| K46.- | Implantation Artery Thoracic Heart |
| W71.4 | Implantation Articular Structure Chondrocyte Autologous Open |
| M55.2 | Implantation Bladder Outlet Female Urinary Sphincter Artificial |
| M64.2 | Implantation Bladder Outlet Male Urinary Sphincter Artificial |
| W05.3 | Implantation Bone Endoprosthesis |
| W05.2 | Implantation Bone Endoprosthesis Massive |

| | |
|---|---|
| K59.- | Implantation Cardioverter Defibrillator |
| K59.6 | Implantation Cardioverter Defibrillator Three Electrode Leads |
| U19.1 | Implantation Electrocardiography Loop Recorder |
| A54.3 | Implantation Intrathecal Drug Delivery Device Adjacent Spinal Cord |
| F11.- | Implantation Jaw |
| W85.3 | Implantation Joint Knee Chondrocyte Autologous |
| | Implantation Neurostimulator – see Neurostimulator site |
| K61.7 | Implantation Pacemaker Cardiac Biventricular |
| K61.6 | Implantation Pacemaker Cardiac Dual Chamber |
| K60.6 | Implantation Pacemaker Cardiac Dual Chamber Intravenous |
| | |
| K60.1 | Implantation Pacemaker Cardiac Intravenous NEC |
| K61.1 | Implantation Pacemaker Cardiac NEC |
| K61.5 | Implantation Pacemaker Cardiac Single Chamber |
| K60.5 | Implantation Pacemaker Cardiac Single Chamber Intravenous |
| T02.2 | Implantation Pectus Excavatum Correction Silicone |
| M70.6 | Implantation Prostate Seed Radioactive |
| M71.2 | Implantation Prostate Substance Radioactive |
| | Implantation Prosthesis – see Prosthesis site |
| Y36.3 | Implantation Seed Radioactive NOC |
| | Implantation Stent – see also Insertion site Stent |
| | |
| | Implantation Stimulator – see Stimulator site |
| | Implantation System – see System |
| F08.- | Implantation Tooth |
| Q13.1 | Implantation Uterus Egg Fertilised |
| P20.5 | Implantation Vagina Radioactive |
| K54.1 | Implantation Ventricular Assist Device Open |
| P06.4 | Implantation Vulva Radioactive |
| E85.3 | Improvement Ventilation Efficiency |
| | Improving – see Improvement |
| Y96.- | In Vitro Fertilisation |
| | |
| U22.2 | Inactivation Functional Brain Hemisphere Single Test |
| | Incision & Curettage – see Curettage |
| | Incision & Drainage – see Drainage |
| | Incision – see also Exploration |
| H56.3 | Incision Anus Septum |
| K52.6 | Incision Atria Tissue |
| D08.4 | Incision Auditory Canal External |
| J33.- | Incision Bile Duct |
| M56.2 | Incision Bladder Outlet Female Endoscopic |
| M66.2 | Incision Bladder Outlet Male Endoscopic |
| | |
| B33.- | Incision Breast |
| H16.- | Incision Caecum |
| H16.- | Incision Colon |
| C41.- | Incision Conjunctiva |
| C49.- | Incision Cornea |
| G53.5 | Incision Duodenum NEC |
| D15.- | Incision Eardrum |
| C10.5 | Incision Eyebrow Lesion |
| C10.5 | Incision Eyebrow Skin Lesion |
| C19.- | Incision Eyelid |

| | |
|---|---|
| C19.- | Incision Eyelid Skin |
| Q31.- | Incision Fallopian Tube |
| J21.- | Incision Gall Bladder |
| K53.- | Incision Heart NEC |
| K32.- | Incision Heart Valve Closed |
| K31.- | Incision Heart Valve NEC |
| K31.- | Incision Heart Valve Open |
| P15.4 | Incision Hymen |
| C62.- | Incision Iris |
| G63.2 | Incision Jejunum |
| | |
| W81.4 | Incision Joint NEC |
| M06.- | Incision Kidney |
| M06.- | Incision Kidney Pelvis |
| C24.5 | Incision Lacrimal Gland |
| C26.4 | Incision Lacrimal Sac |
| Y08.6 | Incision Laser NOC |
| L87.6 | Incision Leg Vein Varicose |
| C73.- | Incision Lens Capsule |
| Y30.1 | Incision Lesion NOC |
| J05.- | Incision Liver |
| | |
| E57.4 | Incision Lung NEC |
| F42.2 | Incision Mouth NEC |
| S70.2 | Incision Nail |
| S66.3 | Incision Nail Bed |
| E27.3 | Incision Nasopharynx NEC |
| Y30.- | Incision NOC |
| E03.5 | Incision Nose Septum |
| G09.- | Incision Oesophagus |
| C06.- | Incision Orbit |
| X55.2 | Incision Organ Unspecified |
| | |
| F32.3 | Incision Palate |
| J62.- | Incision Pancreas |
| N32.3 | Incision Penis NEC |
| K69.- | Incision Pericardium |
| N24.4 | Incision Periurethral Tissue Male |
| E27.3 | Incision Pharynx NEC |
| G40.- | Incision Pylorus |
| F46.- | Incision Salivary Gland |
| | Incision Scar – see Incision Skin Lesion |
| C55.- | Incision Sclera |
| | |
| N22.2 | Incision Seminal Vesicle |
| S47.- | Incision Skin |
| J38.- | Incision Sphincter Oddi Endoscopic |
| J35.- | Incision Sphincter Oddi NEC |
| G38.5 | Incision Stomach NEC |
| S47.- | Incision Subcutaneous Tissue |
| B10.4 | Incision Thyroglossal Cyst |
| B12.3 | Incision Thyroid Lesion |
| F24.- | Incision Tongue |
| F26.3 | Incision Tongue Frenulum |

| | |
|---|---|
| M23.- | Incision Ureter |
| M32.5 | Incision Ureterocele Endoscopic |
| Q09.6 | Incision Uterus NEC |
| P14.- | Incision Vagina Introitus |
| L93.2 | Incision Vein NEC |
| C60.2 | Inclusion Iris |
| | Incomplete Operations – refer to Tabular List Introduction |
| G48.3 | Induction Emesis |
| X35.1 | Induction Labour Intravenous |
| R15.1 | Induction Labour Medical |
| | |
| R15.1 | Induction Labour Misoprostol |
| R15.- | Induction Labour NEC |
| R15.1 | Induction Labour Oxytocin |
| R15.1 | Induction Labour Prostaglandin |
| R14.- | Induction Labour Surgical |
| Q56.1 | Infertility Investigation Female NEC |
| Q41.- | Infertility Investigation Female Tubal Patency |
| N34.1 | Infertility Investigation Male NEC |
| S49.1 | Inflation Expander Skin |
| S49.1 | Inflation Expander Skin Breast |
| | |
| K37.- | Infundibulectomy Heart |
| X29.3 | Infusion Fluids Subcutaneous |
| X29.1 | Infusion Insulin Subcutaneous Pump |
| X29.- | Infusion Therapeutic Continuous |
| X28.- | Infusion Therapeutic Intermittent |
| X39.4 | Inhalation Administration Therapeutic Substance |
| | Injection – see also Insertion |
| | Injection – see also Introduction |
| Q14.- | Injection Amniotic Cavity Prostaglandin |
| Y82.2 | Injection Anaesthetic Local NEC |
| | |
| X30.6 | Injection Anaesthetic NEC |
| X35.5 | Injection Antimicrobial Therapy Intravenous |
| K50.3 | Injection Artery Coronary Transluminal Percutaneous NEC |
| M43.4 | Injection Bladder Nerve Neurolytic Endoscopic |
| M56.3 | Injection Bladder Outlet Female Inert Endoscopic |
| M66.3 | Injection Bladder Outlet Male Inert Endoscopic |
| M49.5 | Injection Bladder Wall Substance Therapeutic |
| C65.2 | Injection Bleb Following Glaucoma Surgery |
| B37.2 | Injection Breast |
| T62.5 | Injection Bursa |
| | |
| A54.- | Injection Cerebrospinal Fluid |
| Y09.2 | Injection Destructive NOC |
| D23.1 | Injection Ear Inner Transtympanic |
| D20.7 | Injection Ear Middle Transtympanic |
| Y81.- | Injection Epidural Anaesthetic |
| A52.- | Injection Epidural Therapeutic |
| C69.3 | Injection Eye Anterior Chamber |
| C86.7 | Injection Eye Around Therapeutic Substance |
| C89.3 | Injection Eye Posterior Segment NEC |
| C89.2 | Injection Eye Posterior Segment Steroid |

| | |
|---|---|
| C89.3 | Injection Eye Posterior Segment Substance Therapeutic |
| C22.4 | Injection Eyelid |
| Q38.2 | Injection Fallopian Tube Access Minimal |
| Q38.2 | Injection Fallopian Tube Endoscopic |
| Y39.1 | Injection Fistula Radiocontrast NOC |
| G43.4 | Injection G.I.Tract Upper Lesion Sclerosing Agent |
| G43.6 | Injection G.I.Tract Upper Lesion Therapy Fibreoptic Endoscopic |
| F48.5 | Injection Gland Salivary Therapeutic Substance |
| X30.- | Injection Globulin |
| H52.3 | Injection Haemorrhoid NEC |
| | |
| H52.3 | Injection Haemorrhoid Sclerosing |
| X38.3 | Injection Hormone NEC |
| Y39.3 | Injection Inert NOC |
| | Injection Intra-amniotic – see Injection Uterine Cavity |
| S53.- | Injection Intradermal NEC |
| X37.- | Injection Intramuscular NEC |
| A54.- | Injection Intrathecal |
| | Injection Intrauterine – see Injection Uterine Cavity |
| X35.- | Injection Intravenous NEC |
| W90.- | Injection Joint |
| | |
| M13.- | Injection Kidney Pelvis Percutaneous |
| M13.- | Injection Kidney Percutaneous |
| E38.1 | Injection Larynx (vocal cords) |
| L86.- | Injection Leg Vein Varicose |
| Y12.2 | Injection Lesion Destructive NOC |
| Y12.1 | Injection Lesion Sclerosing NOC |
| J10.3 | Injection Liver Transluminal Percutaneous |
| M43.4 | Injection Nerve Bladder Neurolytic Endoscopic |
| A60.5 | Injection Nerve Peripheral Destructive |
| A73.5 | Injection Nerve Peripheral Therapeutic |
| | |
| A57.4 | Injection Nerve Root Spinal Destructive |
| A57.7 | Injection Nerve Root Spinal Therapeutic |
| A81.2 | Injection Nerve Sympathetic Therapeutic |
| Y39.- | Injection NOC |
| C08.4 | Injection Orbit Retrobulbar |
| Y38.- | Injection Organ Substance Therapeutic |
| N32.4 | Injection Penis Substance Therapeutic |
| C86.7 | Injection Peribulbar Substance Therapeutic |
| K71.3 | Injection Pericardium Therapeutic |
| H60.4 | Injection Pilonidal Sinus Radiocontrast |
| | |
| X30.- | Injection Prophylactic NEC |
| X31.3 | Injection Radiocontrast Intravenous NEC |
| X31.- | Injection Radiocontrast NEC |
| Y39.2 | Injection Radiocontrast NOC |
| X30.5 | Injection Sclerosing NEC |
| Y09.1 | Injection Sclerosing NOC |
| X30.3 | Injection Serum Immune NEC |
| Y39.1 | Injection Sinus Track Radiocontrast NOC |
| S53.- | Injection Skin NEC |
| V54.4 | Injection Spinal Facet |

| | |
|---|---|
| X38.2 | Injection Steroid NEC |
| C43.4 | Injection Subconjunctival |
| X38.- | Injection Subcutaneous NEC |
| S51.- | Injection Subcutaneous Tissue Destructive |
| S50.- | Injection Subcutaneous Tissue Inert |
| X38.- | Injection Subcutaneous Tissue Therapeutic |
| C86.7 | Injection Subtenons Therapeutic Substance |
| T74.6 | Injection Tendon Blood Autologous |
| T74.4 | Injection Tendon Therapeutic Substance NEC |
| Y38.1 | Injection Therapeutic Continuous NOC |
| | |
| X30.- | Injection Therapeutic NEC |
| Y38.- | Injection Therapeutic NOC |
| X30.4 | Injection Thrombin NEC |
| L97.7 | Injection Thrombin Pseudoaneurysm |
| X38.1 | Injection Triamcinolone |
| M32.3 | Injection Ureteric Orifice Inert Endoscopic |
| Q14.- | Injection Uterine Cavity Abortifacient |
| Q15.3 | Injection Uterine Cavity NEC |
| Q14.- | Injection Uterine Cavity Prostaglandin |
| C79.- | Injection Vitreous Body |
| | |
| U40.1 | Inoculation Skin Intradermal Diagnostic |
| Q13.- | Insemination Artificial |
| | Insertion – see also Implantation |
| | Insertion – see also Injection |
| | Insertion – see also Introduction |
| L28.- | Insertion Aorta Aneurysmal Stent Endovascular |
| L27.- | Insertion Aorta Aneurysmal Stent Graft Endovascular |
| L26.7 | Insertion Aorta Stent Graft Branched Transluminal NEC |
| L26.6 | Insertion Aorta Stent Graft Fenestrated Transluminal NEC |
| L26.5 | Insertion Aorta Stent Transluminal Percutaneous |
| | |
| L31.4 | Insertion Artery Carotid Stent Transluminal Percutaneous |
| L35.3 | Insertion Artery Cerebral Stent Transluminal Percutaneous |
| L47.4 | Insertion Artery Coeliac Stent Transluminal Percutaneous |
| L69.5 | Insertion Artery Collateral Systemic to Pulmonary Major Stent Transluminal Percutaneous |
| K75.- | Insertion Artery Coronary Stent & Angioplasty Balloon Transluminal Percutaneous |
| K75.3 | Insertion Artery Coronary Stent & Angioplasty NEC |
| K75.1 | Insertion Artery Coronary Stent Drug-eluting & Angioplasty Balloon Transluminal Percutaneous |
| L63.5 | Insertion Artery Femoral Stent Transluminal Percutaneous |
| L54.4 | Insertion Artery Iliac Stent Transluminal Percutaneous |
| L47.4 | Insertion Artery Mesenteric Stent Transluminal Percutaneous |

| | |
|---|---|
| L66.7 | Insertion Artery Peripheral Stent Transluminal Percutaneous |
| L63.5 | Insertion Artery Popliteal Stent Transluminal Percutaneous |
| L13.6 | Insertion Artery Pulmonary Stent Transluminal Percutaneous |
| L43.5 | Insertion Artery Renal Stent Transluminal Percutaneous |
| L66.1 | Insertion Artery Stent & Thrombolysis Transluminal Percutaneous |
| L66.2 | Insertion Artery Stent Reconstruction Transluminal Percutaneous |
| L39.5 | Insertion Artery Subclavian Stent Transluminal Percutaneous |
| L47.4 | Insertion Artery Suprarenal Stent Transluminal Percutaneous |
| D05.1 | Insertion Auricular Fixtures Prosthesis First Stage |
| D05.2 | Insertion Auricular Fixtures Prosthesis Second Stage |
| | |
| M60.1 | Insertion Balloon Male Continence Adjustable |
| R04.5 | Insertion Bladder Fetus Drain Percutaneous |
| M55.6 | Insertion Bladder Outlet Female Balloon Continence Adjustable |
| M55.6 | Insertion Bladder Outlet Female Device Retropubic |
| W28.4 | Insertion Bone Intramedullary Fixator & Cementing |
| D13.1 | Insertion Bone Mastoid Prosthesis Anchored Fixture Hearing First Stage |
| D13.5 | Insertion Bone Mastoid Prosthesis Anchored Fixture Hearing One Stage |
| D13.2 | Insertion Bone Mastoid Prosthesis Anchored Fixture Hearing Second Stage |
| A10.6 | Insertion Brain Neoplasm Wafer Carmustine |
| A09.5 | Insertion Brain Neurostimulator Electrodes |
| | |
| C27.1 | Insertion Canalicular Stent |
| | Insertion Cannula – see Cannulation |
| C77.6 | Insertion Capsule Tension Ring |
| | Insertion Catheter – see Catheterisation |
| | Insertion Clip – see Clip site |
| H24.4 | Insertion Colon Sigmoid Stent Expanding Metal Sigmoidoscope Fibreoptic |
| H27.4 | Insertion Colon Sigmoid Stent Expanding Metal Sigmoidoscope Rigid |
| H21.4 | Insertion Colon Stent Expanding Metal Endoscopic Fibreoptic |
| H31.4 | Insertion Colorectal Stent Image Guided |
| C51.5 | Insertion Cornea Contact Lens Therapeutic |
| | |
| A33.4 | Insertion Cranial Nerve Neurostimulator Electrodes |
| C89.1 | Insertion Eye Posterior Segment Sustained Release Device |
| | Insertion Filter – see Filter site |
| G48.5 | Insertion Gastric Balloon |
| G45.3 | Insertion Gastrointestinal Tract Bravo Ph Capsule Endoscopic |
| G44.5 | Insertion Gastrostomy Endoscopic Fibreoptic Percutaneous |
| | Insertion Implant – see Implantation |
| S53.- | Insertion Intradermal NEC |
| C64.7 | Insertion Iris Hooks |
| W81.7 | Insertion Joint Prosthesis Spacer |
| | |
| J15.- | Insertion Liver Blood Vessel Prosthesis Transluminal Percutaneous |
| V28.- | Insertion Lumbar Interspinous Process Spacer |
| A70.4 | Insertion Nerve Peripheral Neurostimulator Electrodes |
| | Insertion Neurostimulator – see Neurostimulator site |
| G16.3 | Insertion Oesophagus Bravo pH Capsule Endoscopic Fibreoptic |
| G19.2 | Insertion Oesophagus Bravo pH Capsule Endoscopic Rigid |
| G15.7 | Insertion Oesophagus Stent Expanding Metal Covered Endoscopic |
| G15.6 | Insertion Oesophagus Stent Expanding Metal Endoscopic NEC |
| G21.5 | Insertion Oesophagus Stent NEC |
| F14.6 | Insertion Orthodontic Anchorage |

| | |
|---|---|
| F14.- | Insertion Orthodontic Appliance |
| F14.6 | Insertion Orthodontic Screw |
| R04.4 | Insertion Pleural Fetus Drain Percutaneous |
| M68.1 | Insertion Prostate Stent Cystoscopic |
| | Insertion Prosthesis – see Prosthesis site |
| C29.3 | Insertion Punctal Plug |
| H24.4 | Insertion Rectum Stent Expanding Metal Sigmoidoscope Fibreoptic |
| H27.4 | Insertion Rectum Stent Expanding Metal Sigmoidoscope Rigid |
| M60.1 | Insertion Retropubic Male Device Continence |
| | Insertion Seton – see Seton site |
| | |
| | Insertion Shunt – see Shunt site |
| | Insertion Skin Expander – see Expander Skin |
| S53.- | Insertion Skin NEC |
| | Insertion Sling – see Sling site |
| A48.7 | Insertion Spinal Cord Neurostimulator Electrodes |
| | Insertion Stent – see also Placement Stent |
| | Insertion Stent – see also Prosthesis |
| Y14.1 | Insertion Stent Expanding Metal Covered NOC |
| Y14.2 | Insertion Stent Expanding Metal NOC |
| Y14.5 | Insertion Stent Graft NOC |
| | |
| Y14.3 | Insertion Stent Metal NOC |
| Y14.- | Insertion Stent NOC |
| Y14.4 | Insertion Stent Plastic NOC |
| S51.- | Insertion Subcutaneous Tissue Destructive |
| S52.5 | Insertion Subcutaneous Tissue Hormone |
| S50.- | Insertion Subcutaneous Tissue Inert |
| S52.5 | Insertion Subcutaneous Tissue Substance Contraceptive |
| S62.6 | Insertion Subcutaneous Tissue Substance Diagnostic |
| S52.- | Insertion Subcutaneous Tissue Therapeutic |
| | Insertion Suture – see Suture site |
| | |
| | Insertion System – see System |
| T64.- | Insertion Tendon Bone |
| R04.6 | Insertion Tracheal Plug Fetal Percutaneous |
| R01.2 | Insertion Tracheal Plug Fetoscopic |
| | Insertion Tube – see Drainage |
| | Insertion Tube – see Tube |
| M33.1 | Insertion Ureter Stent Metallic Percutaneous |
| M33.5 | Insertion Ureter Stent Percutaneous NEC |
| M33.2 | Insertion Ureter Stent Plastic Percutaneous |
| M27.4 | Insertion Ureter Stent Ureteroscopic |
| | |
| M76.6 | Insertion Urethra Stent Endoscopic |
| P26.- | Insertion Vagina Pessary Supporting |
| P26.2 | Insertion Vagina Ring Pessary |
| L97.6 | Insertion Vascular Closure Device |
| L99.7 | Insertion Vein Central Catheter Peripheral Transluminal Percutaneous |
| L94.3 | Insertion Vein Port Subcutaneous Transluminal Percutaneous |
| J06.2 | Insertion Vein Portal Stent Graft Intrahepatic Transjugular |
| J15.5 | Insertion Vein Portal Stent Graft Transluminal Percutaneous |
| J06.1 | Insertion Vein Portal Stent Intrahepatic Transjugular |
| J15.4 | Insertion Vein Portal Stent Transluminal Percutaneous |

| | |
|---|---|
| L80.4 | Insertion Vein Pulmonary Stent Transluminal Percutaneous |
| L99.3 | Insertion Vein Stent & Thrombolysis Transluminal Percutaneous |
| L99.2 | Insertion Vein Stent Reconstruction Transluminal Percutaneous |
| L94.5 | Insertion Vein Stent Transluminal Percutaneous NEC |
| L79.3 | Insertion Vena Cava Stent NEC |
| | Insertion Wire – see Wiring site |
| K53.1 | Inspection Heart Valve |
| Y37.1 | Instillation Substance Photodynamic NOC |
| | Instrumentation – see also Probing |
| V41.- | Instrumentation Spine Correction Deformity |
| | |
| D22.3 | Insufflation Eustachian Canal |
| Q41.4 | Insufflation Fallopian Tube |
| T13.1 | Insufflation Pleural Cavity Talc NEC |
| | Interposition – see also Anastomosis |
| | Interposition Arthroplasty – see Arthroplasty site |
| L29.6 | Interposition Extracranial to Intracranial High Flow |
| G05.- | Interposition Oesophagus NEC |
| L82.2 | Interposition Vein Valve |
| | Intervention Coronary Percutaneous – see Angioplasty Artery Coronary Balloon & Insertion Stent Transluminal Percutaneous |
| | Intervention Coronary Percutaneous – see Angioplasty Artery Coronary Balloon Transluminal Percutaneous |
| | |
| N35.- | Intervention Genitalia Male Non-operative |
| Z99.- | Intervertebral Disc site |
| Z28.- | Intestine Large site |
| G79.- | Intestine Small Operations Endoscopic Therapeutic NEC |
| G82.- | Intestine Small Operations NEC |
| G78.- | Intestine Small Operations Open NEC |
| Z27.7 | Intestine Small site |
| W71.- | Intra-articular Structure Operations NEC |
| X39.3 | Intranasal Administration Therapeutic Subtance |
| | Introduction – see also Injection |
| | |
| | Introduction – see also Insertion |
| Q14.- | Introduction Amniotic Cavity Abortifacient |
| M53.6 | Introduction Bladder Female Tape Transobturator |
| M64.7 | Introduction Bladder Male Transobturator Sling |
| M49.4 | Introduction Bladder Substance Therapeutic |
| W35.- | Introduction Bone Substance |
| Y35.1 | Introduction Caesium Radioactive NOC |
| Y36.1 | Introduction Gold Seeds NOC |
| Y36.2 | Introduction Implant Therapeutic NOC |
| S53.- | Introduction Intradermal NEC |

| | |
|---|---|
| | Introduction Intrauterine – see Introduction Uterine Cavity |
| Y35.2 | Introduction Iridium Wire NOC |
| Y36.- | Introduction Material Non-removable NOC |
| Y35.- | Introduction Material Radioactive Removable NOC |
| T48.- | Introduction Peritoneal Cavity Substance |
| | Introduction Pessary – see Pessary site |
| T13.- | Introduction Pleural Cavity Substance |
| Y35.3 | Introduction Radium NOC |
| S53.- | Introduction Skin NEC |
| S51.- | Introduction Subcutaneous Tissue Destructive |
| | |
| S50.- | Introduction Subcutaneous Tissue Inert |
| S52.- | Introduction Subcutaneous Tissue Therapeutic |
| Y37.1 | Introduction Substance Photodynamic NOC |
| Q12.1 | Introduction Uterine Cavity Contraceptive Device |
| Q13.- | Introduction Uterine Cavity Gamete |
| Q15.- | Introduction Uterine Cavity Substance NEC |
| M53.2 | Introduction Vagina Bean Biethium |
| M53.3 | Introduction Vagina Tension Free Tape |
| | Intubation – see also Drainage |
| | Intubation – see also Tube site |
| | |
| M38.2 | Intubation Bladder Suprapubic |
| H62.4 | Intubation Bowel NEC |
| H30.- | Intubation Colon |
| G57.- | Intubation Duodenum |
| D22.2 | Intubation Eustachian Canal |
| G82.- | Intubation Ileum |
| G78.6 | Intubation Ileum Open |
| G82.- | Intubation Intestine Small NEC |
| G78.6 | Intubation Intestine Small Open NEC |
| G67.- | Intubation Jejunum |
| | |
| G63.4 | Intubation Jejunum Open |
| G21.- | Intubation Oesophagus |
| H46.- | Intubation Rectum |
| G47.- | Intubation Stomach |
| X56.- | Intubation Trachea |
| K05.- | Inversion Atrial Transposition Arteries Great |
| Q56.1 | Investigation Fertility Female NEC |
| Q41.- | Investigation Fertility Female Tubal Patency |
| N34.1 | Investigation Fertility Male NEC |
| Q56.1 | Investigation Infertility Female NEC |
| | |
| Q41.- | Investigation Infertility Female Tubal Patency |
| N34.1 | Investigation Infertility Male NEC |
| C59.- | Iridectomy |
| C59.1 | Iridocyclectomy |
| C62.4 | Iridodialysis |
| C60.4 | Iridoplasty NEC |
| C62.1 | Iridosclerotomy |
| C62.- | Iridotomy |
| C60.- | Iris Operations Filtering |
| C64.- | Iris Operations NEC |

| | |
|---|---|
| Z18.4 | Iris site |
| D08.5 | Irrigation Auditory Canal External NEC |
| D07.1 | Irrigation Auditory Canal External Wax |
| M47.1 | Irrigation Bladder Urethral |
| W33.7 | Irrigation Bone NEC |
| H62.5 | Irrigation Bowel NEC |
| E48.6 | Irrigation Bronchus Endoscopic NEC |
| E50.6 | Irrigation Bronchus Endoscopic Rigid |
| E52.1 | Irrigation Bronchus NEC |
| E48.6 | Irrigation Carina Endoscopic NEC |
| | |
| E50.6 | Irrigation Carina Endoscopic Rigid |
| H30.5 | Irrigation Colon |
| D07.1 | Irrigation Ear Wax |
| C69.4 | Irrigation Eye Anterior Chamber |
| W80.- | Irrigation Joint |
| W85.2 | Irrigation Joint Knee Endoscopic |
| M16.1 | Irrigation Kidney |
| C27.3 | Irrigation Lacrimal Duct |
| E48.6 | Irrigation Lung Endoscopic NEC |
| E50.6 | Irrigation Lung Endoscopic Rigid |
| | |
| E12.3 | Irrigation Maxillary Antrum Approach Sublabial |
| E13.6 | Irrigation Maxillary Antrum NEC |
| C27.3 | Irrigation Nasolacrimal Duct |
| Y22.3 | Irrigation NOC |
| T46.3 | Irrigation Peritoneal Cavity |
| E48.6 | Irrigation Respiratory Tract Lower Endoscopic NEC |
| E50.6 | Irrigation Respiratory Tract Lower Endoscopic Rigid |
| | Irrigation Shunt – see Shunt site |
| G47.3 | Irrigation Stomach |
| E48.6 | Irrigation Trachea Endoscopic NEC |
| | |
| E50.6 | Irrigation Trachea Endoscopic Rigid |
| E52.1 | Irrigation Trachea NEC |
| Z75.4 | Ischium site |
| B08.5 | Isthmectomy Thyroid |

# J

| | |
|---|---|
| V19.- | Jaw Operations NEC |
| Z65.- | Jaw site |
| G58.- | Jejunectomy |
| G65.- | Jejunoscopy NEC |
| G62.- | Jejunoscopy Open |
| G60.- | Jejunostomy |
| G64.- | Jejunum Operations Endoscopic Therapeutic |
| G67.- | Jejunum Operations NEC |
| G62.- | Jejunum Operations Open Endoscopic |
| G63.- | Jejunum Operations Open NEC |
| | |
| Z27.5 | Jejunum site |
| Z81.- | Joint Arm site NEC |
| Z67.1 | Joint Atlanto-occipital site |
| Z67.2 | Joint Atlantoaxial site |
| Z87.3 | Joint Capsule site |
| W85.- | Joint Cavity Knee Operations Endoscopic Therapeutic |
| W86.- | Joint Cavity Operations Endoscopic Therapeutic NEC |
| Z83.- | Joint Finger site |
| Z86.- | Joint Foot site NEC |
| Z82.- | Joint Hand site NEC |
| | |
| Z67.- | Joint Intervertebral site |
| W85.- | Joint Knee Operations Endoscopic Therapeutic |
| Z85.- | Joint Leg Lower site |
| Z84.- | Joint Leg Upper site |
| Z87.2 | Joint Ligament site |
| Z67.6 | Joint Lumbosacral site |
| W77.- | Joint Operations Blocking Stabilising Joint |
| W86.- | Joint Operations Endoscopic Therapeutic NEC |
| W92.- | Joint Operations NEC |
| W81.- | Joint Operations Open NEC |
| | |
| W77.- | Joint Operations Stabilising |
| Z84.- | Joint Pelvis site |
| Z81.- | Joint Shoulder Girdle site |
| Z87.4 | Joint site NEC |
| W84.- | Joint Structure Knee Operations Endoscopic Therapeutic NEC |
| W84.- | Joint Structure Operations Endoscopic Therapeutic NEC |
| W69.- | Joint Synovial Membrane Operations Open |
| Z85.- | Joint Tarsus site NEC |
| V21.- | Joint Temporomandibular Operations NEC |
| Z65.2 | Joint Temporomandibular site |
| | |
| W79.- | Joint Toe Operations Soft Tissue |
| Z82.- | Joint Wrist site |
| Z40.4 | Jugular Body site |

# K

# L

| | |
|---|---|
| D26.- | Labyrinthectomy |
| C29.- | Lacrimal Apparatus Operations NEC |
| Z16.7 | Lacrimal Apparatus site |
| C24.- | Lacrimal Gland Operations |
| Z16.5 | Lacrimal Gland site |
| C26.- | Lacrimal Sac Operations NEC |
| Z16.6 | Lacrimal Sac site |
| | Laminectomy – see also Excision Disc Intervertebral |
| V49.- | Laminectomy Exploratory |
| Y48.- | Laminectomy Spine Approach |
| | |
| V22.7 | Laminoplasty Spine Cervical NEC |
| V23.7 | Laminoplasty Spine Cervical Revisional |
| | Laparoscopic – refer to Index Introduction |
| Y75.- | Laparoscopic Approach NEC |
| T43.- | Laparoscopy |
| Q39.- | Laparoscopy Fallopian Tube |
| Q50.- | Laparoscopy Ovary |
| Y50.2 | Laparotomy Approach NEC |
| T30.- | Laparotomy Exploratory |
| S58.- | Larvae Therapy |
| | |
| E29.- | Laryngectomy Open |
| E35.6 | Laryngectomy Partial Endoscopic |
| E29.5 | Laryngofissure & Chordectomy Vocal Chord |
| E36.- | Laryngoscopy |
| E31.2 | Laryngotracheoplasty NEC |
| E33.3 | Larynx Cartilage Operations NEC |
| E34.- | Larynx Operations Endoscopic Microtherapeutic |
| E35.- | Larynx Operations Endoscopic Therapeutic NEC |
| E38.- | Larynx Operations NEC |
| E33.- | Larynx Operations Open NEC |
| | |
| Z24.2 | Larynx site |
| Y08.- | Laser NOC |
| Y71.- | Late Operations NOC |
| Z94.- | Laterality Operations |
| | Lavage – see also Irrigation |
| E49.- | Lavage Respiratory Tract Lower Endoscopic Fibreoptic |
| E49.- | Lavage Respiratory Tract Lower Endoscopic NEC |
| | Laying Open – see Opening |
| Z94.3 | Left Sided Operations |
| Z90.- | Leg Region site NEC |

| | |
|---|---|
| O13.- | Leg Region site Other NEC (Z) |
| W17.- | Lengthening Bone |
| C35.2 | Lengthening Eye Muscle Slide |
| T70.5 | Lengthening Muscle |
| C35.2 | Lengthening Muscle Eye Slide |
| T70.5 | Lengthening Tendon |
| C77.- | Lens Operations NEC |
| Z19.1 | Lens site |
| C74.3 | Lensectomy Mechanical |
| C74.3 | Lensectomy Pars Plana |
| | |
| X32.7 | Leucopheresis |
| A10.1 | Leucotomy NEC |
| A03.1 | Leucotomy Stereotactic |
| V55.- | Levels Spine |
| | Lift – see also Elevation |
| S01.4 | Lift Brow |
| S03.1 | Lift Buttock |
| S01.- | Lift Face |
| S03.2 | Lift Thigh |
| Q52.- | Ligament Broad Uterus Operations NEC |
| | |
| W76.- | Ligament Operations NEC |
| Z87.2 | Ligament site |
| Q54.- | Ligament Uterus Operations NEC |
| | Ligation – see also Occlusion |
| L75.2 | Ligation Arteriovenous Fistula Acquired |
| L75.1 | Ligation Arteriovenous Malformation Congenital |
| L38.2 | Ligation Artery Axillary |
| L38.2 | Ligation Artery Brachial |
| L30.2 | Ligation Artery Carotid |
| L33.3 | Ligation Artery Cerebral Aneurysmal |
| | |
| L33.3 | Ligation Artery Circle Willis Aneurysmal |
| L46.3 | Ligation Artery Coeliac |
| E12.1 | Ligation Artery Maxillary Approach Sublabial |
| L46.3 | Ligation Artery Mesenteric |
| L70.3 | Ligation Artery NEC |
| E05.2 | Ligation Artery Nose Internal |
| L62.3 | Ligation Artery Popliteal Aneurysmal |
| L12.6 | Ligation Artery Pulmonary |
| L42.3 | Ligation Artery Renal |
| L38.2 | Ligation Artery Subclavian |
| | |
| L46.3 | Ligation Artery Suprarenal |
| L38.2 | Ligation Artery Vertebral |
| L02.2 | Ligation Ductus Arteriosus Patent |
| Q27.1 | Ligation Fallopian Tube Bilateral Open |
| Q28.- | Ligation Fallopian Tube Open NEC |
| G43.7 | Ligation Gastrointestinal Tract Upper Rubber Band Endoscopic Fibreoptic |
| H52.4 | Ligation Haemorrhoid |
| L85.- | Ligation Leg Vein Varicose |
| E57.2 | Ligation Lung Bulla |
| T89.3 | Ligation Lymphatic Duct |

| | |
|---|---|
| Y07.1 | Ligation NOC |
| E05.2 | Ligation Nose Internal Artery |
| G10.4 | Ligation Oesophagus Varices Local |
| G43.7 | Ligation Oesophagus Varices Rubber Band Endoscopic Fibreoptic |
| F52.1 | Ligation Parotid Duct |
| T19.3 | Ligation Patent Processus Vaginalis |
| F52.- | Ligation Salivary Duct |
| K55.1 | Ligation Sinus Valsalva |
| F52.2 | Ligation Submandibular Duct |
| N19.1 | Ligation Varicocele |
| | |
| N17.2 | Ligation Vas Deferens NEC |
| L93.3 | Ligation Vein NEC |
| L83.2 | Ligation Vein Perforating Leg Subfascial Open |
| | Ligature – see Ligation |
| | Ligature Removal – see Removal from site Ligature |
| S12.- | Light Therapy Skin Ultraviolet |
| L91.3 | Linogram Venous Catheter Central |
| F06.- | Lip Mucosa Operations NEC |
| F06.- | Lip Operations NEC |
| Z25.1 | Lip site |
| | |
| F06.- | Lip Skin Operations NEC |
| Z25.1 | Lip Skin site |
| S02.2 | Lipectomy Abdominal |
| S03.3 | Lipectomy NEC |
| S01.3 | Lipectomy Submental |
| B37.5 | Lipofilling Breast |
| Y39.4 | Lipofilling Organ Injection |
| S62.- | Liposuction Subcutaneous Tissue |
| M44.1 | Lithopaxy Endoscopic |
| | Lithotripsy – see also Fragmentation |
| | |
| N27.4 | Lithotripsy Penis Lesion Extracorporeal Shockwave |
| T74.5 | Lithotripsy Tendon Calculus Extracorporeal Shockwave |
| J11.- | Liver Blood Vessel Operations Transjugular Intrahepatic |
| J06.- | Liver Blood Vessel Operations Transjugular Intrahepatic Other |
| J10.- | Liver Blood Vessel Operations Transluminal |
| J77.- | Liver Blood Vessel Operations Transluminal Other |
| X43.- | Liver Failure Compensation |
| J08.- | Liver Operations Endoscopic Therapeutic |
| J08.- | Liver Operations Laparoscope |
| J16.- | Liver Operations NEC |
| | |
| J07.- | Liver Operations Open NEC |
| J13.- | Liver Operations Percutaneous Diagnostic |
| J12.- | Liver Operations Percutaneous Therapeutic NEC |
| J08.- | Liver Operations Peritonoscope |
| Z30.1 | Liver site |
| A01.- | Lobectomy Brain |
| E54.- | Lobectomy Lung |
| B08.4 | Lobectomy Thyroid NEC |
| Z10.- | Lumbar Plexus site |
| B28.3 | Lumpectomy Breast |

| | |
|---|---|
| Z72.3 | Lunate site |
| E48.- | Lung Operations Endoscopic NEC |
| E50.- | Lung Operations Endoscopic Rigid |
| E59.- | Lung Operations NEC |
| E57.- | Lung Operations Open NEC |
| Z24.6 | Lung site |
| T91.- | Lymph Node Operations Sentinel |
| O14.2 | Lymph Node Sentinal (Z) |
| Z61.- | Lymph Node site |
| O14.- | Lymph Node site Other (Z) |
| | |
| T90.- | Lymphangiography |
| T89.- | Lymphatic Duct Operations |
| Z62.2 | Lymphatic Duct site |
| T92.- | Lymphatic Tissue Operations NEC |
| Z62.3 | Lymphatic Tissue site |

# M

| | |
|---|---|
| H57.2 | Maintenance Anal Sphincter Artificial NEC |
| | Maintenance Pack – see Packing |
| | Maintenance Prosthesis – see Prosthesis site |
| | Maintenance Shunt – see Shunt site |
| H57.6 | Maintenance Sphincter Dynamic Graciloplasty |
| Y15.1 | Maintenance Stent NOC |
| | Maintenance System – see System |
| Z78.4 | Malleolus Lateral site |
| Z77.3 | Malleolus Medial site |
| B34.- | Mammary Duct Operations |
| | |
| U18.3 | Mammography |
| B31.- | Mammoplasty |
| V19.- | Mandible Operations NEC |
| Z65.1 | Mandible site |
| V14.- | Mandibulectomy |
| | Manipulation – see also Remanipulation |
| W26.- | Manipulation Bone Fracture |
| W25.- | Manipulation Bone Fracture & Fixation External |
| V09.2 | Manipulation Bone Nose Fracture |
| H17.- | Manipulation Caecum Intra-abdominal |
| | |
| H17.- | Manipulation Colon Intra-abdominal |
| Y42.1 | Manipulation External NOC |
| G76.- | Manipulation Ileum Intra-abdominal |
| G76.- | Manipulation Intestine Small Intra-abdominal NEC |
| V19.5 | Manipulation Jaw NEC |
| W66.- | Manipulation Joint Dislocation Fracture |
| W66.- | Manipulation Joint Dislocation NEC |
| W91.- | Manipulation Joint NEC |
| W91.3 | Manipulation Joint Prosthetic NEC |
| W91.1 | Manipulation Joint Traction NEC |
| | |
| V19.5 | Manipulation Mandible NEC |
| Y42.- | Manipulation NOC |
| H44.- | Manipulation Rectum |
| V50.- | Manipulation Spine |
| Q20.3 | Manipulation Uterus Manual |
| L72.2 | Manometry Arterial NEC |
| M49.8 | Manometry Bladder |
| A11.3 | Manometry Brain Tissue |
| A20.3 | Manometry Brain Ventricle |
| H30.2 | Manometry Colon |

| | |
|---|---|
| H30.2 | Manometry Intestine NEC |
| T83.5 | Manometry Muscle Compartment Catheter |
| Y44.2 | Manometry NOC |
| G21.- | Manometry Oesophagus |
| H46.3 | Manometry Rectum |
| A55.3 | Manometry Spinal |
| G47.- | Manometry Stomach |
| J11.7 | Manometry Vein Hepatic Intrahepatic Transjugular |
| L95.2 | Manometry Vein NEC |
| J11.6 | Manometry Vein Portal Intrahepatic Transjugular |
| | |
| | Mapping – see Study |
| A11.4 | Mapping Cortical |
| | Marsupialisation – see also Deroofing |
| | Marsupialisation – see also Excision |
| P03.2 | Marsupialisation Bartholin Gland |
| C29.4 | Marsupialisation Canaliculus |
| F18.2 | Marsupialisation Jaw Lesion Dental |
| J02.5 | Marsupialisation Liver Lesion |
| Y06.1 | Marsupialisation NOC |
| Q43.3 | Marsupialisation Ovary Lesion |
| | |
| J70.2 | Marsupialisation Spleen Lesion |
| P17.3 | Marsupialisation Vagina Lesion |
| X61.3 | Massage Body |
| K55.2 | Massage Heart Chest Open |
| M70.5 | Massage Prostate |
| H44.5 | Massage Rectum |
| B27.- | Mastectomy |
| D12.- | Mastoid Operations NEC |
| Z20.3 | Mastoid site |
| D10.- | Mastoidectomy |
| | |
| B31.3 | Mastopexy |
| Z64.4 | Maxilla site |
| E12.- | Maxillary Antrum Operations Approach Sublabial |
| E13.- | Maxillary Antrum Operations NEC |
| Z23.1 | Maxillary Antrum site |
| V06.- | Maxillectomy |
| | Measurement – see Manometry |
| | Measurement – see Study |
| D03.4 | Meatoplasty Ear External |
| M81.2 | Meatoplasty Urethra |
| | |
| M32.2 | Meatotomy Ureteric Orifice Endoscopic |
| M81.3 | Meatotomy Urethral Orifice External |
| E35.7 | Medialisation Vocal Cord Endoscopic |
| E33.6 | Medialisation Vocal Cord Using Biological Implant |
| E33.5 | Medialisation Vocal Cord Using Implant |
| E63.- | Mediastinoscopy |
| E63.- | Mediastinoscopy Cervical |
| E61.4 | Mediastinotomy NEC |
| E62.- | Mediastinum Operations Endoscopic Therapeutic |
| E61.- | Mediastinum Operations Open |

| | |
|---|---|
| Z24.7 | Mediastinum site |
| C80.- | Membrane Retina Operations |
| C73.1 | Membranectomy Lens |
| W82.- | Meniscectomy Endoscopic |
| V21.1 | Meniscectomy Joint Temporomandibular |
| W70.- | Meniscectomy NEC |
| T38.- | Mesentery Colon Operations |
| T37.- | Mesentery Intestine Small Operations |
| Z53.6 | Mesentery site |
| Q17.5 | Metroplasty Endoscopic |
| | |
| Q09.5 | Metroplasty Open |
| V29.6 | Microdiscectomy Disc Intervertebral Cervical NEC |
| V30.6 | Microdiscectomy Disc Intervertebral Cervical Revisional |
| V33.7 | Microdiscectomy Disc Intervertebral Lumbar NEC |
| V34.7 | Microdiscectomy Disc Intervertebral Lumbar Revisional |
| B34.4 | Microdochotomy |
| W84.5 | Microfracture Bone Cartilage Articular Repair |
| E37.- | Microlaryngoscopy |
| | Microwave – see Destruction |
| K38.3 | Mitral Subvalvar Apparatus Operations |
| | |
| H62.2 | Mobilisation Bowel NEC |
| | Monitoring – see also Establishing |
| U19.6 | Monitoring Cardiomemo Electrocardiographic |
| | Monitoring Pressure – see Manometry |
| W83.7 | Mosaicplasty Endoscopic |
| F42.- | Mouth Operations NEC |
| F40.5 | Mouth Removal Suture NEC |
| Z25.- | Mouth site |
| X61.4 | Movement Therapy |
| | Muscle – see also site Muscle |
| | |
| Z60.3 | Muscle Abdominal Wall Anterior site |
| Z54.- | Muscle Arm Upper site |
| Z60.4 | Muscle Back site |
| Z60.5 | Muscle Chest site |
| E28.- | Muscle Cricopharyngeus Operations |
| C31.- | Muscle Eye Operations Combined |
| C37.- | Muscle Eye Operations NEC |
| Z17.- | Muscle Eye site NEC |
| Z60.1 | Muscle Face site |
| Z59.- | Muscle Foot site |
| | |
| Z55.- | Muscle Forearm site |
| Z56.- | Muscle Hand site |
| Z57.- | Muscle Hip site |
| Z58.- | Muscle Leg Lower site |
| Z60.2 | Muscle Neck site |
| T83.- | Muscle Operations NEC |
| Z54.- | Muscle Shoulder site |
| Z60.- | Muscle site NEC |
| Z57.- | Muscle Thigh site |
| Z60.5 | Muscle Thorax site |

| | |
|---|---|
| Z87.- | Musculoskeletal System site NEC |
| K24.6 | Myectomy Ventricular Outflow Tract |
| A55.2 | Myelography Spinal NEC |
| A45.3 | Myelotomy Spinal Cord |
| A45.3 | Myelotomy Spinal Tract |
| Q09.2 | Myomectomy Open |
| E28.1 | Myotomy Cricopharyngeal |
| M41.6 | Myotomy Detrusor |
| T83.2 | Myotomy NEC |
| K24.7 | Myotomy Ventricular Outflow Tract |
| | |
| D14.- | Myringoplasty |
| D15.- | Myringotomy |

# N

| | |
|---|---|
| S66.- | Nail Bed Operations NEC |
| Z51.1 | Nail Bed site |
| S70.- | Nail Operations NEC |
| Z51.- | Nail site |
| E17.- | Nasal Sinus Operations NEC |
| Z23.- | Nasal Sinus site |
| C27.- | Nasolacrimal Duct Operations |
| E21.- | Nasopharyngoplasty |
| E25.- | Nasopharyngoscopy |
| E24.- | Nasopharynx Operations Endoscopic Therapeutic |
| | |
| E27.- | Nasopharynx Operations NEC |
| E23.- | Nasopharynx Operations Open NEC |
| Z22.6 | Nasopharynx site |
| Z79.3 | Navicular site |
| E89.3 | Nebuliser NEC |
| J57.6 | Necrosectomy Pancreatic |
| C65.1 | Needling Bleb Following Glaucoma Surgery |
| C71.1 | Needling Lens Cataract |
| A47.1 | Needling Spinal Cord Cervical Substantia Gelatinosa |
| M02.- | Nephrectomy NEC |
| | |
| M03.- | Nephrectomy Partial NEC |
| M06.1 | Nephrolithotomy |
| M16.4 | Nephrolithotomy Percutaneous NEC |
| M05.3 | Nephropexy |
| M11.- | Nephroscopy |
| M15.1 | Nephrostomography |
| | Nephrostomy – see also Drainage Kidney |
| M06.- | Nephrostomy |
| M13.6 | Nephrostomy Tube Insertion Percutaneous |
| M02.- | Nephroureterectomy |
| | |
| Z09.- | Nerve Arm Peripheral site |
| Y82.1 | Nerve Block Anaesthetic |
| | Nerve Block Destructive – see Denervation site |
| | Nerve Block Destructive – see Destruction Nerve |
| Y82.1 | Nerve Block NEC |
| Z09.1 | Nerve Circumflex site |
| A84.3 | Nerve Conduction Studies |
| A36.- | Nerve Cranial Operations NEC |
| Z04.- | Nerve Cranial site NEC |
| Z03.- | Nerve Cranial Upper site |

| | |
|---|---|
| Z10.3 | Nerve Cutaneous Lateral Thigh site |
| Z09.- | Nerve Digital Finger site |
| Z12.5 | Nerve Digital Toe site |
| Z10.1 | Nerve Femoral site |
| Z09.- | Nerve Finger site |
| Z10.5 | Nerve Iliohypogastric site |
| Z10.4 | Nerve Ilioinguinal site |
| Z09.6 | Nerve Interosseous Anterior site |
| Z09.5 | Nerve Interosseous Posterior site |
| Z12.6 | Nerve Leg Peripheral site NEC |
| | |
| Z09.2 | Nerve Median site |
| Z10.2 | Nerve Obturator site |
| Z09.- | Nerve Peripheral Arm site |
| Z12.6 | Nerve Peripheral Leg site NEC |
| A73.- | Nerve Peripheral Operations NEC |
| Z12.- | Nerve Peripheral site |
| Z12.4 | Nerve Plantar site |
| Z12.1 | Nerve Popliteal site |
| Z09.3 | Nerve Radial site |
| A57.- | Nerve Root Spinal Ganglion Operations |
| | |
| A57.- | Nerve Root Spinal Operations |
| Z07.- | Nerve Root Spinal site |
| Z11.2 | Nerve Sacral site |
| Z11.1 | Nerve Sciatic site |
| Z12.- | Nerve site NEC |
| Z12.3 | Nerve Sural site |
| A81.- | Nerve Sympathetic Operations NEC |
| Z12.7 | Nerve Sympathetic site |
| Z10.3 | Nerve Thigh Cutaneous Lateral site |
| Z12.2 | Nerve Tibial Posterior site |
| | |
| Z12.5 | Nerve Toe Digital site |
| Z09.4 | Nerve Ulna site |
| D24.4 | Neurectomy Cochlea |
| A59.- | Neurectomy NEC |
| E12.4 | Neurectomy Nerve Vidian Transantral Approach Sublabial |
| D26.4 | Neurectomy Vestibular Apparatus |
| | Neurolysis – see also Release Nerve Entrapment |
| A31.- | Neurolysis Nerve Cranial Intracranial Stereotactic |
| A68.- | Neurolysis Nerve Peripheral NEC |
| A69.- | Neurolysis Nerve Peripheral Revision |
| | |
| A84.- | Neurophysiological Operations |
| | Neurostimulation – see Neurostimulator |
| A09.- | Neurostimulator Brain |
| A33.- | Neurostimulator Nerve Cranial |
| A70.- | Neurostimulator Nerve Peripheral |
| A48.- | Neurostimulator Spinal Cord |
| A36.4 | Neurotomy Optic Radial (ii) |
| B35.- | Nipple Operations |
| B35.4 | Nipple Operations Plastic |
| Z15.6 | Nipple site |

| | |
|---|---|
| B36. | Nipple Skin Operations |
| Z15.6 | Nipple Skin site |
| Y90.- | Non-operations NEC |
| E09.- | Nose External Operations |
| Z22.- | Nose External site |
| E09.- | Nose External Skin Operations |
| Z22.- | Nose External Skin site |
| E08.- | Nose Internal Operations NEC |
| E10.- | Nose Operations NEC |
| E02.- | Nose Operations Plastic |
| | |
| E07.- | Nose Operations Plastic Other |
| E03.- | Nose Septum Operations |
| E16.- | Nose Sinuses Endoscopic Examination Diagnostic |
| Z22.- | Nose site NEC |
| E04.- | Nose Turbinate Operations |
| U23.- | Nuclear Medicine Haematological Tests |

# O

| | |
|---|---|
| L33.4 | Obliteration Artery Cerebral Aneurysmal NEC |
| L33.4 | Obliteration Artery Circle Willis Aneurysmal NEC |
| Y07.- | Obliteration Cavity NOC |
| Y07.4 | Obliteration Diverticulum NOC |
| Y07.3 | Obliteration Fistula NOC |
| D12.1 | Obliteration Mastoid |
| Y07.3 | Obliteration Sinus Track NOC |
| P18.- | Obliteration Vagina NEC |
| R34.- | Obstetric Operations NEC |
| | Occlusion – see also Ligation |
| | |
| L08.7 | Occlusion Artery Anastomosis Subclavian Pulmonary Transluminal Percutaneous |
| L66.4 | Occlusion Artery Balloon Test Transluminal Percutaneous |
| L69.1 | Occlusion Artery Collateral Systemic to Pulmonary Major |
| K78.1 | Occlusion Artery Mammary Left Internal Side Branch Transluminal Percutaneous |
| L07.5 | Occlusion Artery Shunt Subclavian Pulmonary Transluminal Percutaneous |
| L66.3 | Occlusion Artery Transluminal Percutaneous |
| H31.- | Occlusion Colorectal Fistula Image Guided |
| H31.1 | Occlusion Colorectal Fistula Percutaneous Image Guided |
| H31.2 | Occlusion Colorectal Fistula Transluminal Image Guided |
| L03.1 | Occlusion Ductus Arteriosus Patent Prosthetic Transluminal Percutaneous |
| | |
| Q35.- | Occlusion Fallopian Tube Bilateral Access Minimal |
| Q35.- | Occlusion Fallopian Tube Bilateral Endoscopic NEC |
| Q27.- | Occlusion Fallopian Tube Bilateral Open |
| Q36.- | Occlusion Fallopian Tube Endoscopic NEC |
| Q28.- | Occlusion Fallopian Tube Open NEC |
| C29.3 | Occlusion Lacrimal Punctum |
| Y07.5 | Occlusion NOC |
| Y44.3 | Occlusion Organ Temporary |
| L99.6 | Occlusion Vein Balloon Test Transluminal Percutaneous |
| L99.5 | Occlusion Vein Transluminal Percutaneous |
| | |
| Y44.3 | Occlusion Vessel Temporary |
| G03.- | Oesophagectomy NEC |
| G03.- | Oesophagectomy Partial |
| G02.- | Oesophagectomy Total |
| G01.- | Oesophagogastrectomy |
| G09.2 | Oesophagomyotomy NEC |
| G16.- | Oesophagoscopy Fibreoptic |
| G16.- | Oesophagoscopy NEC |
| G08.- | Oesophagostomy |
| Y51.1 | Oesophagostomy Approach |

| | |
|---|---|
| O15.- | Oesophagus Operations Endoscopic Fibreoptic Therapeutic NEC |
| G18.- | Oesophagus Operations Endoscopic Therapeutic NEC |
| G21.- | Oesophagus Operations NEC |
| G13.- | Oesophagus Operations Open NEC |
| Z27.1 | Oesophagus site |
| G10.- | Oesophagus Varices Operations Open |
| T36.1 | Omentectomy |
| T36.- | Omentum Operations |
| Z53.5 | Omentum site |
| Q48.- | Oocyte Recovery |
| | |
| Q48.- | Oocyte Recovery Access Minimal |
| Q22.3 | Oophorectomy Bilateral NEC |
| Q24.3 | Oophorectomy NEC |
| Q23.- | Oophorectomy Unilateral NEC |
| | Opening – see also Exteriorisation |
| | Opening – see also Reopening |
| T30.- | Opening Abdomen |
| T30.- | Opening Abdominal Wall |
| H55.- | Opening Anal Fistula |
| Y52.- | Opening Artificial Approach NEC |
| | |
| T03.- | Opening Chest |
| T03.- | Opening Chest Wall |
| V01.3 | Opening Cranial Suture |
| V03.- | Opening Cranium |
| G75.- | Opening Ileum Artificial Attention |
| G74.- | Opening Ileum Artificial Creation |
| G75.- | Opening Intestine Small Artificial Attention NEC |
| G74.- | Opening Intestine Small Artificial Creation NEC |
| G60.- | Opening Jejunum Artificial |
| G08.- | Opening Oesophagus Artificial |
| | |
| T30.- | Opening Peritoneal Cavity |
| T30.- | Opening Peritoneum |
| H60.2 | Opening Pilonidal Sinus |
| T03.- | Opening Pleura |
| T03.- | Opening Pleural Cavity |
| S47.- | Opening Skin |
| G34.- | Opening Stomach Artificial NEC |
| S47.- | Opening Subcutaneous Tissue |
| | Operations Abandoned – refer to Tabular List Introduction |
| H57.- | Operations Anal Sphincter Incontinence Control Other |
| | |
| L69.- | Operations Arteries Collateral Systemic to Pulmonary Major |
| K78.- | Operations Artery Mammary Internal Side Branch Transluminal |
| L66.- | Operations Artery Therapeutic Transluminal Other |
| Z94.1 | Operations Bilateral |
| Y70.- | Operations Early NOC |
| Y70.1 | Operations Emergency NOC |
| C89.- | Operations Eye Posterior Segment |
| Y73.- | Operations Facilitating NOC |
| | Operations Failed – refer to Tabular List Introduction |
| Y70.2 | Operations Immediate NOC |

| | |
|---|---|
| | Operations Incomplete – refer to Tabular List Introduction |
| Y71.- | Operations Late NOC |
| Z94.- | Operations Laterality |
| Z94.3 | Operations Left Sided |
| Y44.- | Operations Methods NOC |
| Y70.4 | Operations Primary NOC |
| | Operations Radical – refer to Tabular List Introduction |
| Y71.3 | Operations Revisional NOC |
| Y71.6 | Operations Revisional Second NOC |
| Y71.7 | Operations Revisional Third or Greater NOC |
| | |
| Z94.2 | Operations Right Sided |
| Y71.2 | Operations Secondary NOC |
| Y70.3 | Operations Staged First NOC |
| Y71.1 | Operations Staged Subsequent NOC |
| Y70.5 | Operations Temporary |
| | Operations Unfinished – refer to Tabular List Introduction |
| Z94.4 | Operations Unilateral |
| C87.5 | Ophthalmoscopy Retina Scanning Laser |
| X39.1 | Oral Administration Therapeutic Substance |
| F11.- | Oral Surgery Preprosthetic |
| | |
| C08.- | Orbit Operations NEC |
| Z16.1 | Orbit site |
| C06.- | Orbitotomy |
| N05.- | Orchidectomy Bilateral |
| N06.- | Orchidectomy NEC |
| N08.- | Orchidopexy Bilateral |
| N09.- | Orchidopexy NEC |
| X55.- | Organ Unspecified Operations NEC |
| F14.- | Orthodontic Appliance |
| F14.- | Orthodontic Operations |
| | |
| F15.- | Orthodontic Operations NEC |
| Z79.2 | Os Calcis site |
| W06.- | Ostectomy NEC |
| W11.1 | Osteoclasis Closed |
| W10.- | Osteoclasis NEC |
| W10.- | Osteoclasis Open |
| E16.1 | Osteoplasty Frontal Sinus |
| V10.- | Osteotomy Bone Face NEC |
| W15.7 | Osteotomy Bone Foot & Fixation |
| W13.3 | Osteotomy Cuneiform NEC |
| | |
| W13.4 | Osteotomy Derotation & Relocation |
| W14.- | Osteotomy Diaphyseal |
| W13.2 | Osteotomy Displacement |
| V16.- | Osteotomy Jaw NEC |
| V16.1 | Osteotomy Mandible & Advancement |
| V16.2 | Osteotomy Mandible & Retrusion |
| V16.3 | Osteotomy Mandible Dentoalveolar Level |
| V16.- | Osteotomy Mandible NEC |
| V10.5 | Osteotomy Maxilla Dentoalveolar Level |
| V10.- | Osteotomy Maxilla NEC |

| | |
|---|---|
| W15.- | Osteotomy Metatarsal |
| W03.2 | Osteotomy Metatarsal Multiple |
| W03.6 | Osteotomy Metatarsals Multiple & Fixation |
| W16.- | Osteotomy Multiple NEC |
| W16.- | Osteotomy NEC |
| X25.1 | Osteotomy Os Calcis Body |
| X22.- | Osteotomy Pelvis Correction Hip Deformity Congenital |
| W12.- | Osteotomy Periarticular Angulation |
| W13.1 | Osteotomy Periarticular Rotation |
| W77.5 | Osteotomy Periarticular Stabilising Joint |
| | |
| W15.6 | Osteotomy Phalanx Proximal Cuneiform & Resection First Metatarsal Head |
| W15.6 | Osteotomy Phalanx Proximal Wedge & Resection First Metatarsal Head |
| W13.4 | Osteotomy Relocation & Derotation |
| V54.3 | Osteotomy Spine NEC |
| W15.- | Osteotomy Tarsal |
| W13.3 | Osteotomy Wedge NEC |
| E04.7 | Outfracture Nose Turbinate Surgical |
| Q45.2 | Ovariopexy |
| Q49.- | Ovary Operations Endoscopic Therapeutic |
| Q47.- | Ovary Operations Open NEC |
| | |
| Q51.- | Ovary Operations Other |
| Z46.3 | Ovary site |
| M43.3 | Overdistension Bladder Endoscopic NEC |
| | Oversewing – see Closure |
| E91.1 | Oximetry Assessment |
| E91.2 | Oximetry Continuous |
| E91.3 | Oximetry Overnight |
| E91.- | Oximetry Testing |
| E87.3 | Oxygen Ambulatory |
| E87.1 | Oxygen Support Home |
| | |
| X52.- | Oxygen Therapy |
| E87.2 | Oxygen Therapy Long Term |
| X58.1 | Oxygenation Extracorporeal Membrane |

# P

| | |
|---|---|
| J04.3 | Packing Liver Laceration |
| D12.- | Packing Mastoid Cavity |
| E06.- | Packing Nose Cavity |
| F16.3 | Packing Tooth Socket |
| F32.- | Palate Operations NEC |
| Z25.6 | Palate site |
| J68.- | Pancreas Operations NEC |
| J65.- | Pancreas Operations Open NEC |
| J67.- | Pancreas Operations Percutaneous Diagnostic |
| J66.- | Pancreas Operations Percutaneous Therapeutic |
| | |
| Z31.1 | Pancreas site |
| J57.- | Pancreatectomy NEC |
| J55.- | Pancreatectomy Total |
| J42.- | Pancreatic Duct Operations Endoscopic Therapeutic Retrograde |
| J60.- | Pancreatic Duct Operations Open NEC |
| Z31.2 | Pancreatic Duct site |
| J56.- | Pancreaticoduodenectomy |
| J67.2 | Pancreatography & Puncture Pancreatic Duct Percutaneous |
| J45.- | Pancreatography Endoscopic Retrograde |
| J63.- | Pancreatography Open |
| | |
| H04.- | Panproctocolectomy & Anastomosis Ileum Anus |
| H04.1 | Panproctocolectomy & Ileostomy |
| Q55.- | Papanicolau Smear |
| J39.- | Papilla Vater Operations Endoscopic Therapeutic NEC |
| J36.- | Papilla Vater Operations NEC |
| Z30.6 | Papilla Vater site |
| K38.1 | Papillary Muscle Operations |
| T46.1 | Paracentesis Abdominis Ascites |
| T12.2 | Paracentesis Chest |
| C69.2 | Paracentesis Eye Anterior Chamber |
| | |
| B16.- | Parathyroid Operations NEC |
| Z13.5 | Parathyroid site |
| B14.- | Parathyroidectomy |
| F58.1 | Parotid Duct Operations NEC |
| F53.1 | Parotid Duct Operations Open NEC |
| Z26.5 | Parotid Duct site |
| Z26.1 | Parotid Gland site |
| F44.- | Parotidectomy |
| G30.2 | Partitioning Stomach NEC |
| G30.3 | Partitioning Stomach Using Band |

| | |
|---|---|
| G30.1 | Partitioning Stomach Using Staples |
| A52.3 | Patch Epidural Blood |
| U27.- | Patch Test Skin |
| Z78.7 | Patella site |
| Q41.5 | Patency Fallopian Tube NEC |
| C80.1 | Peel Epiretinal Fibroglial Membrane |
| C80.1 | Peel Epiretinal Membrane |
| C80.2 | Peel Retina Internal Limiting Membrane |
| Z75.- | Pelvis site |
| O16.1 | Pelvis site NEC (Z) |
| | |
| N32.6 | Penis Operations Erectile Dysfunction NEC |
| N32.- | Penis Operations NEC |
| N28.- | Penis Operations Plastic |
| Z42.7 | Penis site |
| N32.- | Penis Skin Operations NEC |
| N28.- | Penis Skin Operations Plastic |
| Z42.7 | Penis Skin site |
| K35.6 | Perforation Valve Pulmonary Transluminal Percutaneous & Dilation |
| L97.3 | Perfusion Limb Isolated |
| J07.2 | Perfusion Liver Cannula Insertion Open |
| | |
| J16.1 | Perfusion Liver Localised |
| H55.- | Perianal Region Operations NEC |
| Z29.3 | Perianal Tissue site |
| K68.2 | Pericardiocentesis NEC |
| K77.1 | Pericardiocentesis Transluminal |
| K71.- | Pericardium Operations NEC |
| Z33.5 | Pericardium site |
| P13.3 | Perineoplasty Female |
| P13.2 | Perineorrhaphy Female |
| P13.5 | Perineotomy Female NEC |
| | |
| P13.- | Perineum Female Operations NEC |
| Z44.4 | Perineum Female site |
| N24.- | Perineum Male Operations |
| Z43.6 | Perineum Male site |
| P13.- | Perineum Skin Female Operations NEC |
| Z44.4 | Perineum Skin Female site |
| N24.- | Perineum Skin Male Operations |
| Z43.6 | Perineum Skin Male site |
| C41.1 | Peritomy |
| T48.- | Peritoneal Cavity Introduction Substance |
| | |
| T42.- | Peritoneal Cavity Operations Endoscopic Therapeutic |
| T48.- | Peritoneal Cavity Operations NEC |
| T41.- | Peritoneal Cavity Operations Open NEC |
| Z53.4 | Peritoneal Cavity site |
| T43.- | Peritoneoscopy |
| T42.- | Peritoneum Operations Endoscopic Therapeutic |
| T48.- | Peritoneum Operations NEC |
| T41.- | Peritoneum Operations Open NEC |
| T39.- | Peritoneum Posterior Operations |
| Z53.3 | Peritoneum site |

| | |
|---|---|
| F36.- | Peritonsillar Region Operations |
| Z25.7 | Peritonsillar Region site |
| P13.6 | Periurethral Tissue Female Operations NEC |
| Q14.6 | Pessary Abortifacient NEC |
| Q14.5 | Pessary Prostaglandin |
| P26.- | Pessary Vagina Supporting |
| C71.2 | Phacoemulsification Lens |
| E23.2 | Pharyngeal Pouch Operations |
| E19.- | Pharyngectomy |
| E21.- | Pharyngoplasty |
| | |
| E25.- | Pharyngoscopy |
| E24.- | Pharynx Operations Endoscopic Therapeutic |
| E27.- | Pharynx Operations NEC |
| E23.- | Pharynx Operations Open NEC |
| Z24.1 | Pharynx site |
| S64.2 | Phenolisation Nail Bed |
| L87.7 | Phlebectomy Transilluminated Powered Leg Vein Varicose |
| S12.- | Photochemotherapy Skin |
| S12.- | Photochemotherapy Skin Combined & Light Therapy Ultraviolet |
| C66.4 | Photocoagulation Ciliary Body Laser |
| C81.- | Photocoagulation Retina Detachment |
| C82.6 | Photocoagulation Retina Lesion Laser NEC |
| C82.5 | Photocoagulation Retina Lesion Laser Panretinal |
| C82.- | Photocoagulation Retina NEC |
| S09.- | Photocoagulation Skin Lesion Infrared |
| | Photodestruction – see also Destruction |
| S09.- | Photodestruction Skin Lesion NEC |
| S09.- | Photodestruction Subcutaneous Tissue Lesion NEC |
| J41.4 | Photodynamic Therapy Bile Duct Lesion Laser Endoscopic Retrograde |
| J48.4 | Photodynamic Therapy Bile Duct Lesion Percutaneous |
| | |
| G42.2 | Photodynamic Therapy Gastrointestinal Tract Upper Lesion Endo. Fibreoptic |
| G42.2 | Photodynamic Therapy Gastrointestinal Tract Upper Lesion Endoscopic NEC |
| Y13.6 | Photodynamic Therapy NOC |
| G14.7 | Photodynamic Therapy Oesophagus Lesion Endoscopic Fibreoptic |
| E48.7 | Photodynamic Therapy Respiratory Tract Lower Lesion Endoscopic Fibreoptic |
| S07.- | Photodynamic Therapy Skin |
| C88.2 | Photodynamic Therapy Subretina Lesion |
| F42.4 | Photography Mouth |
| U27.7 | Photopatch Testing Skin |
| U28.- | Phototesting Skin |
| | |
| S12.- | Phototherapy Skin |
| H60.- | Pilonidal Sinus Operations NEC |
| B06.- | Pineal Operations |
| Z14.2 | Pineal site |
| D03.3 | Pinnaplasty |
| W19.1 | Pinning & Plating Femur Neck Fracture NEC |
| W24.1 | Pinning Femur Neck Fracture NEC |
| B04.- | Pituitary Operations NEC |
| Z14.1 | Pituitary site |
| B04.5 | Pituitary Stalk Operations |

| | |
|---|---|
| H57.1 | Placement Anal Sphincter Artificial NEC |
| J40.- | Placement Bile Duct Stent Endoscopic Retrograde |
| C51.5 | Placement Cornea Therapeutic Contact Lens |
| A11.1 | Placement Depth Electrodes Electroencephalography |
| D05.5 | Placement Ear External Hearing Implant |
| D20.4 | Placement Ear Middle Hearing Implant |
| Q35.4 | Placement Intrafallopian Implant Bilateral Endoscopic |
| Q36.2 | Placement Intrafallopian Implant Solitary Endoscopic |
| | Placement Prosthesis – see Prosthesis site |
| H57.5 | Placement Sphincter Dynamic Gracioplasty |
| | |
| L89.- | Placement Stent Coated Endovascular |
| L89.- | Placement Stent Drug-eluting Endovascular |
| L76.- | Placement Stent Endovascular |
| O20.1 | Placement Stent Graft Branched One Endovascular (L) |
| O20.- | Placement Stent Graft Endovascular (L) |
| O20.2 | Placement Stent Graft Fenestrated One Endovascular (L) |
| O20.3 | Placement Stent Graft One Endovascular NEC (L) |
| O20.5 | Placement Stent Graft Three Endovascular (L) |
| O20.4 | Placement Stent Graft Two Endovascular (L) |
| L76.- | Placement Stent Metallic Endovascular |
| | |
| L89.- | Placement Stent Other Endovascular |
| L76.- | Placement Stent Plastic Endovascular |
| A11.2 | Placement Surface Electrodes Electroencephalography |
| N08.- | Placement Testis Scrotum Bilateral |
| N09.- | Placement Testis Scrotum NEC |
| Z45.4 | Placenta site |
| X48.- | Plaster Cast |
| | Plastic Reconstruction – see Reconstruction site Plastic |
| | Plastic Repair – see Repair site Plastic |
| S23.- | Plasty W |
| | |
| S23.- | Plasty Z |
| W19.1 | Plating & Pinning Femur Neck Fracture NEC |
| T10.- | Pleura Operations Endoscopic Therapeutic |
| T14.- | Pleura Operations NEC |
| T09.- | Pleura Operations Open NEC |
| Z52.1 | Pleura site |
| T13.- | Pleural Cavity Introduction Substance |
| T14.- | Pleural Cavity Operations NEC |
| Z52.2 | Pleural Cavity site |
| T07.- | Pleurectomy |
| | |
| T10.- | Pleurodesis Access Minimal |
| T10.- | Pleurodesis Endoscopic |
| T09.- | Pleurodesis Open |
| | Plication – see also Tucking |
| H42.2 | Plication Anal Sphincter & Muscle Levator Ani Perineal |
| W81.6 | Plication Capsule Joint |
| T16.2 | Plication Diaphragm |
| C33.- | Plication Eye Muscle |
| G46.1 | Plication Gastro-oesophageal Junction Endoluminal Endoscopic Fibreoptic |
| N11.2 | Plication Hydrocele Sac |

| | |
|---|---|
| G76.4 | Plication Ileum |
| M05.4 | Plication Kidney |
| C33.- | Plication Muscle Eye |
| H42.2 | Plication Muscle Levator Ani & Anal Sphincter Perineal |
| N28.3 | Plication Penis Corpora |
| Q54.2 | Plication Uterus Ligament Round |
| L79.2 | Plication Vena Cava |
| E54.- | Pneumonectomy |
| F16.7 | Polishing Teeth |
| W01.2 | Pollicisation Finger |
| | |
| | Polypectomy – see also Excision Lesion |
| E08.1 | Polypectomy Nose Internal |
| U33.1 | Polysomnography |
| Z22.6 | Postnasal Space site |
| P31.- | Pouch Douglas Operations |
| Z44.6 | Pouch Douglas site |
| X68.- | Preparation Brachytherapy |
| X67.- | Preparation Radiotherapy External Beam |
| F17.6 | Preparation Teeth Bridge |
| F17.1 | Preparation Tooth Crown Dental |
| | |
| F11.- | Preprosthetic Oral Surgery |
| N30.- | Prepuce Operations |
| Z42.6 | Prepuce site |
| N30.- | Prepuce Skin Operations |
| Z42.6 | Prepuce Skin site |
| N30.1 | Prepuceplasty |
| E85.2 | Pressure Airway Continuous Positive Support |
| E85.2 | Pressure Chest-wall Continuous Negative Support |
| | Pressure Monitoring – see Manometry |
| Y70.4 | Primary Operations NOC |
| | |
| C27.5 | Probing Nasolacrimal Duct NEC |
| H55.6 | Probing Perineal Fistula |
| | Procedures – see Operation site |
| M33.- | Procedures Ureter Stent Percutaneous |
| H33.2 | Proctectomy & Anastomosis Colon Anus |
| H41.4 | Proctectomy Mucosal Peranal & Anastomosis Endoanal |
| H04.1 | Proctocolectomy NEC |
| H62.6 | Proctoscopy |
| X70.- | Procurement Chemotherapy Neoplasm Drugs Bands 1–5 |
| X71.- | Procurement Chemotherapy Neoplasm Drugs Bands 6–10 |
| | |
| L60.- | Profundoplasty Artery Femoral |
| L60.- | Profundoplasty Artery Popliteal |
| M67.- | Prostate Operations Endoscopic Therapeutic NEC |
| M62.- | Prostate Operations Open NEC |
| M71.- | Prostate Operations Other NEC |
| Z42.2 | Prostate site |
| M61.- | Prostatectomy NEC |
| M62.3 | Prostatotomy |
| | Prosthesis – see also Replacement |
| Y03.6 | Prosthesis Adjustment NOC |

| | |
|---|---|
| G25.2 | Prosthesis Angelchick Adjustment |
| G24.6 | Prosthesis Angelchick Insertion |
| G25.3 | Prosthesis Angelchick Removal |
| L22.- | Prosthesis Aorta Attention |
| L74.1 | Prosthesis Arteriovenous Insertion |
| K43.- | Prosthesis Artery Coronary |
| Y03.- | Prosthesis Attention NOC |
| J40.- | Prosthesis Bile Duct Endoscopic Retrograde |
| J47.- | Prosthesis Bile Duct Insertion Percutaneous |
| J48.- | Prosthesis Bile Duct Insertion Percutaneous Attention |
| | |
| J31.- | Prosthesis Bile Duct Open |
| M55.- | Prosthesis Bladder Outlet Female Collar |
| M64.- | Prosthesis Bladder Outlet Male Collar |
| O09.- | Prosthesis Bone (W) |
| H24.3 | Prosthesis Bowel Lower Tubal Insertion Sigmoidoscope Fibreoptic |
| B30.- | Prosthesis Breast |
| B30.4 | Prosthesis Breast Renewal |
| T02.- | Prosthesis Chest Wall |
| D24.- | Prosthesis Cochlear |
| H24.3 | Prosthesis Colon Sigmoid Tubal Insertion Endoscopic NEC |
| | |
| H24.3 | Prosthesis Colon Sigmoid Tubal Insertion Sigmoidoscope Fibreoptic |
| H27.3 | Prosthesis Colon Sigmoid Tubal Insertion Sigmoidoscope Rigid |
| H24.3 | Prosthesis Colon Tubal Insertion Sigmoidoscope Fibreoptic |
| C40.4 | Prosthesis Conjunctiva |
| Y03.5 | Prosthesis Conversion NOC |
| C46.4 | Prosthesis Cornea Insertion |
| Y03.3 | Prosthesis Correction Displaced NOC |
| V01.4 | Prosthesis Cranium Removal |
| F63.- | Prosthesis Dental |
| T16.1 | Prosthesis Diaphragm Repair |
| | |
| G44.1 | Prosthesis Duodenum Proximal Insertion & Exam. U.G.I. Tract Endoscope Fibreoptic |
| G44.1 | Prosthesis Duodenum Proximal Insertion & Exam. U.G.I. Tract Endoscope NEC |
| G54.3 | Prosthesis Duodenum Tubal Insertion Endoscopic NEC |
| G53.4 | Prosthesis Duodenum Tubal Insertion Open |
| C04.- | Prosthesis Eye Attention |
| C03.- | Prosthesis Eye Insertion |
| Q26.- | Prosthesis Fallopian Tube |
| G44.1 | Prosthesis Gastrointestinal Tract Upper Insertion Endoscope Fibreoptic |
| G44.1 | Prosthesis Gastrointestinal Tract Upper Insertion Endoscopic NEC |
| K02.- | Prosthesis Heart |
| | |
| J40.- | Prosthesis Hepatic Duct Endoscopic Retrograde |
| J47.- | Prosthesis Hepatic Duct Insertion Percutaneous |
| J31.- | Prosthesis Hepatic Duct Open |
| J29.- | Prosthesis Hepatic Duct Open & Anastomosis Jejunum |
| G79.3 | Prosthesis Ileum Tubal Insertion Endoscopic |
| G79.3 | Prosthesis Intestine Small Tubal Insertion Endoscopic NEC |
| G64.3 | Prosthesis Jejunum Tubal Insertion Endoscopic |
| | Prosthesis Joint – see Replacement Joint |
| M06.4 | Prosthesis Kidney Attention |
| E31.- | Prosthesis Larynx |

| | |
|---|---|
| E31.3 | Prosthesis Larynx Insertion & Division Stenosis |
| E35.4 | Prosthesis Larynx Removal Endoscopic |
| C75.- | Prosthesis Lens |
| X05.- | Prosthesis Limb Attention |
| X05.- | Prosthesis Limb Implantation |
| J15.- | Prosthesis Liver Blood Vessel Insertion Transluminal |
| Y03.1 | Prosthesis Maintenance NOC |
| Y02.- | Prosthesis NOC |
| E03.7 | Prosthesis Nose Septum Perforation |
| G44.1 | Prosthesis Oesophagus Insertion & Exam. U.G.I. Tract Endoscopic Fibreoptic |
| G44.1 | Prosthesis Oesophagus Insertion & Exam. U.G.I. Tract Endoscopic NEC |
| G11.- | Prosthesis Oesophagus Open |
| G15.4 | Prosthesis Oesophagus Tubal Insertion Endoscopic Fibreoptic |
| G18.4 | Prosthesis Oesophagus Tubal Insertion Endoscopic NEC |
| C03.- | Prosthesis Orbit |
| C04.- | Prosthesis Orbit Attention |
| C04.- | Prosthesis Orbit Revision |
| D16.- | Prosthesis Ossicular Chain |
| J42.- | Prosthesis Pancreatic Duct Endoscopic Retrograde |
| J60.- | Prosthesis Pancreatic Duct Tubal Insertion |
| N29.- | Prosthesis Penis |
| M68.- | Prosthesis Prostate Insertion Endoscopic |
| G44.1 | Prosthesis Pylorus Insertion Endoscopic Fibreoptic |
| G44.1 | Prosthesis Pylorus Insertion Endoscopic NEC |
| H24.3 | Prosthesis Rectum Tubal Insertion Endoscopic NEC |
| H24.3 | Prosthesis Rectum Tubal Insertion Sigmoidoscope Fibreoptic |
| H27.3 | Prosthesis Rectum Tubal Insertion Sigmoidoscope Rigid |
| Y03.7 | Prosthesis Removal NOC |
| Y03.2 | Prosthesis Renewal NOC |
| Y03.4 | Prosthesis Resiting NOC |
| O09.1 | Prosthesis Rib Vertical Expanding Titanium (W) |
| C54.- | Prosthesis Sclera for Attachment of Retina Attention |
| G44.1 | Prosthesis Stomach Insertion Endoscopic Fibreoptic |
| G44.1 | Prosthesis Stomach Insertion Endoscopic NEC |
| G38.2 | Prosthesis Stomach Insertion Open |
| G18.4 | Prosthesis Stomach Tubal Insertion Gastroscope Rigid |
| T74.2 | Prosthesis Tendon Removal |
| N10.- | Prosthesis Testis |
| E41.- | Prosthesis Trachea |
| M29.- | Prosthesis Ureter Tubal Endoscopic NEC |
| M26.4 | Prosthesis Ureter Tubal Insertion Nephroscopic |
| M29.5 | Prosthesis Ureter Tubal Renewal Endoscopic |
| M75.2 | Prosthesis Urethra Bulb Male Compression |
| L73.- | Protection Blood Vessel Mechanical Embolic |
| Z75.5 | Pubis Ramus site |
| M73.5 | Pull Through Urethra |
| | Pump – see also Cannulation |
| Y73.1 | Pump Cardiovascular |
| | Puncture – see also Drainage |
| | Puncture – see also Injection |

| | |
|---|---|
| W36.- | Puncture Bone Diagnostic |
| W36.- | Puncture Bone NEC |
| W36.- | Puncture Bone Percutaneous NEC |
| W35.5 | Puncture Bone Percutaneous Therapeutic |
| W35.- | Puncture Bone Therapeutic |
| A22.2 | Puncture Brain Cistern |
| A10.5 | Puncture Brain Tissue NEC |
| W90.- | Puncture Joint |
| M13.- | Puncture Kidney Pelvis Percutaneous |
| M13.- | Puncture Kidney Percutaneous |
| | |
| J14.- | Puncture Liver NEC |
| A55.9 | Puncture Lumbar NEC |
| E13.6 | Puncture Maxillary Antrum |
| Y33.- | Puncture NOC |
| J67.2 | Puncture Pancreatic Duct Percutaneous & Pancreatography |
| T12.- | Puncture Pleura |
| A55.- | Puncture Spinal Diagnostic |
| A54.- | Puncture Spinal Therapeutic |
| W36.4 | Puncture Sternum Diagnostic |
| E41.4 | Puncture Tracheo-oesophageal Speech Prosthesis Insertion |
| | |
| A20.8 | Puncture Ventricle NEC |
| C60.4 | Pupilloplasty |
| M13.5 | Pyelography Antegrade |
| X31.2 | Pyelography Intravenous |
| M30.1 | Pyelography Retrograde Endoscopic |
| M06.1 | Pyelolithotomy |
| M10.2 | Pyeloplasty Endoscopic |
| M05.- | Pyeloplasty Open |
| M12.1 | Pyeloureterodynamics Percutaneous |
| G40.1 | Pyloromyotomy |
| | |
| G40.- | Pyloroplasty |
| G41.- | Pylorus Operations NEC |
| Z27.3 | Pylorus site |

# Q

| | |
|---|---|
| B28.1 | Quadrantectomy Breast |
| T79.2 | Quadricepsplasty |

# R

|  | Radical Operations – refer to Tabular List Introduction |
| A55.1 | Radiculography |
| Y35.- | Radioactive Material Removable Introduction NOC |
| Y36.3 | Radioactive Seed Implantation NEC |
| Y53.1 | Radiological Control Approach |
| U08.- | Radiology Abdomen Diagnostic |
| U04.1 | Radiology Bitewing |
| U05.- | Radiology Central Nervous System Diagnostic |
| U07.- | Radiology Chest Diagnostic |
| Y97.- | Radiology Contrast |
|  |  |
| U06.- | Radiology Face & Neck Diagnostic |
| K63.- | Radiology Heart Contrast |
| U10.- | Radiology Heart Diagnostic |
| U04.4 | Radiology Jaw Lateral Oblique |
| T90.- | Radiology Lymphatic Tissue Contrast |
| U13.- | Radiology Musculoskeletal Diagnostic |
| U04.3 | Radiology Occlusal |
| U09.- | Radiology Pelvis Diagnostic |
| U04.2 | Radiology Periapical |
| Y98.- | Radiology Procedures |
|  |  |
| U12.- | Radiology Urinary Diagnostic |
| U11.- | Radiology Vascular Diagnostic |
| A10.7 | Radiosurgery Brain Tissue Stereotactic |
| X65.- | Radiotherapy Delivery |
| Y91.- | Radiotherapy External Beam |
| J12.3 | Radiotherapy Liver Lesion Selective Internal Using Microspheres |
| Y90.2 | Radiotherapy NEC |
| A61.3 | Radiotherapy Nerve Peripheral Lesion |
| C82.3 | Radiotherapy Retina Lesion External Beam |
| C82.3 | Radiotherapy Retina Lesion NEC |
|  |  |
| C82.4 | Radiotherapy Retina Lesion Plaque |
| Z72.1 | Radius & Ulna Shaft Combination site |
| Z70.- | Radius site NEC |
|  | Re-excision – see also Excision |
| B28.4 | Re-excision Breast Margins |
| T60.- | Re-excision Ganglion |
| S06.6 | Re-excision Skin Margins Head Neck |
| S06.7 | Re-excision Skin Margins NEC |
|  | Re-exploration – see also Exploration |
|  | Re-exploration – see also Reopening |

| | |
|---|---|
| Y32.- | Re-exploration & Arrest Bleeding Postoperative Surgical NOC |
| Y32.- | Re-exploration & Packing NOC |
| Y32.- | Re-exploration & Repair NOC |
| Y32.- | Re-exploration NOC |
| E94.3 | Reactivity Bronchial |
| X12.- | Reamputation |
| J32.2 | Reanastomosis Bile Duct |
| Q29.1 | Reanastomosis Fallopian Tube NEC |
| H50.4 | Reanastomosis Rectum Anal Canal Correction Rectum Atresia Congenital |
| | Reattachment – see also Repair |
| | |
| W84.- | Reattachment Ligament Intra-articular Endoscopic |
| W84.- | Reattachment Ligament Knee Intra-articular Endoscopic |
| Y04.1 | Reattachment Microvascular NOC |
| H62.1 | Recanalisation Bowel Laser NEC |
| Q41.6 | Recanalisation Fallopian Tube |
| C31.- | Recession Eye Muscle & Resection |
| C31.- | Recession Eye Muscle Bilateral |
| C32.- | Recession Eye Muscle NEC |
| C31.- | Recession Muscle Eye & Resection |
| C31.- | Recession Muscle Eye Bilateral |
| | |
| C32.- | Recession Muscle Eye NEC |
| | Reconstruction – see also Refashioning |
| | Reconstruction – see also Reformation |
| L65.1 | Reconstruction Aorta Revision |
| K17.3 | Reconstruction Aortopulmonary Procedure |
| B36.- | Reconstruction Areola |
| L37.- | Reconstruction Artery Axillary |
| L37.8 | Reconstruction Artery Axillary Graft |
| L37.- | Reconstruction Artery Brachial |
| L37.8 | Reconstruction Artery Brachial Graft |
| | |
| L29.- | Reconstruction Artery Carotid |
| L34.1 | Reconstruction Artery Cerebral |
| L34.1 | Reconstruction Artery Circle Willis |
| L45.- | Reconstruction Artery Coeliac |
| L60.- | Reconstruction Artery Femoral |
| L65.3 | Reconstruction Artery Femoral Revision |
| L52.- | Reconstruction Artery Iliac |
| L65.2 | Reconstruction Artery Iliac Revision |
| L45.- | Reconstruction Artery Mesenteric |
| L60.- | Reconstruction Artery Popliteal |
| | |
| L65.3 | Reconstruction Artery Popliteal Revision |
| L41.- | Reconstruction Artery Renal |
| L65.- | Reconstruction Artery Revision |
| L66.2 | Reconstruction Artery Stent Transluminal Percutaneous |
| L37.- | Reconstruction Artery Subclavian |
| L37.8 | Reconstruction Artery Subclavian Graft |
| L45.- | Reconstruction Artery Suprarenal |
| L37.- | Reconstruction Artery Vertebral |
| L37.8 | Reconstruction Artery Vertebral Graft |
| K05.- | Reconstruction Atrium Transposition Arteries Great |

| | |
|---|---|
| D08.2 | Reconstruction Auditory Canal External |
| J32.1 | Reconstruction Bile Duct |
| M37.8 | Reconstruction Bladder NEC |
| M54.2 | Reconstruction Bladder Neck Female NEC |
| M64.6 | Reconstruction Bladder Neck Male NEC |
| V13.1 | Reconstruction Bone Face |
| W17.- | Reconstruction Bone NEC |
| W17.5 | Reconstruction Bone Revision |
| B29.- | Reconstruction Breast |
| B39.- | Reconstruction Breast Flap Abdominal |
| | |
| B39.5 | Reconstruction Breast Flap Free Omental |
| B39.4 | Reconstruction Breast Flap Pedicled Omental |
| B39.3 | Reconstruction Breast Free Flap Deep Inferior Epigastric Perforator |
| B39.1 | Reconstruction Breast Free Flap Transverse Rectus Abdominis Myocutaneous |
| B39.2 | Reconstruction Breast Pedicled Flap Transverse Rectus Abdominis Myocutaneous |
| B29.5 | Reconstruction Breast Revision |
| B38.- | Reconstruction Breast Skin Flap Buttock |
| E44.- | Reconstruction Carina |
| W02.- | Reconstruction Carpus |
| T02.- | Reconstruction Chest Wall |
| | |
| X21.7 | Reconstruction Club Hand Radial |
| D03.- | Reconstruction Ear External |
| D03.- | Reconstruction Ear External Skin |
| C14.- | Reconstruction Eyelid |
| Q30.1 | Reconstruction Fallopian Tube |
| W03.- | Reconstruction Forefoot Complex |
| W02.- | Reconstruction Hand Complex NEC |
| W02.- | Reconstruction Hand Soft Tissue Complex NEC |
| W04.- | Reconstruction Hindfoot Complex |
| V19.1 | Reconstruction Jaw NEC |
| | |
| W57.- | Reconstruction Joint Excision |
| W02.- | Reconstruction Joint Hand Multiple NEC |
| W56.- | Reconstruction Joint Interposition Natural Tissue |
| W56.- | Reconstruction Joint Interposition NEC |
| W55.- | Reconstruction Joint Interposition Prosthetic |
| W58.- | Reconstruction Joint NEC |
| O10.- | Reconstruction Joint Shoulder Complex (W) |
| V20.- | Reconstruction Joint Temporomandibular |
| E31.1 | Reconstruction Laryngotracheal Graft Cartilage |
| E31.- | Reconstruction Larynx |
| | |
| W77.6 | Reconstruction Ligament Annular |
| O27.1 | Reconstruction Ligament Extra-articular Stabilisation Joint (W) |
| W74.- | Reconstruction Ligament NEC |
| F04.- | Reconstruction Lip NEC |
| F04.- | Reconstruction Lip Skin NEC |
| T89.1 | Reconstruction Lymphatic Duct |
| V19.1 | Reconstruction Mandible |
| Y24.1 | Reconstruction Microvascular NOC |
| F39.- | Reconstruction Mouth NEC |
| B36.- | Reconstruction Nipple |

| | |
|---|---|
| Y26.1 | Reconstruction NOC |
| E02.- | Reconstruction Nose |
| C05.1 | Reconstruction Orbit Cavity |
| D16.- | Reconstruction Ossicular Chain |
| N28.2 | Reconstruction Penis |
| N03.6 | Reconstruction Scrotum |
| T72.1 | Reconstruction Tendon Sheath |
| W01.- | Reconstruction Thumb |
| W01.- | Reconstruction Thumb Complex |
| E40.- | Reconstruction Trachea |
| | |
| M73.4 | Reconstruction Urethra |
| P32.1 | Reconstruction Vagina Interposition Bowel |
| P21.2 | Reconstruction Vagina NEC |
| P32.2 | Reconstruction Vagina Pelvic Peritoneal Graft |
| P32.3 | Reconstruction Vagina Urethral Dissection |
| L99.2 | Reconstruction Vein Stent Transluminal Percutaneous |
| U19.5 | Recording Holter Extended Electrocardiographic |
| F42.5 | Recording Jaw Relationships |
| Z29.4 | Rectosigmoid site |
| H33.- | Rectosigmoidectomy |
| | |
| H33.3 | Rectosigmoidectomy & Anastomosis Colon |
| H41.1 | Rectosigmoidectomy & Anastomosis Peranal |
| H33.5 | Rectosigmoidectomy & Closure Rectal Stump & Exteriorisation Bowel |
| H42.- | Rectum Mucosa Prolapse Operations Perineal |
| H27.- | Rectum Operations Endoscopic NEC |
| H27.- | Rectum Operations Endoscopic Sigmoidoscope Rigid NEC |
| | Rectum Operations NEC – see also Bowel Operations NEC |
| H46.- | Rectum Operations NEC |
| H24.- | Rectum Operations Therapeutic Sigmoidoscope Fibreoptic NEC |
| H40.- | Rectum Operations Through Anal Sphincter |
| | |
| H41.- | Rectum Operations Through Anus NEC |
| H36.- | Rectum Prolapse Operations Abdominal NEC |
| H42.- | Rectum Prolapse Operations Perineal |
| Z29.1 | Rectum site |
| D05.3 | Reduction Auricular Soft Tissue Prosthesis |
| V09.- | Reduction Bone Face Fracture NEC |
| W25.- | Reduction Bone Fracture Closed & Fixation External |
| W24.- | Reduction Bone Fracture Closed & Fixation Internal |
| W26.- | Reduction Bone Fracture Closed NEC |
| O17.- | Reduction Bone Fracture Closed Secondary & Fixation Internal (W) |
| | |
| W21.- | Reduction Bone Fracture Intra-articular Open |
| W19.- | Reduction Bone Fracture Open & Fixation Intramedullary |
| W20.- | Reduction Bone Fracture Open & Fixation NEC |
| W22.- | Reduction Bone Fracture Open NEC |
| W19.- | Reduction Bone Fracture Open Primary & Fixation Intramedullary |
| W20.- | Reduction Bone Fracture Open Primary & Fixation NEC |
| W22.- | Reduction Bone Fracture Open Primary NEC |
| W23.- | Reduction Bone Fracture Open Secondary |
| W24.- | Reduction Bone Fragment Closed & Fixation |
| O17.5 | Reduction Bone Fragment Closed Secondary & Fixation Internal (W) |

| | |
|---|---|
| W19.- | Reduction Bone Fragment Open & Fixation |
| D13.3 | Reduction Bone Mastoid Soft Tissue Prosthesis Anchored Hearing |
| V09.- | Reduction Bone Nose Fracture |
| H17.1 | Reduction Caecum Intussusception Open |
| H17.2 | Reduction Caecum Volvulus Open |
| P01.2 | Reduction Clitoris |
| H17.1 | Reduction Colon Intussusception Open |
| H30.1 | Reduction Colon Intussusception Radiological Enema Barium |
| H30.3 | Reduction Colon Sigmoid Volvulus Flatus Tube |
| H17.3 | Reduction Colon Sigmoid Volvulus Open |
| | |
| H17.4 | Reduction Colon Volvulus Open NEC |
| | Reduction Dislocation – see Reduction Joint |
| W48.5 | Reduction Femur Head Prosthesis Dislocated Closed |
| X25.3 | Reduction Foot Gigantism |
| | Reduction Fracture – see Reduction Bone |
| G44.4 | Reduction Gastroenterostomy Intussusception Endoscopic Fibreoptic |
| G33.4 | Reduction Gastroenterostomy Intussusception Open |
| | Reduction Gigantism – see Reduction site |
| H53.3 | Reduction Haemorrhoid Prolapsed Manual |
| X21.1 | Reduction Hand Gigantism |
| | |
| G75.5 | Reduction Ileostomy Prolapse |
| G76.1 | Reduction Ileum Intussusception Open |
| G82.1 | Reduction Ileum Intussusception Radiological Enema Barium |
| G82.1 | Reduction Intestine Small Intussusception Radiol. Enema Barium NEC |
| V15.- | Reduction Jaw Fracture NEC |
| W66.- | Reduction Joint Dislocation Closed |
| W66.4 | Reduction Joint Dislocation Fracture Closed Primary & Fixation Internal |
| W66.- | Reduction Joint Dislocation Manipulative |
| W66.- | Reduction Joint Dislocation NEC |
| W65.- | Reduction Joint Dislocation Open |
| | |
| W67.- | Reduction Joint Dislocation Secondary |
| | Reduction Joint Fracture Dislocation – see Reduction Joint Dislocation |
| W68.- | Reduction Joint Growth Plate Injury |
| X22.1 | Reduction Joint Hip Deformity Congenital Open |
| W39.6 | Reduction Joint Hip Prosthesis Dislocated Closed |
| X23.1 | Reduction Joint Knee Dislocation Congenital Operative |
| V21.2 | Reduction Joint Temporomandibular Dislocation |
| P05.7 | Reduction Labia Major |
| P05.6 | Reduction Labia Minor |
| V15.- | Reduction Mandible Fracture |
| | |
| V08.- | Reduction Maxilla Fracture |
| E04.2 | Reduction Nose Turbinate NEC |
| C08.- | Reduction Orbit Fracture |
| N30.6 | Reduction Prepuce Manual |
| H46.- | Reduction Rectum Intussusception |
| H44.2 | Reduction Rectum Prolapse Manual |
| A49.4 | Reduction Spinal Cord Abnormal Tissue Complex |
| V45.- | Reduction Spine Fracture NEC |
| X19.1 | Reduction Sprengel Deformity |
| G38.6 | Reduction Stomach Volvulus |

| | |
|---|---|
| N13.3 | Reduction Testis Torsion |
| | Refashioning – see also Operation site |
| | Refashioning – see also Revision |
| K20.- | Refashioning Atrium |
| S60.4 | Refashioning Scar NEC |
| Y03.1 | Refilling Pump NOC |
| C69.1 | Reformation Eye Anterior Chamber |
| U52.2 | Rehabilitation Addiction Alcohol |
| U52.1 | Rehabilitation Addiction Drug |
| U51.1 | Rehabilitation Brain Injuries |
| | |
| U53.3 | Rehabilitation Burns |
| U54.1 | Rehabilitation Cardiac Disorders |
| U50.2 | Rehabilitation Hip Fracture |
| U50.3 | Rehabilitation Joint Replacement |
| U50.1 | Rehabilitation Limb Amputation |
| U50.- | Rehabilitation Musculoskeletal Disorders |
| U54.1 | Rehabilitation Myocardial Infarction Acute |
| U51.- | Rehabilitation Neurological Disorders |
| U50.5 | Rehabilitation Osteoarthritis |
| U54.- | Rehabilitation Other Disorders |
| | |
| U51.3 | Rehabilitation Pain Syndromes |
| U52.- | Rehabilitation Psychiatric Disorders |
| U53.- | Rehabilitation Reconstructive Surgery |
| U54.2 | Rehabilitation Respiratory Disorders |
| U50.4 | Rehabilitation Rheumatoid Arthritis |
| U51.2 | Rehabilitation Spinal Cord Injury |
| U54.3 | Rehabilitation Stroke |
| U53.- | Rehabilitation Trauma |
| | Reimplantation – see Replantation |
| W73.- | Reinforcement Ligament Prosthetic |
| | |
| S23.- | Relaxation Skin Contracture Operations Flap |
| X61.2 | Relaxation Therapy Session |
| | Release Adhesions – see Freeing site Adhesions |
| L23.4 | Release Aorta Vascular Ring |
| A65.2 | Release Canal Guyon |
| A65.1 | Release Carpal Tunnel |
| A69.2 | Release Carpal Tunnel Revision |
| A67.1 | Release Cubital Tunnel |
| T51.- | Release Fascia Abdomen |
| T55.- | Release Fascia NEC |
| | |
| T51.2 | Release Fascia Pelvis |
| X24.- | Release Foot Joint Correction Foot Deformity Congenital |
| W04.5 | Release Hindfoot Soft Tissue |
| W78.4 | Release Joint Capsule Contracture Limited |
| W78.- | Release Joint Contracture |
| T80.- | Release Muscle Contracture |
| T80.4 | Release Muscle Sternomastoid |
| T80.- | Release Muscle Tether |
| T80.3 | Release Neck Webbing |
| A31.- | Release Nerve Cranial Intracranial Stereotactic |

| | |
|---|---|
| A67.2 | Release Nerve Lateral Cutaneous Thigh Entrapment |
| A66.- | Release Nerve Peripheral Ankle Entrapment |
| A67.- | Release Nerve Peripheral Entrapment NEC |
| A68.- | Release Nerve Peripheral NEC |
| A69.- | Release Nerve Peripheral Revision |
| A65.- | Release Nerve Peripheral Wrist Entrapment |
| A67.3 | Release Nerve Plantar Digital Entrapment |
| Y18.- | Release NOC |
| X20.- | Release Radius Correction Forearm Deformity Congenital |
| V42.3 | Release Spine Anterolateral & Graft |
| | |
| X27.1 | Release Streeter Band |
| A66.1 | Release Tarsal Tunnel |
| A69.3 | Release Tarsal Tunnel Revision |
| T72.3 | Release Tendon Sheath Constriction |
| T80.2 | Release Tether Cicatricial |
| T80.1 | Release Tether Paralytic |
| X27.2 | Release Toe Syndactyly |
| F26.3 | Release Tongue Tie |
| T80.4 | Release Torticollis |
| X20.- | Release Ulna Correction Forearm Deformity Congenital |
| | |
| H17.6 | Relief Caecum Obstruction Open NEC |
| H17.5 | Relief Caecum Strangulation Open |
| H17.6 | Relief Colon Obstruction Open NEC |
| H17.5 | Relief Colon Strangulation Open |
| G76.3 | Relief Ileum Obstruction Open NEC |
| G76.2 | Relief Ileum Strangulation Open |
| K24.- | Relief Ventricular Outflow Tract Obstruction |
| W25.- | Remanipulation Bone Fracture |
| O17.- | Remanipulation Bone Fracture Closed & Fixation Internal (W) |
| W67.- | Remanipulation Joint Dislocation Fracture |
| | |
| W67.- | Remanipulation Joint Dislocation NEC |
| | Removal – see also Excision |
| | Removal – see also Primary Operation site |
| | Removal – see also Removal from site |
| H57.3 | Removal Anal Sphincter Artificial NEC |
| M60.2 | Removal Balloon Male Continence Adjustable |
| U33.3 | Removal Blood Pressure Monitor Ambulatory |
| | Removal Bypass – see Bypass site |
| K55.3 | Removal Cardiac Thrombus Open |
| K55.4 | Removal Cardiac Vegetations Open NEC |
| | |
| K59.5 | Removal Cardioverter Defibrillator |
| Q12.3 | Removal Contraceptive Device Displaced NEC |
| P31.5 | Removal Contraceptive Device Displaced Pouch Douglas |
| Q12.4 | Removal Contraceptive Device Uterine Cavity |
| U19.7 | Removal Electrocardiography Loop Recorder |
| | Removal Explant – see Explant site |
| | Removal Fixation – see Fixation site |
| | Removal Foreign Body – see also Removal from site Foreign Body |
| Y29.- | Removal Foreign Body NOC |
| | Removal from – see also Evacuation |

| | |
|---|---|
| T31.6 | Removal from Abdominal Wall Anterior Foreign Body |
| T31.6 | Removal from Abdominal Wall Foreign Body NEC |
| T39.8 | Removal from Abdominal Wall Posterior Foreign Body |
| D07.3 | Removal from Auditory Canal External Foreign Body |
| D07.2 | Removal from Auditory Canal External Wax NEC |
| J41.1 | Removal from Bile Duct Calculus Endoscopic Retrograde |
| J33.- | Removal from Bile Duct Calculus Open |
| J49.- | Removal from Bile Duct Calculus T Tube Track Endoscopic |
| J49.- | Removal from Bile Duct Calculus T Tube Track Percutaneous |
| J76.1 | Removal from Bile Duct Calculus Transhepatic Percutaneous |
| | |
| M44.4 | Removal from Bladder Blood Clot Endoscopic |
| M44.2 | Removal from Bladder Calculus Endoscopic NEC |
| M39.1 | Removal from Bladder Calculus Open |
| M44.3 | Removal from Bladder Foreign Body Endoscopic |
| M39.2 | Removal from Bladder Foreign Body Open |
| M55.7 | Removal from Bladder Outlet Female Balloon Continence Adjustable |
| M55.7 | Removal from Bladder Outlet Female Device Retropubic |
| M49.3 | Removal from Bladder Suprapubic Tube |
| W35.3 | Removal from Bone Substance Implanted |
| A07.2 | Removal from Brain Tissue Foreign Body |
| | |
| E48.5 | Removal from Bronchus Foreign Body Endoscopic NEC |
| E50.5 | Removal from Bronchus Foreign Body Endoscopic Rigid |
| H21.3 | Removal from Caecum Foreign Body Endoscopic Fibreoptic |
| H21.3 | Removal from Caecum Foreign Body Endoscopic NEC |
| H19.4 | Removal from Caecum Foreign Body Open |
| E48.5 | Removal from Carina Foreign Body Endoscopic NEC |
| E50.5 | Removal from Carina Foreign Body Endoscopic Rigid |
| T01.2 | Removal from Chest Wall Plombage |
| T05.4 | Removal from Chest Wall Wire |
| H21.3 | Removal from Colon Foreign Body Endoscopic Fibreoptic |
| | |
| H21.3 | Removal from Colon Foreign Body Endoscopic NEC |
| H19.4 | Removal from Colon Foreign Body Open |
| H24.8 | Removal from Colon Sigmoid Foreign Body Endoscopic NEC |
| H27.2 | Removal from Colon Sigmoid Foreign Body Sigmoidoscope Rigid |
| H31.5 | Removal from Colorectum Stent Image Guided |
| C43.3 | Removal from Conjunctiva Foreign Body |
| C48.- | Removal from Cornea Foreign Body |
| G54.8 | Removal from Duodenum Foreign Body Endoscopic NEC |
| G53.3 | Removal from Duodenum Foreign Body Open |
| G44.2 | Removal from Duodenum Prox. Foreign Body & Exam. U.G.I. Tract Endo. NEC |
| | |
| G44.2 | Removal from Duodenum Prox. Foreign Body & Exam. U.G.I. Tract Fibreoptic |
| D05.7 | Removal from Ear External Hearing Implant |
| D20.6 | Removal from Ear Middle Hearing Implant |
| C86.4 | Removal from Eye Foreign Body NEC |
| C22.3 | Removal from Eyelid Foreign Body |
| Q37.1 | Removal from Fallopian Tube Clip Access Minimal |
| Q37.1 | Removal from Fallopian Tube Clip Endoscopic |
| Q29.2 | Removal from Fallopian Tube Clip Open NEC |
| Q31.1 | Removal from Fallopian Tube Products Conception NEC |
| Q29.2 | Removal from Fallopian Tube Ring Open NEC |

| | |
|---|---|
| J08.1 | Removal from Gall Bladder Calculus Access Minimal |
| J08.1 | Removal from Gall Bladder Calculus Endoscopic NEC |
| J08.1 | Removal from Gall Bladder Calculus Laparoscopic |
| J21.1 | Removal from Gall Bladder Calculus Open |
| J08.1 | Removal from Gall Bladder Calculus Peritoneoscope |
| G44.2 | Removal from Gastrointestinal Tract Upper Foreign Body Endoscopic Fibreoptic |
| G44.2 | Removal from Gastrointestinal Tract Upper Foreign Body Endoscopic NEC |
| K57.3 | Removal from Heart Foreign Body Transluminal Percutaneous |
| K55.3 | Removal from Heart Thrombus |
| K37.- | Removal from Heart Valve Structure Adjacent Obstruction |
| | |
| K55.4 | Removal from Heart Vegetations |
| T27.- | Removal from Hernia Abdominal Wall Material Prosthetic Repair NEC |
| T23.4 | Removal from Hernia Femoral Material Prosthetic Repair |
| T26.4 | Removal from Hernia Incisional Material Prosthetic Repair |
| T21.4 | Removal from Hernia Inguinal Material Prosthetic Repair |
| T24.4 | Removal from Hernia Umbilical Material Prosthetic Repair |
| T27.4 | Removal from Hernia Ventral Material Prosthetic Repair |
| G78.3 | Removal from Ileum Foreign Body |
| G78.3 | Removal from Intestine Small Foreign Body NEC |
| C64.5 | Removal from Iris Foreign Body |
| | |
| W85.1 | Removal from Joint Knee Loose Body Endoscopic |
| W86.1 | Removal from Joint Loose Body Endoscopic NEC |
| W81.2 | Removal from Joint Loose Body Open |
| M09.4 | Removal from Kidney Calculus Endoscopic NEC |
| M06.1 | Removal from Kidney Calculus Open |
| M06.1 | Removal from Kidney Pelvis Calculus Open |
| E35.5 | Removal from Larynx Foreign Body Endoscopic |
| C77.- | Removal from Lens Foreign Body |
| J08.1 | Removal from Liver Calculus Access Minimal |
| J08.1 | Removal from Liver Calculus Endoscopic NEC |
| | |
| J08.1 | Removal from Liver Calculus Laparoscope |
| J05.2 | Removal from Liver Calculus Open |
| J12.2 | Removal from Liver Calculus Percutaneous |
| J08.1 | Removal from Liver Calculus Peritoneoscope |
| J04.1 | Removal from Liver Fragment Lacerated |
| E48.5 | Removal from Lung Foreign Body Endoscopic NEC |
| E50.5 | Removal from Lung Foreign Body Endoscopic Rigid |
| F40.5 | Removal from Mouth Suture NEC |
| S70.3 | Removal from Nail Foreign Body |
| E27.4 | Removal from Nasopharynx Foreign Body |
| | |
| E08.5 | Removal from Nose Cavity Foreign Body |
| G44.2 | Removal from Oesophagus Foreign Body & Exam. U.G.I. Tract Endoscopic NEC |
| G44.2 | Removal from Oesophagus Foreign Body & Exam. U.G.I. Tract Fibreoptic Endoscopic |
| G15.1 | Removal from Oesophagus Foreign Body Endoscopic Fibreoptic |
| G18.1 | Removal from Oesophagus Foreign Body Endoscopic NEC |
| G18.1 | Removal from Oesophagus Foreign Body NEC |
| G13.2 | Removal from Oesophagus Foreign Body Open |
| C06.4 | Removal from Orbit Foreign Body |
| Y44.4 | Removal from Organ Calculus |
| F32.2 | Removal from Palate Foreign Body |

| | |
|---|---|
| J60.- | Removal from Pancreatic Duct Calculus |
| J42.3 | Removal from Pancreatic Duct Calculus Endoscopic Retrograde |
| F56.1 | Removal from Parotid Duct Calculus Manipulative |
| F51.1 | Removal from Parotid Duct Calculus Open |
| N32.5 | Removal from Penis Constricting Object |
| T42.4 | Removal from Peritoneum Foreign Body Access Minimal |
| T42.4 | Removal from Peritoneum Foreign Body Endoscopic |
| T41.4 | Removal from Peritoneum Foreign Body NEC |
| F36.4 | Removal from Peritonsillar Region Foreign Body |
| E27.4 | Removal from Pharynx Foreign Body |
| | |
| P31.5 | Removal from Pouch Douglas Contraceptive Device Intrauterine |
| P31.6 | Removal from Pouch Douglas Foreign Body NEC |
| M67.4 | Removal from Prostate Calculus Endoscopic |
| M68.2 | Removal from Prostate Stent Cystoscopic |
| G44.2 | Removal from Pylorus Foreign Body Endoscopic Fibreoptic |
| G44.2 | Removal from Pylorus Foreign Body Endoscopic NEC |
| H44.1 | Removal from Rectum Foreign Body Manual |
| H27.2 | Removal from Rectum Foreign Body Sigmoidoscope Rigid |
| E48.5 | Removal from Respiratory Tract Lower Foreign Body Endoscopic NEC |
| E50.5 | Removal from Respiratory Tract Lower Foreign Body Endoscopic Rigid |
| | |
| F56.- | Removal from Salivary Duct Calculus Manipulative |
| F51.- | Removal from Salivary Duct Calculus Open |
| N03.5 | Removal from Scrotum Foreign Body |
| S54.2 | Removal from Skin Burnt Slough Head |
| S55.2 | Removal from Skin Burnt Slough NEC |
| S54.2 | Removal from Skin Burnt Slough Neck |
| S43.- | Removal from Skin Clip |
| S44.- | Removal from Skin Foreign Body Inorganic NEC |
| S45.- | Removal from Skin Foreign Body NEC |
| S43.- | Removal from Skin Repair Material |
| | |
| S56.2 | Removal from Skin Slough Head NEC |
| S57.2 | Removal from Skin Slough NEC |
| S56.2 | Removal from Skin Slough Neck NEC |
| S44.- | Removal from Skin Substance Inorganic NEC |
| S45.- | Removal from Skin Substance NEC |
| S43.- | Removal from Skin Suture |
| A45.5 | Removal from Spinal Cord Foreign Body |
| A45.5 | Removal from Spinal Tract Foreign Body |
| V46.5 | Removal from Spine Fixation Device |
| V40.5 | Removal from Spine Instrumentation |
| | |
| G44.2 | Removal from Stomach Foreign Body Endoscopic Fibreoptic |
| G44.2 | Removal from Stomach Foreign Body Endoscopic NEC |
| G18.1 | Removal from Stomach Foreign Body Gastroscope Rigid |
| G38.4 | Removal from Stomach Foreign Body Open |
| G38.7 | Removal from Stomach Gastric Band |
| S54.2 | Removal from Subcutaneous Tissue Burnt Slough Head |
| S55.2 | Removal from Subcutaneous Tissue Burnt Slough NEC |
| S54.2 | Removal from Subcutaneous Tissue Burnt Slough Neck |
| S43.- | Removal from Subcutaneous Tissue Clip |
| S44.- | Removal from Subcutaneous Tissue Foreign Body Inorganic NEC |

| | |
|---|---|
| S45.- | Removal from Subcutaneous Tissue Foreign Body NEC |
| S62.5 | Removal from Subcutaneous Tissue Implant Hormone |
| S62.4 | Removal from Subcutaneous Tissue Pack |
| S43.- | Removal from Subcutaneous Tissue Repair Material |
| S56.2 | Removal from Subcutaneous Tissue Slough Head NEC |
| S57.2 | Removal from Subcutaneous Tissue Slough NEC |
| S56.2 | Removal from Subcutaneous Tissue Slough Neck NEC |
| S44.- | Removal from Subcutaneous Tissue Substance Inorganic NEC |
| S62.3 | Removal from Subcutaneous Tissue Substance Inserted NEC |
| S45.- | Removal from Subcutaneous Tissue Substance NEC |
| | |
| F56.2 | Removal from Submandibular Duct Calculus Manipulative |
| N13.6 | Removal from Testis Foreign Body |
| F24.2 | Removal from Tongue Foreign Body |
| F36.4 | Removal from Tonsil Foreign Body |
| E48.5 | Removal from Trachea Foreign Body Endoscopic NEC |
| E50.5 | Removal from Trachea Foreign Body Endoscopic Rigid |
| M28.- | Removal from Ureter Calculus Endoscopic NEC |
| M26.3 | Removal from Ureter Calculus Nephroscopic |
| M27.3 | Removal from Ureter Calculus Ureteroscopic |
| M22.2 | Removal from Ureter Ligature |
| | |
| M33.6 | Removal from Ureter Stent Percutaneous NEC |
| M27.5 | Removal from Ureter Stent Ureteroscopic |
| M75.4 | Removal from Urethra Calculus Open |
| M76.2 | Removal from Urethra Foreign Body Endoscopic |
| M76.7 | Removal from Urethra Stent Endoscopic |
| M86.1 | Removal from Urinary Diversion Calculus Endoscopic |
| M83.3 | Removal from Urinary Tract Foreign Body NEC |
| Q12.4 | Removal from Uterine Cavity Contraceptive Device |
| Q15.4 | Removal from Uterine Cavity Substance Therapeutic |
| R28.- | Removal from Uterus Delivered Products Conception Instrument |
| | |
| R29.- | Removal from Uterus Delivered Products Conception Manual |
| Q09.1 | Removal from Uterus Products Conception Open |
| P29.4 | Removal from Vagina Foreign Body |
| M53.5 | Removal from Vagina Tension Free Tape Partial |
| M53.4 | Removal from Vagina Tension Free Tape Total |
| L90.- | Removal from Vein Thrombus Open |
| L96.- | Removal from Vein Thrombus Percutaneous |
| L79.5 | Removal from Vena Cava Filter |
| C79.7 | Removal from Vitreous Body Internal Tamponade Agent |
| | Removal from Wound – see Removal from Skin |
| | |
| G38.7 | Removal Gastric Band |
| | Removal Grommet – see Grommet site |
| | Removal Implant – see Implantation site |
| A54.5 | Removal Intrathecal Drug Delivery Device Adjacent Spinal Cord |
| | Removal Ligature – see Ligature site |
| Y44.8 | Removal Material Radioactive Removable NOC |
| E11.5 | Removal Nasal Prosthesis Fixtures Attachment |
| F14.7 | Removal Orthodontic Anchorage |
| F14.4 | Removal Orthodontic Appliance NEC |
| F14.7 | Removal Orthodontic Screw |

| | |
|---|---|
| | Removal Pack – see Packing |
| R29.1 | Removal Placenta Uterus Delivered Manual |
| X48.3 | Removal Plaster Cast |
| | Removal Prosthesis – see Prosthesis site |
| C80.6 | Removal Retina Band |
| C80.6 | Removal Retina Membrane NEC |
| C80.5 | Removal Retina Membrane Vascular |
| M55.7 | Removal Retropubic Device Female |
| M60.2 | Removal Retropubic Male Device Continence |
| | Removal Shunt – see Shunt site |
| | |
| | Removal site – see Excision site |
| | Removal Snare – see Resection site |
| | Removal Spacer Prosthesis Joint – see Attention site Joint |
| H57.7 | Removal Sphincter Dynamic Graciloplasty |
| A48.6 | Removal Spinal Cord Adjacent Neurostimulator |
| | Removal Stent – see also Prosthesis |
| Y15.7 | Removal Stent NOC |
| C80.6 | Removal Subretinal Band |
| C80.6 | Removal Subretinal Membrane NEC |
| C80.5 | Removal Subretinal Vascular Membrane |
| | |
| | Removal Suture – see also Suture site |
| C65.4 | Removal Suture Releasable Following Glaucoma Surgery |
| | Removal System – see System site |
| F17.5 | Removal Tooth Crown Dental |
| F09.- | Removal Tooth Surgical |
| M53.7 | Removal Transobturator Tape |
| | Removal Tube – see Drainage site |
| | Removal Tube – see Tube site |
| K54.2 | Removal Ventricular Assist Device Open |
| | Removal Wire – see Removal from site |
| | |
| X40.- | Renal Failure Compensation NEC |
| Z41.4 | Renal Pelvis site NEC |
| | Renewal Pack – see Packing |
| | Renewal Prosthesis – see Prosthesis site |
| | Renewal Shunt – see Shunt site |
| | Renewal Stent – see Stent |
| Y15.2 | Renewal Stent NOC |
| | Renewal Tube – see Tube |
| T05.8 | Renewal Wire Chest Wall |
| U12.6 | Renogram Mercaptoacetyltriglycine |
| | |
| U12.5 | Renogram Static |
| | Reopening – see also Re-exploration |
| T30.- | Reopening Abdomen & Arrest Bleeding Intra-abdominal Postoperative Surgery |
| T30.- | Reopening Abdomen & Re-exploration Intra-abdominal Operation |
| T30.3 | Reopening Abdomen NEC |
| T03.- | Reopening Chest & Arrest Bleeding Intrathoracic Postoperative Surgical |
| T03.- | Reopening Chest & Re-exploration Intrathoracic Operation |
| T03.- | Reopening Chest NEC |
| V03.- | Reopening Cranium |
| V03.- | Reopening Cranium & Arrest Bleeding Intracranial Postoperative Surg. |

| | |
|---|---|
| V03.- | Reopening Cranium & Re-exploration Intracranial Operation |
| E08.7 | Reopening Nares Anterior Surgical |
| T30.3 | Reopening Peritoneum NEC |
| | Repair – see also Closure |
| | Repair – see also Correction |
| T28.- | Repair Abdominal Wall NEC |
| T28.8 | Repair Abdominal Wall with Prosthetic Insertion |
| H55.7 | Repair Anal Fistula Plug |
| H50.- | Repair Anus |
| L23.- | Repair Aorta Plastic |
| | |
| L23.7 | Repair Aortic Arch Interrupted |
| L23.- | Repair Aortic Coarctation |
| L23.- | Repair Aortic Hypoplasia |
| F15.6 | Repair Appliance Orthodontic |
| L75.2 | Repair Arteriovenous Fistula Acquired |
| L38.1 | Repair Artery Axillary NEC |
| L38.1 | Repair Artery Brachial NEC |
| L31.3 | Repair Artery Carotid Endovascular |
| L30.1 | Repair Artery Carotid NEC |
| K47.- | Repair Artery Coronary |
| | |
| K47.3 | Repair Artery Coronary Aneurysmal |
| K47.2 | Repair Artery Coronary Fistula Arteriovenous |
| K47.5 | Repair Artery Coronary Malformation Arteriovenous |
| K47.4 | Repair Artery Coronary Rupture |
| L62.1 | Repair Artery Femoral NEC |
| K06.- | Repair Artery Great Transposition |
| L53.1 | Repair Artery Iliac NEC |
| L68.- | Repair Artery NEC |
| L62.1 | Repair Artery Popliteal NEC |
| L10.- | Repair Artery Pulmonary |
| | |
| L01.3 | Repair Artery Pulmonary Origin Anomalous from Ascending Aorta |
| L10.4 | Repair Artery Pulmonary Sling |
| L41.- | Repair Artery Renal |
| L38.1 | Repair Artery Subclavian NEC |
| L38.1 | Repair Artery Vertebral NEC |
| K22.2 | Repair Atrium NEC |
| J32.- | Repair Bile Duct |
| K17.5 | Repair Biventricular Hypoplastic Left Heart Syndrome |
| M37.- | Repair Bladder NEC |
| E47.3 | Repair Bronchus NEC |
| | |
| C29.1 | Repair Canaliculus |
| W82.3 | Repair Cartilage Semilunar Endoscopic |
| W70.3 | Repair Cartilage Semilunar NEC |
| Q05.1 | Repair Cervix Uteri NEC |
| T05.3 | Repair Chest Wall NEC |
| C40.- | Repair Conjunctiva |
| K20.3 | Repair Cor Triatriatum |
| V05.4 | Repair Cranium Fracture NEC |
| V01.- | Repair Cranium Plastic |
| F63.4 | Repair Denture |

| | |
|---|---|
| T16.- | Repair Diaphragm NEC |
| T15.- | Repair Diaphragm Rupture |
| G23.- | Repair Diaphragmatic Hernia |
| A39.- | Repair Dura |
| D06.- | Repair Ear External |
| D14.- | Repair Eardrum |
| P23.4 | Repair Enterocele NEC |
| M73.2 | Repair Epispadias |
| T28.1 | Repair Exomphalos HFQ |
| C86.2 | Repair Eye Injury Penetrating |
| | |
| C37.4 | Repair Eye Muscle NEC |
| C17.- | Repair Eyelid NEC |
| C16.- | Repair Eyelid Plastic NEC |
| C17.- | Repair Eyelid Skin NEC |
| Q30.- | Repair Fallopian Tube NEC |
| T57.3 | Repair Fascia |
| M37.5 | Repair Fistula Bladder |
| M62.4 | Repair Fistula Rectoprostatic |
| J20.- | Repair Gall Bladder |
| J20.3 | Repair Gall Bladder Perforation |
| | |
| T28.1 | Repair Gastroschisis HFQ |
| C86.2 | Repair Globe |
| K55.6 | Repair Heart Injury Traumatic |
| K17.- | Repair Heart Univentricular |
| K29.- | Repair Heart Valve Plastic NEC |
| K30.- | Repair Heart Valve Plastic Revision |
| K23.3 | Repair Heart Wall NEC |
| L01.3 | Repair Hemitruncus Arteriosus |
| T27.- | Repair Hernia Abdominal Wall NEC |
| T98.- | Repair Hernia Abdominal Wall Recurrent |
| | |
| T16.4 | Repair Hernia Diaphragmatic Congenital |
| G23.- | Repair Hernia Diaphragmatic NEC |
| T22.- | Repair Hernia Femoral NEC |
| T23.- | Repair Hernia Femoral Recurrent |
| T25.- | Repair Hernia Incisional NEC |
| T26.- | Repair Hernia Incisional Recurrent |
| T20.- | Repair Hernia Inguinal NEC |
| T21.- | Repair Hernia Inguinal Recurrent |
| T24.- | Repair Hernia Umbilical |
| T97.- | Repair Hernia Umbilical Recurrent |
| | |
| T27.- | Repair Hernia Ventral |
| T98.1 | Repair Hernia Ventral Insert Material Natural Recurrent |
| T98.2 | Repair Hernia Ventral Insert Material Prosthetic Recurrent |
| T98.3 | Repair Hernia Ventral Sutures Recurrent |
| P15.3 | Repair Hymen |
| K17.- | Repair Hypoplastic Left Heart Syndrome |
| M73.1 | Repair Hypospadias |
| G75.2 | Repair Ileostomy Prolapse |
| P15.8 | Repair Introitus |
| O27.- | Repair Joint Capsule Glenohumeral & Labrum (W) |

| | |
|---|---|
| W77.- | Repair Joint Capsule NEC |
| M05.- | Repair Kidney Open |
| W84.7 | Repair Labrum Superior Tear Anterior Posterior Endoscopic |
| W84.- | Repair Ligament Intra-articular Endoscopic |
| W84.- | Repair Ligament Knee Intra-articular Endoscopic |
| W75.- | Repair Ligament NEC |
| W75.- | Repair Ligament Open |
| F05.- | Repair Lip NEC |
| F05.- | Repair Lip Skin NEC |
| J04.- | Repair Liver |
| | |
| E57.1 | Repair Lung |
| A39.1 | Repair Meningoencephalocele |
| T38.4 | Repair Mesentery Colon |
| T37.4 | Repair Mesentery Intestine Small |
| Y24.- | Repair Microvascular NOC |
| F40.- | Repair Mouth NEC |
| T79.- | Repair Muscle |
| C37.4 | Repair Muscle Eye NEC |
| H36.- | Repair Muscle Levator Ani |
| H36.1 | Repair Muscle Pelvic Floor NEC |
| | |
| S66.2 | Repair Nail Bed |
| E21.- | Repair Nasopharynx |
| A30.- | Repair Nerve Cranial |
| A62.- | Repair Nerve Peripheral Microsurgical |
| A62.- | Repair Nerve Peripheral Multiple Microsurgical |
| A64.- | Repair Nerve Peripheral NEC |
| Y26.- | Repair NOC |
| R32.- | Repair Obstetric Laceration |
| R32.- | Repair Obstetric Tear |
| F63.4 | Repair Obturator |
| | |
| G23.- | Repair Oesophageal Hiatus |
| G07.- | Repair Oesophagus |
| C05.- | Repair Orbit Plastic |
| K09.4 | Repair Ostium Primum Persistent |
| Q45.- | Repair Ovary |
| F29.- | Repair Palate Cleft |
| F29.- | Repair Palate Cleft Plastic |
| F30.- | Repair Palate NEC |
| F30.- | Repair Palate Plastic NEC |
| P23.5 | Repair Paravaginal |
| | |
| H36.1 | Repair Pelvic Floor Muscle NEC |
| N28.6 | Repair Penis Fracture |
| K71.2 | Repair Pericardium |
| R32.5 | Repair Perineum Sphincter Mucosa Anus Obstetric Laceration |
| E21.- | Repair Pharynx |
| Y26.2 | Repair Plastic NOC |
| G40.2 | Repair Pylorus Atresia Congenital |
| G41.2 | Repair Pylorus Perforation |
| E07.1 | Repair Pyriform Aperture Stenosis |
| P25.3 | Repair Rectovaginal Fistula |

| | |
|---|---|
| H42.6 | Repair Rectum Prolapse Perineal NEC |
| T79.3 | Repair Rotator Cuff Revisional |
| T79.- | Repair Rotator Cuff Shoulder Plastic |
| F48.3 | Repair Salivary Gland NEC |
| C57.2 | Repair Sclera |
| K13.- | Repair Septum Atrial Defect Transluminal Percutaneous |
| K09.- | Repair Septum Atrioventricular Defect |
| K12.- | Repair Septum Heart Defect NEC |
| K13.- | Repair Septum Heart Defect Transluminal |
| K10.- | Repair Septum Interatrial Defect NEC |
| | |
| K11.- | Repair Septum Interventricular Defect NEC |
| K13.- | Repair Septum Ventricular Defect Transluminal Percutaneous |
| T79.4 | Repair Shoulder Rotator Cuff Multiple Tears Plastic |
| T79.5 | Repair Shoulder Rotator Cuff Multiple Tears Revisional |
| K20.4 | Repair Sinus Coronary Abnormality |
| E15.3 | Repair Sinus Sphenoidal |
| N18.- | Repair Spermatic Cord |
| J34.- | Repair Sphincter Oddi Plastic |
| A49.- | Repair Spina Bifida |
| J72.4 | Repair Spleen |
| | |
| G36.- | Repair Stomach NEC |
| K37.3 | Repair Subaortic Stenosis |
| K37.4 | Repair Supra-aortic Stenosis |
| V21.8 | Repair Temporomandibular Joint NEC |
| T67.- | Repair Tendon NEC |
| T67.- | Repair Tendon Primary |
| T68.- | Repair Tendon Secondary |
| N13.7 | Repair Testis Rupture |
| K04.- | Repair Tetralogy Fallot |
| M22.- | Repair Ureter |
| | |
| M73.- | Repair Urethra |
| P25.2 | Repair Urethrovaginal Fistula |
| P25.4 | Repair Uterovaginal Fistula |
| P25.- | Repair Vagina NEC |
| P32.- | Repair Vagina Other Plastic |
| P21.- | Repair Vagina Plastic |
| P22.- | Repair Vagina Prolapse & Amputation Cervix Uteri |
| P23.- | Repair Vagina Prolapse NEC |
| P24.- | Repair Vagina Vault |
| K38.6 | Repair Valsalva Aneurysm Aortic Sinus |
| | |
| K26.- | Repair Valve Aortic Plastic |
| K25.- | Repair Valve Mitral Plastic |
| K28.- | Repair Valve Pulmonary Plastic |
| K27.- | Repair Valve Tricuspid Plastic |
| K29.6 | Repair Valve Truncal Plastic |
| L79.6 | Repair Vein Caval Anomalous Connection |
| L80.1 | Repair Vein Pulmonary Stenosis |
| L82.- | Repair Vein Valve |
| K24.4 | Repair Ventricle Aneurysmal Left |
| K24.3 | Repair Ventricle Aneurysmal Right |

| | |
|---|---|
| K08.- | Repair Ventricle Outlet Double |
| K24.2 | Repair Ventricle Right Double Chambered |
| M37.2 | Repair Vesicocolic Fistula |
| P25.1 | Repair Vesicovaginal Fistula |
| P07.- | Repair Vulva |
| P07.- | Repair Vulva Skin |
| | Replacement – see also Autoreplacement |
| | Replacement – see also Prosthesis |
| | Replacement – see also Renewal |
| L18.- | Replacement Aorta Segment Aneurysmal Emergency |
| | |
| L19.- | Replacement Aorta Segment Aneurysmal NEC |
| L20.- | Replacement Aorta Segment Emergency NEC |
| L21.- | Replacement Aorta Segment NEC |
| K33.- | Replacement Aortic Root |
| K33.1 | Replacement Aortic Root Autograft Valve Pulmonary |
| L29.1 | Replacement Artery Carotid Graft |
| K42.- | Replacement Artery Coronary Allograft |
| K41.- | Replacement Artery Coronary Autograft NEC |
| K40.- | Replacement Artery Coronary Graft Vein Saphenous |
| K44.- | Replacement Artery Coronary NEC |
| | |
| K43.- | Replacement Artery Coronary Prosthetic |
| K44.2 | Replacement Artery Coronary Revision |
| L56.- | Replacement Artery Femoral Aneurysmal Emergency |
| L57.- | Replacement Artery Femoral Aneurysmal NEC |
| L58.- | Replacement Artery Femoral Emergency NEC |
| L59.- | Replacement Artery Femoral NEC |
| L48.- | Replacement Artery Iliac Aneurysmal Emergency |
| L49.- | Replacement Artery Iliac Aneurysmal NEC |
| L50.- | Replacement Artery Iliac Emergency NEC |
| L51.- | Replacement Artery Iliac NEC |
| | |
| L56.- | Replacement Artery Popliteal Aneurysmal Emergency |
| L57.- | Replacement Artery Popliteal Aneurysmal NEC |
| L58.- | Replacement Artery Popliteal Emergency NEC |
| L59.- | Replacement Artery Popliteal NEC |
| W52.- | Replacement Bone Articulation Prosthetic Cemented NEC |
| W54.- | Replacement Bone Articulation Prosthetic NEC |
| W53.- | Replacement Bone Articulation Prosthetic Uncemented NEC |
| W05.- | Replacement Bone Prosthetic |
| C09.- | Replacement Canthal Tendon |
| K18.7 | Replacement Conduit Cardiac Valved |
| | |
| C40.4 | Replacement Conjunctiva Prosthetic |
| V36.- | Replacement Disc Intervertebral Prosthetic |
| W46.- | Replacement Femur Head Prosthetic Cemented |
| W48.- | Replacement Femur Head Prosthetic NEC |
| W47.- | Replacement Femur Head Prosthetic Uncemented |
| K29.- | Replacement Heart Valve NEC |
| K30.- | Replacement Heart Valve Revision |
| W49.- | Replacement Humerus Head Prosthetic Cemented |
| W51.- | Replacement Humerus Head Prosthetic NEC |
| W50.- | Replacement Humerus Head Prosthetic Uncemented |

| O23.4 | Replacement Joint Elbow Prosthetic Total Attention NEC (W) |
| O21.0 | Replacement Joint Elbow Prosthetic Total Cemented Conversion From (W) |
| O21.2 | Replacement Joint Elbow Prosthetic Total Cemented Conversion To (W) |
| O21.- | Replacement Joint Elbow Prosthetic Total Cemented NEC (W) |
| O21.1 | Replacement Joint Elbow Prosthetic Total Cemented Primary (W) |
| O21.3 | Replacement Joint Elbow Prosthetic Total Cemented Revision (W) |
| O23.0 | Replacement Joint Elbow Prosthetic Total Conversion From NEC (W) |
| O23.2 | Replacement Joint Elbow Prosthetic Total Conversion To NEC (W) |
| O23.- | Replacement Joint Elbow Prosthetic Total NEC (W) |
| O21.4 | Replacement Joint Elbow Prosthetic Total One Component Cemented Revision (W) |
| | |
| O23.5 | Replacement Joint Elbow Prosthetic Total One Component Revision NEC (W) |
| O22.4 | Replacement Joint Elbow Prosthetic Total One Component Uncemented Revision (W) |
| O23.1 | Replacement Joint Elbow Prosthetic Total Primary NEC (W) |
| O23.3 | Replacement Joint Elbow Prosthetic Total Revision NEC (W) |
| O22.0 | Replacement Joint Elbow Prosthetic Total Uncemented Conversion From (W) |
| O22.2 | Replacement Joint Elbow Prosthetic Total Uncemented Conversion To (W) |
| O22.- | Replacement Joint Elbow Prosthetic Total Uncemented NEC (W) |
| O22.1 | Replacement Joint Elbow Prosthetic Total Uncemented Primary (W) |
| O22.3 | Replacement Joint Elbow Prosthetic Total Uncemented Revision (W) |
| W93.- | Replacement Joint Hip Hybrid Prosthetic Cemented Acetabular Component |
| | |
| W94.- | Replacement Joint Hip Hybrid Prosthetic Cemented Femoral Component |
| W95.- | Replacement Joint Hip Hybrid Prosthetic Cemented NEC |
| W37.- | Replacement Joint Hip Prosthetic Total Cemented |
| W39.- | Replacement Joint Hip Prosthetic Total NEC |
| W38.- | Replacement Joint Hip Prosthetic Total Uncemented |
| O18.- | Replacement Joint Knee Hybrid Prosthetic Cemented (W) |
| O18.4 | Replacement Joint Knee Hybrid Prosthetic Cemented Attention (W) |
| O18.0 | Replacement Joint Knee Hybrid Prosthetic Cemented Conversion From (W) |
| O18.2 | Replacement Joint Knee Hybrid Prosthetic Cemented Conversion To (W) |
| O18.1 | Replacement Joint Knee Hybrid Prosthetic Cemented Primary (W) |
| | |
| O18.3 | Replacement Joint Knee Hybrid Prosthetic Cemented Revision (W) |
| W40.- | Replacement Joint Knee Prosthetic Total Cemented |
| W42.- | Replacement Joint Knee Prosthetic Total NEC |
| W41.- | Replacement Joint Knee Prosthetic Total Uncemented |
| W43.- | Replacement Joint Prosthetic Total Cemented NEC |
| W45.- | Replacement Joint Prosthetic Total NEC |
| W44.- | Replacement Joint Prosthetic Total Uncemented NEC |
| O07.- | Replacement Joint Shoulder Hybrid Prosthetic Cemented Glenoid Component (W) |
| O06.- | Replacement Joint Shoulder Hybrid Prosthetic Cemented Humeral Component (W) |
| O08.- | Replacement Joint Shoulder Hybrid Prosthetic Cemented NEC (W) |
| | |
| W96.- | Replacement Joint Shoulder Prosthetic Total Cemented |
| W98.- | Replacement Joint Shoulder Prosthetic Total NEC |
| W96.5 | Replacement Joint Shoulder Prosthetic Total Reverse Polarity Cemented Primary |
| W96.6 | Replacement Joint Shoulder Prosthetic Total Reverse Polarity Cemented Revision |
| W98.6 | Replacement Joint Shoulder Prosthetic Total Reverse Polarity Primary NEC |
| W98.7 | Replacement Joint Shoulder Prosthetic Total Reverse Polarity Revision NEC |
| W97.5 | Replacement Joint Shoulder Prosthetic Total Reverse Polarity Uncemented Primary |
| W97.6 | Replacement Joint Shoulder Prosthetic Total Reverse Polarity Uncemented Revision |
| W97.- | Replacement Joint Shoulder Prosthetic Total Uncemented |
| V20.- | Replacement Joint Temporomandibular Prosthetic |

| | |
|---|---|
| W72.- | Replacement Ligament Prosthetic |
| J01.3 | Replacement Liver Transplant |
| E98.- | Replacement Nicotine Therapy |
| Y01.- | Replacement NOC |
| D16.- | Replacement Ossicular Chain |
| O26.4 | Replacement Radius Head Prosthetic Attention NEC (W) |
| O24.- | Replacement Radius Head Prosthetic Cemented (W) |
| O24.0 | Replacement Radius Head Prosthetic Cemented Conversion From (W) |
| O24.2 | Replacement Radius Head Prosthetic Cemented Conversion To (W) |
| O24.1 | Replacement Radius Head Prosthetic Cemented Primary (W) |
| | |
| O24.3 | Replacement Radius Head Prosthetic Cemented Revision (W) |
| O26.0 | Replacement Radius Head Prosthetic Conversion From NEC (W) |
| O26.2 | Replacement Radius Head Prosthetic Conversion To NEC (W) |
| O26.- | Replacement Radius Head Prosthetic NEC (W) |
| O26.1 | Replacement Radius Head Prosthetic Primary NEC (W) |
| O26.3 | Replacement Radius Head Prosthetic Revision NEC (W) |
| O25.- | Replacement Radius Head Prosthetic Uncemented (W) |
| O25.0 | Replacement Radius Head Prosthetic Uncemented Conversion From (W) |
| O25.2 | Replacement Radius Head Prosthetic Uncemented Conversion To (W) |
| O25.1 | Replacement Radius Head Prosthetic Uncemented Primary (W) |
| | |
| O25.3 | Replacement Radius Head Prosthetic Uncemented Revision (W) |
| S52.6 | Replacement Subcutaneous Tissue Hormone |
| C09.- | Replacement Tendon Canthus |
| | Replacement Testis – see also Placement Testis |
| N10.- | Replacement Testis Prosthetic |
| | Replacement Tube – see Tube |
| M21.- | Replacement Ureter NEC |
| M33.3 | Replacement Ureteric Stent Metallic NEC |
| M33.4 | Replacement Ureteric Stent Plastic NEC |
| Q12.2 | Replacement Uterine Cavity Contraceptive Device |
| | |
| K26.- | Replacement Valve Aortic |
| K25.- | Replacement Valve Mitral |
| K28.- | Replacement Valve Pulmonary |
| K35.7 | Replacement Valve Pulmonary Transluminal Percutaneous |
| K27.- | Replacement Valve Tricuspid |
| K29.7 | Replacement Valve Truncal |
| L94.4 | Replacement Vein Port Subcutaneous Transluminal Percutaneous |
| A73.6 | Replantation & Transfer Nerve Peripheral |
| L45.2 | Replantation Artery Coeliac |
| L45.2 | Replantation Artery Mesenteric |
| | |
| L41.3 | Replantation Artery Renal |
| L45.2 | Replantation Artery Suprarenal |
| J27.1 | Replantation Bile Duct Common Duodenum & Excision Ampulla Vater |
| Q30.2 | Replantation Fallopian Tube |
| X02.- | Replantation Limb Lower |
| X01.- | Replantation Limb Upper |
| A57.6 | Replantation Nerve Spinal Into Spinal Cord |
| Y04.- | Replantation NOC |
| X03.- | Replantation Organ NEC |
| Q45.1 | Replantation Ovary |

| | |
|---|---|
| J69.1 | Replantation Spleen Fragments & Excision Total |
| F08.3 | Replantation Tooth |
| M20.- | Replantation Ureter |
| | Repositioning – see also Resiting |
| K06.- | Repositioning Arteries Great Transposed |
| F08.4 | Repositioning Tooth |
| R30.1 | Repositioning Uterus Delivered Inverted |
| R12.3 | Repositioning Uterus Gravid Retroverted |
| K27.5 | Repositioning Valve Tricuspid |
| L79.4 | Repositioning Vena Cava Filter |
| | |
| A48.5 | Reprogramming Spinal Cord Neurostimulator |
| | Resection – see also Excision |
| M42.1 | Resection Bladder Lesion Endoscopic |
| M42.1 | Resection Bladder Lesion Transurethral |
| M56.1 | Resection Bladder Outlet Female Endoscopic |
| M55.1 | Resection Bladder Outlet Female Open |
| M65.- | Resection Bladder Outlet Male Endoscopic |
| M64.1 | Resection Bladder Outlet Male Open |
| H23.6 | Resection Bowel Lower Lesion Sigmoidoscope Fibreoptic NEC |
| H23.1 | Resection Bowel Lower Lesion Snare Sigmoidoscope Fibreoptic |
| | |
| H23.5 | Resection Bowel Lower Lesion Submucosal Sigmoidoscope Fibreoptic |
| E48.1 | Resection Bronchus Lesion Snare Endoscopic NEC |
| E50.1 | Resection Bronchus Lesion Snare Endoscopic Rigid |
| E46.1 | Resection Bronchus Sleeve & Anastomosis |
| H20.1 | Resection Caecum Lesion Snare Endoscopic Fibreoptic |
| H20.1 | Resection Caecum Lesion Snare Endoscopic NEC |
| E48.1 | Resection Carina Lesion Snare Endoscopic NEC |
| E50.1 | Resection Carina Lesion Snare Endoscopic Rigid |
| W82.- | Resection Cartilage Semilunar Endoscopic |
| H20.1 | Resection Colon Lesion Snare Endoscopic Fibreoptic |
| | |
| H20.1 | Resection Colon Lesion Snare Endoscopic NEC |
| H23.1 | Resection Colon Lesion Snare Sigmoidoscope Fibreoptic |
| H20.5 | Resection Colon Lesion Submucosal Endoscopic Fibreoptic |
| H26.7 | Resection Colon Sigmoid Lesion Sigmoidoscope Rigid NEC |
| H23.1 | Resection Colon Sigmoid Lesion Snare Endoscopic NEC |
| H23.1 | Resection Colon Sigmoid Lesion Snare Sigmoidoscope Fibreoptic |
| H26.1 | Resection Colon Sigmoid Lesion Snare Sigmoidoscope Rigid |
| H23.5 | Resection Colon Sigmoid Lesion Submucosal Sigmoidoscope Fibreoptic |
| H26.6 | Resection Colon Sigmoid Lesion Submucosal Sigmoidoscope Rigid |
| G54.1 | Resection Duodenum Lesion Snare NEC |
| | |
| G43.1 | Resection Duodenum Prox. Lesion Snare & Exam. U.G.I. Tract Endoscopic Fibreoptic |
| G43.1 | Resection Duodenum Prox. Lesion Snare & Exam. U.G.I. Tract Endoscopic NEC |
| C31.- | Resection Eye Muscle & Recession |
| C31.- | Resection Eye Muscle Bilateral |
| C33.- | Resection Eye Muscle NEC |
| G43.1 | Resection Gastrointestinal Tract Upper Lesion Snare Endo. Fibreoptic |
| G43.1 | Resection Gastrointestinal Tract Upper Lesion Snare Endoscopic NEC |
| G42.1 | Resection Gastrointestinal Tract Upper Lesion Submucosal Endo. Fibreoptic |
| G42.1 | Resection Gastrointestinal Tract Upper Lesion Submucosal Endoscopic NEC |
| K55.5 | Resection Heart Tumour |

| | |
|---|---|
| H07.1 | Resection Ileocaecal |
| G73.4 | Resection Ileocolic Anastomosis |
| G73.3 | Resection Ileostomy |
| M10.1 | Resection Kidney Lesion Endoscopic |
| E34.- | Resection Larynx Lesion Endoscopic Microtherapeutic |
| J02.3 | Resection Liver Section |
| J02.3 | Resection Liver Segment |
| E48.1 | Resection Lung Lesion Snare Endoscopic NEC |
| E50.1 | Resection Lung Lesion Snare Endoscopic Rigid |
| C31.- | Resection Muscle Eye & Recession |
| | |
| C31.- | Resection Muscle Eye Bilateral |
| C33.- | Resection Muscle Eye NEC |
| G43.1 | Resection Oesophagus Lesion Snare & Exam. U.G.I. Tract Endo. Fibreoptic |
| G43.1 | Resection Oesophagus Lesion Snare & Exam. U.G.I. Tract Endoscopic NEC |
| G14.1 | Resection Oesophagus Lesion Snare Endoscopic Fibreoptic |
| G14.1 | Resection Oesophagus Lesion Snare Endoscopic NEC |
| G14.6 | Resection Oesophagus Lesion Submucosal Endoscopic Fibreoptic |
| Y05.4 | Resection Organ Ante Situm Hypothermic NOC |
| Y05.4 | Resection Organ Ex Vivo NOC |
| T42.1 | Resection Peritoneum Lesion Access Minimal |
| | |
| T42.1 | Resection Peritoneum Lesion Endoscopic |
| M65.- | Resection Prostate Endoscopic |
| M65.- | Resection Prostate Transurethral |
| H33.- | Resection Rectum Anterior & Anastomosis |
| H23.1 | Resection Rectum Lesion Snare Endoscopic NEC |
| H23.1 | Resection Rectum Lesion Snare Sigmoidoscope Fibreoptic |
| H26.1 | Resection Rectum Lesion Snare Sigmoidoscope Rigid |
| H23.5 | Resection Rectum Lesion Submucosal Sigmoidoscope Fibreoptic |
| H26.6 | Resection Rectum Lesion Submucosal Sigmoidoscope Rigid |
| H33.7 | Resection Rectum Perineal |
| | |
| E48.1 | Resection Respiratory Tract Lower Lesion Snare Endoscopic NEC |
| E50.1 | Resection Respiratory Tract Lower Lesion Snare Endoscopic Rigid |
| C53.1 | Resection Sclera Punch |
| H26.6 | Resection Sigmoid Colon Lesion Submucosal Sigmoidoscope Rigid |
| G43.1 | Resection Stomach Lesion Snare Endoscopic Fibreoptic |
| G43.1 | Resection Stomach Lesion Snare Endoscopic NEC |
| G17.1 | Resection Stomach Lesion Snare Gastroscope Rigid |
| E48.1 | Resection Trachea Lesion Snare Endoscopic NEC |
| E50.1 | Resection Trachea Lesion Snare Endoscopic Rigid |
| M32.6 | Resection Ureteric Orifice Transurethral Endoscopic |
| | |
| Q17.1 | Resection Uterus Lesion Endoscopic |
| A12.5 | Reservoir Cerebrospinal Fluid Subcutaneous Creation |
| V04.- | Reshaping Cranium |
| | Resiting – see also Repositioning |
| K60.2 | Resiting Cardiac Pacemaker System Lead Intravenous |
| K61.2 | Resiting Cardiac Pacemaker System Lead NEC |
| K59.3 | Resiting Cardioverter Defibrillator Lead |
| | Resiting Prosthesis – see Prosthesis site |
| Y15.4 | Resiting Stent NOC |
| L91.3 | Resiting Venous Catheter Central |

| | |
|---|---|
| E48.- | Respiratory Tract Lower Operations Endoscopic NEC |
| E50.- | Respiratory Tract Lower Operations Endoscopic Rigid |
| Z24.- | Respiratory Tract site NEC |
| E94.- | Response Bronchodilator |
| F13.- | Restoration Crown |
| F13.- | Restoration Tooth |
| | Resurfacing Arthroplasty – see Arthroplasty Joint Resurfacing |
| | Resurfacing Hemiarthroplasty Head of Humerus – see Hemiarthroplasty |
| X50.- | Resuscitation External |
| | Resuture – see also Suture |
| | |
| T28.3 | Resuture Abdominal Wall |
| Y25.- | Resuture NOC |
| C80.- | Retina Membrane Operations NEC |
| C54.- | Retina Operations Buckling Attachment |
| C84.- | Retina Operations NEC |
| Z19.3 | Retina site |
| C84.6 | Retinectomy Relieving |
| C81.2 | Retinopexy Laser for Detachment |
| C85.- | Retinopexy NEC |
| C84.6 | Retinotomy NEC |
| | |
| V16.2 | Retrusion Mandible & Osteotomy |
| K23.4 | Revascularisation Heart NEC |
| K23.4 | Revascularisation Heart Wall |
| L97.1 | Revascularisation Impotence |
| | Reversal – see Primary Operation site |
| | Revision – see Operation Revision |
| | Revision – see Primary Operation |
| | Revision Anastomosis – see Anastomosis site |
| C65.3 | Revision Bleb Following Glaucoma Surgery |
| | Revision Bypass – see Bypass site |
| | |
| | Revision Connection – see Connection site |
| H66.2 | Revision Ileoanal Pouch |
| C65.3 | Revision Iris Bleb |
| E11.4 | Revision Nasal Prosthesis Fixtures Attachment |
| | Revision Neurolysis   see Neurolysis site |
| | Revision Prosthesis – see Prosthesis site |
| | Revision Reconstruction – see Reconstruction site |
| | Revision Release – see Release site |
| Y71.- | Revisional Operations NOC |
| E02.- | Rhinoplasty |
| | |
| E17.4 | Rhinotomy Nasal Sinus Lateral NEC |
| A57.2 | Rhizotomy Nerve Root Spinal |
| Z74.- | Rib Cage site NEC |
| Z74.- | Rib site |
| Z94.2 | Right Sided Operations |
| Q36.- | Ringing Fallopian Tube Access Minimal NEC |
| Q35.3 | Ringing Fallopian Tube Bilateral Access Minimal |
| Q35.3 | Ringing Fallopian Tube Bilateral Endoscopic |
| Q27.2 | Ringing Fallopian Tube Bilateral Open |
| Q36.- | Ringing Fallopian Tube Endoscopic NEC |

| Q28.- | Ringing Fallopian Tube Open NEC |
| F12.2 | Root Canal Tooth Therapy |
| X23.6 | Rotation Plasty Ankle Correction Leg Deformity Congenital Reversal |
| R14.1 | Rupture Amniotic Membrane Forewater |
| R14.2 | Rupture Amniotic Membrane Hindwater |
| M10.5 | Rupture Kidney Pelviureteric Junction Stenosis Endoscopic Endoluminal Balloon |
| M27.6 | Rupture Ureter Stenosis Ureteroscopic Endoluminal Balloon |

# S

| | |
|---|---|
| Z11.- | Sacral Plexus site |
| A59.- | Sacrifice Nerve Peripheral |
| T65.1 | Sacrifice Tendon |
| P24.2 | Sacrocolpopexy |
| Q54.5 | Sacrohysteropexy |
| Z75.- | Sacrum site |
| Z26.- | Salivary Apparatus site |
| F58.- | Salivary Duct Operations NEC |
| F53.- | Salivary Duct Operations Open NEC |
| Z26.7 | Salivary Duct site |
| | |
| F48.- | Salivary Gland Operations NEC |
| Z26.4 | Salivary Gland site |
| Q22.2 | Salpingectomy Bilateral NEC |
| Q24.2 | Salpingectomy NEC |
| Q25.- | Salpingectomy Partial |
| Q23.- | Salpingectomy Unilateral NEC |
| Q41.1 | Salpingography |
| Q22.1 | Salpingoophorectomy Bilateral |
| Q24.1 | Salpingoophorectomy NEC |
| Q23.- | Salpingoophorectomy Unilateral |
| | |
| Q30.4 | Salpingostomy |
| Q31.- | Salpingotomy |
| H25.2 | Sampling Bowel Lower Bacterial Overgrowth NEC |
| R10.- | Sampling Chorionic Villus NEC |
| R05.3 | Sampling Chorionic Villus Percutaneous |
| R02.- | Sampling Fetal Blood Fetoscopic |
| R05.2 | Sampling Fetal Blood Percutaneous |
| T86.- | Sampling Lymph Nodes |
| M30.3 | Sampling Urine Ureteric Endoscopic |
| X36.3 | Sampling Venous NEC |
| | |
| J77.1 | Sampling Venous Portal Transhepatic Percutaneous |
| W18.2 | Saucerisation Bone |
| F16.4 | Scaling Tooth |
| | Scan – see also Imaging |
| R37.1 | Scan Biophysical Profile |
| U14.- | Scan Bone Nuclear |
| U10.7 | Scan Cardiac Multiple Gated Acquisition |
| R40.2 | Scan Cervix Length |
| R36.1 | Scan Dating |
| U13.1 | Scan Dual Emission X-ray Absorptiometry |

| | |
|---|---|
| R37.5 | Scan Fetal Ascites |
| R37.3 | Scan Fetal Biometry |
| R37.3 | Scan Growth NEC |
| U16.1 | Scan Hepatobiliary Nuclear |
| R38.2 | Scan Liquor Volume |
| U15.1 | Scan Lung Perfusion NEC |
| U15.2 | Scan Lung Ventilation NEC |
| T91.2 | Scan Lymph Node Sentinel |
| U17.1 | Scan Meckel's |
| R36.3 | Scan Mid Trimester |
| | |
| U10.6 | Scan Myocardial Perfusion |
| R37.4 | Scan Nuchal Translucency |
| R37.- | Scan Obstetric Non-routine Fetal Observations |
| R38.- | Scan Obstetric Non-routine Other |
| R36.- | Scan Obstetric Routine |
| R38.1 | Scan Placenta Localisation |
| R37.6 | Scan Rhesus Detailed |
| R37.2 | Scan Structural Detailed |
| U06.5 | Scan Thyroid Gland |
| U15.3 | Scan Ventilation Perfusion |
| | |
| R36.2 | Scan Viability |
| U23.2 | Scan White Cell Indium 111 |
| U23.3 | Scan White Cell Technetium 99 |
| | Scanning – see Scan |
| Y90.3 | Scanning NEC |
| Z72.2 | Scaphoid site |
| U18.1 | Scintimammography |
| C57.- | Sclera Operations NEC |
| Z18.3 | Sclera site |
| C52.1 | Sclerectomy Deep with Spacer |
| | |
| C52.2 | Sclerectomy Deep Without Spacer |
| C54.1 | Scleroplasty Overlay |
| G43.4 | Sclerotherapy Gastrointestinal Tract Upper Lesion Endoscopic Fibreoptic |
| G43.4 | Sclerotherapy Gastrointestinal Tract Upper Lesion Endoscopic NEC |
| H52.3 | Sclerotherapy Haemorrhoid |
| N11.6 | Sclerotherapy Hydrocele Sac Injection |
| L86.1 | Sclerotherapy Leg Vein Varicose |
| L86.2 | Sclerotherapy Leg Vein Varicose Foam Ultrasound Guided |
| Y12.1 | Sclerotherapy Lesion NOC |
| G14.4 | Sclerotherapy Oesophagus Varices Injection Endoscopic Fibreoptic |
| | |
| G14.4 | Sclerotherapy Oesophagus Varices Injection Endoscopic NEC |
| G10.5 | Sclerotherapy Oesophagus Varices Injection Open |
| G17.4 | Sclerotherapy Stomach Varices Injection Gastroscope Rigid |
| C55.- | Sclerotomy |
| M17.1 | Screening Kidney Live Donor |
| N03.- | Scrotum Operations NEC |
| Z43.1 | Scrotum site |
| N03.- | Scrotum Skin Operations NEC |
| Z43.1 | Scrotum Skin site |
| Y71.2 | Secondary Operations NOC |

| | |
|---|---|
| C49.1 | Section Cornea |
| Y84.2 | Sedation NEC |
| C80.4 | Segmentation Epiretinal Fibrovascular Membrane |
| D26.- | Semi-circular Canal Operations |
| N22.- | Seminal Vesicle Operations |
| Z43.5 | Seminal Vesicle site |
| C67.1 | Separation Ciliary Body |
| X25.4 | Separation Tarsal Coalition |
| X17.- | Separation Twins Conjoined |
| K14.4 | Septation Atrial Surgical |
| | |
| K14.3 | Septectomy Atrial |
| E07.2 | Septodermoplasty Nose |
| E03.6 | Septoplasty Nose NEC |
| E07.3 | Septorhinoplasty NEC |
| E02.4 | Septorhinoplasty Using Graft |
| E02.3 | Septorhinoplasty Using Implant |
| K15.2 | Septostomy Atrial Closed |
| K14.2 | Septostomy Atrial NEC |
| K16.- | Septostomy Atrial Transluminal Percutaneous |
| W18.3 | Sequestrectomy Bone |
| | |
| U08.4 | Series Gastrointestinal Upper Imaging |
| H55.4 | Seton Anal Fistula High Insertion & Laying Open Track Partial HFQ |
| X15.- | Sexual Transformation Operations |
| B36.- | Sharing Nipple |
| F06.3 | Shave Lip |
| F06.3 | Shave Lip Mucosa |
| F06.3 | Shave Lip Skin |
| E09.4 | Shave Nose Skin |
| W83.3 | Shaving Cartilage Articular Endoscopic |
| C84.4 | Sheathotomy Retinal Vascular |
| | |
| X12.3 | Shortening Amputation Stump |
| W17.4 | Shortening Bone |
| T70.- | Shortening Tendon |
| Q52.3 | Shortening Uterus Ligament Broad |
| | Shunt – see also Anastomosis |
| | Shunt – see also Connection |
| L06.- | Shunt Aortopulmonary NEC |
| L05.- | Shunt Aortopulmonary Prosthesis Interposition Tube Creation |
| L74.- | Shunt Arteriovenous |
| L08.- | Shunt Artery Subclavian Pulmonary NEC |
| | |
| L07.- | Shunt Artery Subclavian Pulmonary Prosthesis Tube Creation |
| A14.- | Shunt Cerebroventricular Attention NEC |
| A13.- | Shunt Cerebroventricular Catheter Maintenance |
| A13.- | Shunt Cerebroventricular Component Attention |
| A12.1 | Shunt Cerebroventricular Creation |
| A14.4 | Shunt Cerebroventricular Irrigation |
| A14.- | Shunt Cerebroventricular NEC |
| A14.3 | Shunt Cerebroventricular Removal |
| R04.- | Shunt Fetal Insertion Percutaneous |
| A53.6 | Shunt Lumbar Subcutaneous |

| | |
|---|---|
| A53.- | Shunt Lumboperitoneal |
| L77.- | Shunt Mesocaval |
| L81.- | Shunt Peritoneovenous |
| L81.- | Shunt Peritovenous |
| L77.- | Shunt Portocaval |
| L77.- | Shunt Portosystemic |
| J11.4 | Shunt Portosystemic Intrahepatic Transjugular |
| A53.8 | Shunt Spinal Attention |
| L77.- | Shunt Splenorenal |
| A53.- | Shunt Syringoperitoneal |
| | |
| A53.- | Shunt Thecoperitoneal |
| A13.- | Shunt Ventricle Brain Catheter Maintenance |
| A12.- | Shunt Ventricle Brain Creation |
| A14.- | Shunt Ventricle Brain Removal |
| A12.2 | Shunt Ventriculoatrial Creation |
| A13.- | Shunt Ventriculoperitoneal Catheter Maintenance |
| A12.4 | Shunt Ventriculoperitoneal Creation |
| A14.- | Shunt Ventriculoperitoneal Removal |
| A13.- | Shunt Ventriculopleural Catheter Maintenance |
| A12.3 | Shunt Ventriculopleural Creation |
| | |
| A14.- | Shunt Ventriculopleural Removal |
| A13.- | Shunt Ventriculovascular Catheter Maintenance |
| A12.2 | Shunt Ventriculovascular Creation |
| A14.- | Shunt Ventriculovascular Removal |
| F48.4 | Sialography |
| H25.- | Sigmoidoscopy Fibreoptic |
| H25.- | Sigmoidoscopy NEC |
| H28.- | Sigmoidoscopy Rigid |
| Y39.1 | Sinogram NOC |
| H60.4 | Sinography Pilonidal Sinus |
| | |
| Z50.7 | Skin Ankle site |
| Z50.1 | Skin Arm site |
| Z49.2 | Skin Axilla site |
| Z49.1 | Skin Breast site |
| Z49.5 | Skin Buttock site |
| | Skin Ear External – see also Ear External Skin |
| D06.- | Skin Ear External Operations NEC |
| Z20.1 | Skin Ear External site |
| | Skin Eyebrow – see also Eyebrow |
| C10.- | Skin Eyebrow Operations |
| | |
| Z16.2 | Skin Eyebrow site |
| | Skin Eyelid – see also Eyelid Skin |
| C22.- | Skin Eyelid Operations NEC |
| Z16.4 | Skin Eyelid site |
| Z47.- | Skin Face site |
| Z50.3 | Skin Finger site |
| | Skin Flap – see Flap site |
| Z50.5 | Skin Foot site |
| Z49.7 | Skin Groin site |
| Z50.2 | Skin Hand site |

| | |
|---|---|
| Z48.- | Skin Head site NEC |
| Z50.4 | Skin Leg site |
| | Skin Lip – see also Lip |
| F06.- | Skin Lip Operations NEC |
| Z25.1 | Skin Lip site |
| Z48.2 | Skin Neck site |
| | Skin Nipple – see also Nipple |
| B35.- | Skin Nipple Operations |
| Z15.6 | Skin Nipple site |
| | Skin Nose External – see also Nose External Skin |
| | |
| E09.- | Skin Nose External Operations |
| Z22.- | Skin Nose External site |
| S60.- | Skin Operations NEC |
| | Skin Penis – see also Penis Skin |
| N32.- | Skin Penis Operations NEC |
| Z42.7 | Skin Penis site |
| | Skin Perineum Female – see also Perineum Skin Female |
| P13.- | Skin Perineum Female Operations NEC |
| Z44.4 | Skin Perineum Female site |
| | Skin Perineum Male – see also Perineum Skin Male |
| | |
| N24.- | Skin Perineum Male Operations |
| Z43.6 | Skin Perineum Male site |
| N30.- | Skin Prepuce Operations |
| Z42.6 | Skin Prepuce site |
| | Skin Scrotum – see also Scrotum Skin |
| N03.- | Skin Scrotum Operations NEC |
| Z43.1 | Skin Scrotum site |
| Z49.6 | Skin Shoulder site |
| Z50.- | Skin site NEC |
| U27.- | Skin Test Application Diagnostic |
| | |
| U28.- | Skin Test Diagnostic NEC |
| Z50.6 | Skin Toe site |
| Z49.- | Skin Trunk site |
| | Skin Umbilicus – see Umbilicus Skin |
| Z53.2 | Skin Umbilicus site |
| | Skin Vulva – see also Vulva Skin |
| P09.- | Skin Vulva Operations NEC |
| Z44.3 | Skin Vulva site |
| H42.3 | Sling Supralevator Insertion |
| M52.1 | Sling Suprapubic |
| | |
| N30.- | Slit Prepuce |
| Q55.- | Smear Cervical |
| F43.1 | Smear Mucosa Buccal |
| Q55.- | Smear Papanicolau |
| | Snare Removal – see Resection site |
| W79.- | Soft Tissue Operations Joint Toe |
| T96.- | Soft Tissue Operations NEC |
| Z62.- | Soft Tissue site NEC |
| N20.- | Spermatic Cord Operations NEC |
| Z43.4 | Spermatic Cord site |

| | |
|---|---|
| E15.- | Sphenoid Sinus Operations NEC |
| Z23.4 | Sphenoid Sinus site |
| J39.- | Sphincter Oddi Operations Endoscopic Therapeutic NEC |
| J36.- | Sphincter Oddi Operations NEC |
| Z30.5 | Sphincter Oddi site |
| J34.- | Sphincteroplasty Bile Duct Approach Duodenal |
| J34.- | Sphincteroplasty Pancreatic Duct Approach Duodenal |
| J34.- | Sphincteroplasty Papilla Vater |
| J39.1 | Sphincterotomy Ampulla Vater Accessory Endoscopic |
| H56.2 | Sphincterotomy Anus Lateral |
| | |
| J35.- | Sphincterotomy Bile Duct Approach Duodenal |
| M66.1 | Sphincterotomy Bladder Sphincter External Male Endoscopic |
| H51.2 | Sphincterotomy Haemorrhoid Internal Partial |
| J35.- | Sphincterotomy Pancreatic Duct Approach Duodenal |
| J35.- | Sphincterotomy Papilla Vater |
| J38.- | Sphincterotomy Papilla Vater Endoscopic |
| J38.- | Sphincterotomy Sphincter Oddi Endoscopic |
| A51.- | Spinal Cord Meninges Operations NEC |
| Z06.4 | Spinal Cord Meninges site |
| A48.- | Spinal Cord Operations NEC |
| | |
| A45.- | Spinal Cord Operations Open NEC |
| Z06.- | Spinal Cord site |
| Z07.- | Spinal Nerve Root site |
| A45.- | Spinal Tract Operations Open NEC |
| Y48.- | Spine Approach Back |
| Y48.- | Spine Approach Laminectomy |
| Y50.1 | Spine Approach Transperitoneal |
| Y49.2 | Spine Approach Transthoracic |
| V55.- | Spine Levels |
| V54.- | Spine Operations NEC |
| | |
| O16.2 | Spine site NEC (Z) |
| E93.2 | Spirometry |
| J72.- | Spleen Operations NEC |
| Z31.3 | Spleen site |
| J69.- | Splenectomy NEC |
| J70.1 | Splenectomy Partial |
| O30.2 | Splenic Flexure site (Z) |
| X49.- | Splint |
| F63.5 | Splinting Teeth |
| O27.- | Stabilisation Joint Glenohumeral (W) |
| | |
| O27.2 | Stabilisation Joint Glenohumeral Repair Capsule Labrum Anterior & Posterior (W) |
| O27.3 | Stabilisation Joint Glenohumeral Repair Capsule Labrum Anterior (W) |
| O27.4 | Stabilisation Joint Glenohumeral Repair Capsule Labrum Posterior (W) |
| W77.- | Stabilisation Joint NEC |
| V40.- | Stabilisation Spine |
| V40.1 | Stabilisation Spine Non-rigid |
| Y70.3 | Staged Operations First NOC |
| Y71.1 | Staged Operations Subsequent NOC |
| G45.4 | Staining Stomach Mucosa NEC |
| D17.- | Stapedectomy |

| | |
|---|---|
| W27.- | Stapling Epiphysis |
| Y26.3 | Stapling NOC |
| G30.4 | Stapling Stomach |
| Y99.- | Status Donor |
| A81.1 | Stellate Ganglion Blockade |
| | Stent – see Operation site Stent |
| | Stent Graft Insertion – see Insertion site Stent Graft |
| | Stent Implantation – see Implantation site Stent |
| S54.6 | Sterilisation & Cleansing Skin Burnt Head |
| S55.6 | Sterilisation & Cleansing Skin Burnt NEC |
| | |
| S54.6 | Sterilisation & Cleansing Skin Burnt Neck |
| S56.6 | Sterilisation & Cleansing Skin Head |
| S57.6 | Sterilisation & Cleansing Skin NEC |
| S56.6 | Sterilisation & Cleansing Skin Neck |
| | Sterilisation Female – see also Operation |
| Q37.- | Sterilisation Female Reversal Endoscopic |
| Q29.- | Sterilisation Female Reversal Open |
| | Sterilisation Male – see Operation |
| Y49.1 | Sternotomy Median Approach |
| T03.1 | Sternotomy Median Exploratory |
| | |
| Z74.- | Sternum site |
| | Stimulation Nerve – see Neurostimulator |
| W33.- | Stimulator Bone Electromagnetic |
| Y90.1 | Stimulator Nerve Electrical Transcutaneous Application |
| G44.- | Stomach Operations Endoscopic Fibreoptic NEC |
| G44.- | Stomach Operations Endoscopic Therapeutic NEC |
| G18.- | Stomach Operations Gastroscope Rigid NEC |
| G48.- | Stomach Operations NEC |
| G38.- | Stomach Operations Open NEC |
| G30.- | Stomach Operations Plastic |
| | |
| Z27.2 | Stomach site |
| G35.- | Stomach Ulcer Operations |
| Q56.8 | Storage Oocyte |
| U11.5 | Stress Test Thallium |
| H54.1 | Stretching Anorectal |
| P15.5 | Stretching Hymen |
| C64.6 | Stretching Iris |
| T83.3 | Stretching Muscle |
| Y40.2 | Stretching NOC |
| N30.5 | Stretching Prepuce |
| | |
| G78.2 | Strictureplasty Ileum |
| G78.2 | Strictureplasty Intestine Small NEC |
| C09.2 | Strip Periosteal Lateral |
| C09.3 | Strip Periosteal Medial |
| C09.1 | Strip Tarsal Lateral |
| L92.1 | Stripping Catheter |
| T57.4 | Stripping Fascia |
| L87.- | Stripping Leg Vein Varicose |
| W04.4 | Stripping Muscle Os Calcis |
| E93.3 | Study Airways Resistance Body Plethysmographic |

| | |
|---|---|
| E93.4 | Study Airways Resistance Forced Oscillation Technique |
| E92.3 | Study Alveolar Carbon Monoxide |
| E94.- | Study Bronchial Reaction |
| E93.7 | Study Expiratory & Inspiratory Flow Volume Loop |
| E93.1 | Study Expiratory Peak Flow Rate |
| U23.4 | Study Ferrokinetic |
| K58.- | Study Heart Conducting System |
| E93.7 | Study Inspiratory & Expiratory Flow Volume Loop |
| E93.5 | Study Lung Static Volume |
| A84.3 | Study Nerve Conduction |
| | |
| R42.- | Study Obstetric Doppler |
| E91.3 | Study Oxygen Desaturation Index |
| E93.6 | Study Respiratory Muscle Strength |
| E93.- | Study Respiratory NEC |
| U17.2 | Study Selenium 75 Homocholic Acid Taurine |
| A84.7 | Study Sleep NEC |
| M12.- | Study Urinary Tract Upper Percutaneous |
| A22.- | Subarachnoid Space Operations |
| Z49.2 | Subcutaneous Tissue Axilla site |
| Z49.1 | Subcutaneous Tissue Breast site |
| | |
| Z49.5 | Subcutaneous Tissue Buttock site |
| Z47.- | Subcutaneous Tissue Face site |
| Z48.- | Subcutaneous Tissue Head site NEC |
| Z48.2 | Subcutaneous Tissue Neck site |
| S62.- | Subcutaneous Tissue Operations NEC |
| Z50.- | Subcutaneous Tissue site NEC |
| Z49.- | Subcutaneous Tissue Trunk site |
| Z26.3 | Sublingual Gland site |
| F58.2 | Submandibular Duct Operations NEC |
| F53.2 | Submandibular Duct Operations Open NEC |
| | |
| Z26.6 | Submandibular Duct site |
| Z26.2 | Submandibular Gland site |
| | Suction Clearance – see Clearance |
| X58.- | Support Body System Artificial |
| X49.- | Support Bone Fracture External NEC |
| X49.- | Support Limb External NEC |
| E87.1 | Support Oxygen Home |
| Y92.- | Support Radiotherapy |
| E89.- | Support Respiratory Other |
| E95.- | Support Tuberculosis |
| | |
| E85.- | Support Ventilation |
| Y73.3 | Support Ventilatory |
| M52.1 | Suprapubic Operation Sling |
| M49.8 | Suprapubic Tube Operation Through |
| M51.2 | Suspension Bladder Neck Endoscopic |
| M52.2 | Suspension Bladder Neck Retropubic |
| M51.1 | Suspension Urethra Abdominoperineal |
| M51.1 | Suspension Urethra Abdominovaginal |
| Q54.4 | Suspension Uterus Mesh NEC |
| Q54.1 | Suspension Uterus NEC |

| | |
|---|---|
| P24.- | Suspension Vagina |
| | Suture – see also Resuture |
| T28.- | Suture Abdomen |
| T28.- | Suture Abdominal Wall |
| Q01.2 | Suture Cervix Uteri & Excision |
| T05.- | Suture Chest Wall |
| C40.5 | Suture Conjunctiva |
| C47.- | Suture Cornea |
| Q45.4 | Suture Corpus Luteum Rupture |
| T16.5 | Suture Diaphragm NEC |
| | |
| G52.- | Suture Duodenum Ulcer |
| | Suture Encirclement – see Cerclage |
| C35.3 | Suture Eye Muscle Adjustable Insertion |
| C86.3 | Suture Eye NEC |
| C10.4 | Suture Eyebrow |
| C17.1 | Suture Eyelid |
| C20.- | Suture Eyelid Protective |
| C17.1 | Suture Eyelid Skin |
| Q30.5 | Suture Fallopian Tube |
| F20.5 | Suture Gingiva |
| | |
| C65.4 | Suture Glaucoma Surgery Removal |
| F05.3 | Suture Lip |
| F05.4 | Suture Lip Removal |
| C65.5 | Suture Lysis Eye Glaucoma Surgery Laser |
| F40.4 | Suture Mouth NEC |
| C35.3 | Suture Muscle Eye Adjustable Insertion |
| Y25.- | Suture NOC |
| E09.3 | Suture Nose External |
| E09.3 | Suture Nose External Skin |
| Q45.3 | Suture Ovary |
| | |
| F30.7 | Suture Palate |
| H42.- | Suture Perianal Sphincter Insertion |
| H42.- | Suture Perianal Sphincter Removal |
| W33.3 | Suture Periosteum |
| C57.4 | Suture Sclera |
| N03.3 | Suture Scrotum |
| N03.3 | Suture Scrotum Skin |
| S41.- | Suture Skin Head |
| S42.- | Suture Skin NEC |
| S41.- | Suture Skin Neck |
| | |
| S43.- | Suture Skin Removal |
| G35.- | Suture Stomach Ulcer |
| S41.- | Suture Subcutaneous Tissue Head |
| S42.- | Suture Subcutaneous Tissue NEC |
| S41.- | Suture Subcutaneous Tissue Neck |
| S43.- | Suture Subcutaneous Tissue Removal |
| F26.5 | Suture Tongue |
| M22.1 | Suture Ureter |
| P25.5 | Suture Vagina |
| N18.2 | Suture Vas Deferens NEC |

|  | Suture Wound – see Suture Skin |
|---|---|
| Q55.6 | Swab Genital Female |
| K06.1 | Switch Arterial |
| K06.4 | Switch Arterial Double |
| G71.7 | Switch Duodenal Reversal |
| G71.6 | Switch Duodenum |
| G28.4 | Switch Duodenum & Sleeve Gastrectomy |
| A76.- | Sympathectomy Chemical |
| A75.- | Sympathectomy NEC |
| W79.3 | Syndactylisation Toe Lesser |
|  |  |
| W69.- | Synovectomy |
|  | Syringing – see Irrigation |
| A53.1 | Syringostomy Cerebrospinal |
| K60.- | System Cardiac Pacemaker Intravenous |
| K61.- | System Cardiac Pacemaker NEC |
| K56.- | System Heart Assist Transluminal |

# T

| | |
|---|---|
| L06.7 | Takedown Anastomosis Aortopulmonary |
| K17.6 | Takedown Cavopulmonary Connection Total |
| Z79.- | Talus site |
| C79.- | Tamponade Retina Operations |
| N11.5 | Tapping Hydrocele Sac |
| T46.2 | Tapping Peritoneum Ascites NEC |
| T46.9 | Tapping Peritoneum NEC |
| X25.2 | Tarsectomy Wedge Correction Foot Deformity Congenital |
| C18.5 | Tarsomullerectomy |
| C16.- | Tarsorrhaphy |
| | |
| Z79.- | Tarsus site |
| C51.4 | Tattooing Cornea |
| B36.4 | Tattooing Nipple |
| Y39.5 | Tattooing NOC |
| S60.3 | Tattooing Skin |
| U22.1 | Telemetry Electroencephalograph |
| X51.- | Temperature Change |
| Y70.5 | Temporary Operations |
| T74.- | Tendon Operations NEC |
| T72.- | Tendon Sheath Operations NEC |
| | |
| | Tendon site – see Muscle site |
| T64.5 | Tenodesis |
| T69.1 | Tenolysis Primary |
| T69.2 | Tenolysis Revision |
| T71.1 | Tenosynovectomy |
| C34.- | Tenotomy Eye Muscle |
| C34.- | Tenotomy Muscle Eye |
| T70.- | Tenotomy NEC |
| | Terminalisation – see Amputation |
| | Termination Pregnancy – see Operation |
| | |
| U29.5 | Test Adrenal Suppression |
| U29.6 | Test Arginine Vasopressin Response Hypertonic Saline |
| U32.- | Test Blood Diagnostic |
| U32.1 | Test Blood Human Immunodeficiency Virus |
| U25.- | Test Breath |
| E92.1 | Test Carbon Monoxide Transfer |
| U34.1 | Test Cardiac Provocation |
| U30.2 | Test Carotid Sinus Massage |
| E92.5 | Test Cycle Progressive with Measure of Gas Exchange |
| U29.4 | Test Deprivation Water |

| | |
|---|---|
| U33.- | Test Diagnostic Other |
| U22.7 | Test Executive Function Neuropsychology |
| U26.1 | Test Glomerular Filtration Rate |
| U29.3 | Test Glucose Tolerance |
| E95.1 | Test Heaf |
| U29.2 | Test Insulin Secretion Glucagon |
| U22.3 | Test Intelligence Neuropsychology |
| E92.5 | Test Jones Stage 2–4 |
| U22.4 | Test Language Neuropsychology |
| E92.- | Test Lung Function Exercise |
| | |
| E92.5 | Test Lung Function Exercise Complex |
| E92.6 | Test Lung Function Exercise Simple |
| E95.5 | Test Mantoux |
| U22.5 | Test Memory Neuropsychology |
| U22.- | Test Neuropsychology |
| U31.1 | Test Pacemaker Distant |
| U22.6 | Test Perception Neuropsychology |
| U29.1 | Test Pituitary Anterior Function Insulin Stress |
| E92.- | Test Respiratory |
| U26.5 | Test Schilling |
| | |
| U29.7 | Test Short Synacthen |
| U27.- | Test Skin Application Diagnostic |
| U40.- | Test Skin Diagnostic |
| U28.- | Test Skin Diagnostic Other |
| U28.- | Test Skin for Urticaria NEC |
| U28.- | Test Skin Passive Transfer for Urticaria |
| U28.- | Test Skin Reverse Passive Transfer for Urticaria |
| U28.6 | Test Skin Serum Autologous for Urticaria |
| U40.2 | Test Skin Ultraviolet Diagnostic |
| E92.5 | Test Treadmill Progressive with Measure of Gas Exchange |
| | |
| E92.2 | Test Ventilation Distribution |
| U30.- | Testing Cardiovascular Autonomic |
| E91.- | Testing Oximetry |
| U31.- | Testing Pacemaker |
| U30.1 | Testing Table Tilt |
| N13.- | Testis Operations NEC |
| Z43.2 | Testis site |
| N13.2 | Tether Testis |
| X37.1 | Therapy Calcitonin Intramuscular |
| X66.- | Therapy Cognitive Behavioural |
| | |
| X61.- | Therapy Complementary |
| A83.- | Therapy Electroconvulsive |
| X61.1 | Therapy Functional Session |
| X37.2 | Therapy Gold Intramuscular |
| X52.1 | Therapy Hyperbaric |
| X51.1 | Therapy Hypothermia |
| E97.1 | Therapy Inhalation |
| E05.4 | Therapy Internal Nose Laser |
| S58.- | Therapy Larvae |
| Y08.- | Therapy Laser NOC |

| | |
|---|---|
| X61.4 | Therapy Movement NEC |
| E89.3 | Therapy Nebuliser |
| E98.- | Therapy Nicotine Replacement |
| E87.2 | Therapy Oxygen Long-term |
| | Therapy Photodynamic – see Photodynamic Therapy |
| X65.5 | Therapy Radioactive Iodine Oral |
| X61.2 | Therapy Relaxation Session |
| S12.- | Therapy Skin Light Ultraviolet |
| E98.- | Therapy Smoking Cessation |
| E95.3 | Therapy Tuberculosis Directly Observed |
| | |
| V62.- | Thermocoagulation Disc Intervertebral Radiofrequency Percutaneous NEC |
| V62.- | Thermocoagulation Disc Intervertebral Radiofrequency Percutaneous Primary |
| V63.- | Thermocoagulation Disc Intervertebral Radiofrequency Percutaneous Revisional |
| U35.1 | Thermography Blood Flow |
| U01.3 | Thermography Body Whole |
| U18.2 | Thermography Breast |
| U36.1 | Thermography NEC |
| C88.1 | Thermotherapy Retina Lesion Transpupillary |
| C88.1 | Thermotherapy Subretina Lesion Transpupillary |
| S03.2 | Thigh Lift |
| | |
| Y49.- | Thoracic Cavity Approach |
| T12.3 | Thoracocentesis |
| T01.1 | Thoracoplasty |
| | Thoracoscopic – refer to Index Introduction |
| Y74.- | Thoracoscopic Operations NEC |
| T11.- | Thoracoscopy |
| Y49.3 | Thoracotomy Approach NEC |
| T03.- | Thoracotomy Exploratory |
| L25.3 | Thrombectomy Aorta Bifurcation NEC |
| L26.3 | Thrombectomy Aorta Bifurcation Transluminal Percutaneous |
| | |
| L74.5 | Thrombectomy Arteriovenous Fistula |
| L38.3 | Thrombectomy Artery Axillary NEC |
| L39.2 | Thrombectomy Artery Axillary Transluminal Percutaneous |
| L38.3 | Thrombectomy Artery Brachial NEC |
| L39.2 | Thrombectomy Artcry Brachial Transluminal Percutaneous |
| L30.3 | Thrombectomy Artery Carotid NEC |
| L34.3 | Thrombectomy Artery Cerebral NEC |
| L34.3 | Thrombectomy Artery Circle Willis NEC |
| L46.1 | Thrombectomy Artery Coeliac NEC |
| L62.2 | Thrombectomy Artery Femoral NEC |
| | |
| L63.2 | Thrombectomy Artery Femoral Transluminal Percutaneous |
| L53.2 | Thrombectomy Artery Iliac NEC |
| L54.2 | Thrombectomy Artery Iliac Transluminal Percutaneous |
| L46.1 | Thrombectomy Artery Mesenteric NEC |
| L70.1 | Thrombectomy Artery NEC |
| L62.2 | Thrombectomy Artery Popliteal NEC |
| L63.2 | Thrombectomy Artery Popliteal Transluminal Percutaneous |
| L12.4 | Thrombectomy Artery Pulmonary NEC |
| L13.1 | Thrombectomy Artery Pulmonary Transluminal Percutaneous |
| L42.1 | Thrombectomy Artery Renal NEC |

| | |
|---|---|
| L43.2 | Thrombectomy Artery Renal Transluminal Percutaneous |
| L38.3 | Thrombectomy Artery Subclavian NEC |
| L39.2 | Thrombectomy Artery Subclavian Transluminal Percutaneous |
| L46.1 | Thrombectomy Artery Suprarenal NEC |
| L71.2 | Thrombectomy Artery Transluminal Percutaneous |
| L38.3 | Thrombectomy Artery Vertebral NEC |
| L39.2 | Thrombectomy Artery Vertebral Transluminal Percutaneous |
| J10.5 | Thrombectomy Blood Vessel Liver Transluminal Percutaneous NEC |
| J10.5 | Thrombectomy Vein Hepatic Transluminal Percutaneous |
| L90.- | Thrombectomy Vein Open |
| | |
| J11.2 | Thrombectomy Vein Portal Intrahepatic Transjugular |
| J10.5 | Thrombectomy Vein Portal Transluminal Percutaneous |
| L96.2 | Thromboembolectomy Aspiration Percutaneous |
| L96.1 | Thromboembolectomy Mechanical Percutaneous |
| L04.1 | Thromboendarterectomy Artery Pulmonary |
| L66.1 | Thrombolysis Arterial Reconstruction Transluminal Percutaneous |
| L66.1 | Thrombolysis Artery & Placement Stent Transluminal Percutaneous |
| K50.2 | Thrombolysis Artery Coronary Transluminal Percutaneous Streptokinase |
| L71.6 | Thrombolysis Artery Transluminal Percutaneous |
| L71.6 | Thrombolysis Artery Transluminal Percutaneous Streptokinase |
| | |
| J10.6 | Thrombolysis Blood Vessel Liver Transluminal Percutaneous NEC |
| L99.3 | Thrombolysis Vein & Placement Stent Transluminal Percutaneous |
| L99.3 | Thrombolysis Vein Angioplasty Transluminal Percutaneous |
| J10.6 | Thrombolysis Vein Hepatic Transluminal Percutaneous |
| J11.3 | Thrombolysis Vein Portal Intrahepatic Transjugular |
| J10.6 | Thrombolysis Vein Portal Transluminal Percutaneous |
| L99.3 | Thrombolysis Venous Reconstruction Transluminal Percutaneous |
| L99.4 | Thrombolysis Venous Transluminal Percutaneous NEC |
| B18.- | Thymectomy |
| B20.- | Thymus Operations NEC |
| | |
| Z14.3 | Thymus site |
| Z13.3 | Thyroglossal Cyst site |
| B10.- | Thyroglossal Tissue Operations |
| Z13.4 | Thyroglossal Tract site |
| B12.- | Thyroid Operations NEC |
| Z13.1 | Thyroid site |
| B09.- | Thyroid Tissue Aberrant Operations |
| Z13.2 | Thyroid Tissue Aberrant site |
| B08.- | Thyroidectomy |
| | Thyroplasty – see Medialisation Vocal Cord |
| | |
| Z78.1 | Tibia & Fibula Shaft Combination site |
| Z77.- | Tibia site NEC |
| | Tissue Expander – see Expander Skin |
| | Toilet – see also Debridement |
| S54.- | Toilet Skin Burnt Head NEC |
| S55.- | Toilet Skin Burnt NEC |
| S54.- | Toilet Skin Burnt Neck NEC |
| S56.- | Toilet Skin Head NEC |
| S57.- | Toilet Skin NEC |
| S56.- | Toilet Skin Neck NEC |

| | |
|---|---|
| S54.- | Toilet Subcutaneous Tissue Burnt Head NEC |
| S55.- | Toilet Subcutaneous Tissue Burnt NEC |
| S54.- | Toilet Subcutaneous Tissue Burnt Neck NEC |
| S56.- | Toilet Subcutaneous Tissue Head NEC |
| S57.- | Toilet Subcutaneous Tissue NEC |
| S56.- | Toilet Subcutaneous Tissue Neck NEC |
| P27.2 | Toilet Vagina |
| U08.1 | Tomography Abdomen Computed NEC |
| U35.4 | Tomography Arteries Pulmonary Computed |
| U01.1 | Tomography Body Whole Computed |
| | |
| U13.6 | Tomography Bone Computed |
| U05.1 | Tomography Brain Computed |
| U10.1 | Tomography Cardiac Calcium Scoring |
| U10.2 | Tomography Cardiac Computed Angiography |
| U11.4 | Tomography Cerebral Vessels Computed |
| U07.1 | Tomography Chest Computed |
| U17.5 | Tomography Colon Computed |
| U05.1 | Tomography Head Computed |
| U13.6 | Tomography Joint Computed |
| U37.2 | Tomography Kidneys Computed |
| | |
| U10.4 | Tomography Myocardial Positron Emission |
| U09.1 | Tomography Pelvis Computed |
| U21.3 | Tomography Positron Emission |
| U36.2 | Tomography Positron Emission Computed Tomography |
| C87.3 | Tomography Retina Computed |
| U21.4 | Tomography Single Photon Emission Computed |
| U36.3 | Tomography Single Photon Emission Computed Tomography |
| U06.1 | Tomography Sinuses Computed |
| U05.4 | Tomography Spinal Cord Computed |
| U05.4 | Tomography Spine Computed |
| | |
| F26.- | Tongue Operations NEC |
| Z25.5 | Tongue site |
| F36.- | Tonsil Operations NEC |
| Z25.7 | Tonsil site |
| F34.- | Tonsillectomy |
| F34.7 | Tonsillectomy Coblation Bilateral |
| F12.- | Tooth Apex Surgery |
| F17.- | Tooth Bridge Operations |
| F17.- | Tooth Crown Operations |
| F16.- | Tooth Operations NEC |
| | |
| F12.2 | Tooth Root Canal Therapy |
| Z25.3 | Tooth site NEC |
| Z25.2 | Tooth Wisdom site |
| C60.1 | Trabeculectomy |
| C61.1 | Trabeculoplasty Laser |
| C61.2 | Trabeculotomy |
| E48.- | Trachea Operations Endoscopic NEC |
| E50.- | Trachea Operations Endoscopic Rigid |
| E52.- | Trachea Operations NEC |
| E43.- | Trachea Operations Open NEC |

| | |
|---|---|
| E40.- | Trachea Operations Plastic |
| Z24.3 | Trachea site |
| E49.- | Tracheobronchoscopy NEC |
| E43.3 | Tracheopexy |
| E43.2 | Tracheorrhaphy |
| E49.9 | Tracheoscopy NEC |
| E42.- | Tracheostomy |
| Y52.1 | Tracheostomy Approach |
| E42.3 | Tracheotomy |
| W29.- | Traction Bone Skeletal |
| | |
| X49.4 | Traction Skin |
| V50.1 | Traction Skull Halo Ring & Jacket |
| V46.4 | Traction Skull Skeletal Fracture Spine |
| K48.1 | Transection Artery Coronary Muscle Bridge |
| M43.1 | Transection Bladder Endoscopic |
| M41.3 | Transection Bladder Open |
| A28.8 | Transection Nerve Abducens (vi) Extracranial |
| A25.2 | Transection Nerve Abducens (vi) NEC |
| A25.8 | Transection Nerve Accessory (xi) Intracranial |
| A28.2 | Transection Nerve Accessory (xi) NEC |
| | |
| A28.8 | Transection Nerve Acoustic (viii) Extracranial |
| A25.5 | Transection Nerve Acoustic (viii) NEC |
| A28.- | Transection Nerve Cranial Extracranial |
| A25.- | Transection Nerve Cranial Intracranial |
| A25.4 | Transection Nerve Facial (vii) Intracranial |
| A28.8 | Transection Nerve Facial (vii) NEC |
| A28.8 | Transection Nerve Glossopharyngeal (ix) Extracranial |
| A25.6 | Transection Nerve Glossopharyngeal (ix) NEC |
| A28.8 | Transection Nerve Hypoglossal (xii) Extracranial |
| A25.8 | Transection Nerve Hypoglossal (xii) NEC |
| | |
| A28.8 | Transection Nerve Oculomotor (iii) Extracranial |
| A25.2 | Transection Nerve Oculomotor (iii) NEC |
| A28.8 | Transection Nerve Optic (ii) Extracranial |
| A25.1 | Transection Nerve Optic (ii) NEC |
| A60.3 | Transection Nerve Peripheral |
| A25.3 | Transection Nerve Trigeminal (v) Intracranial |
| A28.1 | Transection Nerve Trigeminal (v) NEC |
| A28.8 | Transection Nerve Trochlear (iv) Extracranial |
| A25.2 | Transection Nerve Trochlear (iv) NEC |
| A25.7 | Transection Nerve Vagus (x) Intracranial |
| | |
| A27.- | Transection Nerve Vagus (x) NEC |
| G10.- | Transection Oesophagus |
| A07.5 | Transections Subpial Multiple |
| A73.6 | Transfer & Reimplantation Nerve Peripheral |
| Q13.- | Transfer Embryo |
| T50.1 | Transfer Fascial Tissue |
| Q38.3 | Transfer Gamete Intrafallopian Access Minimal |
| Q38.3 | Transfer Gamete Intrafallopian Endoscopic |
| T76.1 | Transfer Muscle Flap Free Tissue Microvascular |
| W83.7 | Transfer Osteochondral Endoscopic |

| | |
|---|---|
| T64.- | Transfer Tendon |
| W03.- | Transfer Tendon Extensor Hallucis Longus |
| N08.1 | Transfer Testis Scrotum Microvascular Bilateral |
| N09.1 | Transfer Testis Scrotum Microvascular Unilateral |
| W01.5 | Transfer Thumb Opposition |
| W01.1 | Transfer Toe Thumb Microvascular |
| Q21.1 | Transfer Uterus Transmyometrial Embryo |
| X15.- | Transformation Sexual Operations |
| X32.- | Transfusion Blood Exchange |
| X32.1 | Transfusion Blood Exchange Neonatal |
| | |
| X34.4 | Transfusion Blood Expander |
| R01.1 | Transfusion Blood Fetus Fetoscopic |
| R04.3 | Transfusion Blood Fetus Percutaneous |
| X33.1 | Transfusion Blood Intra-arterial |
| X33.- | Transfusion Blood Intravenous |
| X33.- | Transfusion Blood NEC |
| X34.1 | Transfusion Coagulation Factor |
| X34.- | Transfusion Intravenous NEC |
| X32.- | Transfusion Plasma Exchange |
| X34.2 | Transfusion Plasma NEC |
| | |
| X32.6 | Transfusion Red Cell Exchange |
| X34.3 | Transfusion Serum NEC |
| | Translocation – see also Transfer |
| L41.5 | Translocation Artery Renal Branch |
| C83.3 | Translocation Macula Limited |
| C83.3 | Translocation Macula NEC |
| C83.2 | Translocation Macula Three Hundred & Sixty Degrees |
| C83.- | Translocation Retina |
| C83.1 | Translocation Retina Pigment Epithelium |
| | Transplantation – see also Allotransplantation |
| | |
| X04.1 | Transplantation Adrenal Medulla to Brain Caudate Nucleus |
| X04.- | Transplantation Between Systems |
| W34.- | Transplantation Bone Marrow |
| C43.7 | Transplantation Conjunctiva |
| C46.7 | Transplantation Cornea Limbal Cells |
| J54.1 | Transplantation Duodenum & Pancreas |
| T50.- | Transplantation Fascia |
| K01.- | Transplantation Heart & Lung |
| K01.2 | Transplantation Heart & Lung Revision |
| K02.- | Transplantation Heart NEC |
| | |
| K02.4 | Transplantation Heart Piggyback |
| K02.6 | Transplantation Heart Revision NEC |
| G68.- | Transplantation Ileum |
| M01.- | Transplantation Kidney |
| M17.- | Transplantation Kidney Associated Interventions |
| J01.- | Transplantation Liver |
| J01.4 | Transplantation Liver Cells |
| K01.- | Transplantation Lung & Heart |
| E53.1 | Transplantation Lung Double |
| E53.- | Transplantation Lung NEC |

| | |
|---|---|
| E53.2 | Transplantation Lung Single |
| E53.3 | Transplantation Lung Single Lobe |
| T76.- | Transplantation Muscle |
| J54.- | Transplantation Pancreas |
| G68.- | Transplantation Small Intestine NEC |
| J72.1 | Transplantation Spleen |
| X33.- | Transplantation Stem Cells Peripheral |
| B17.- | Transplantation Thymus Gland |
| F08.- | Transplantation Tooth |
| | Transposition – see also Resiting |
| | |
| | Transposition – see also Translocation |
| K05.- | Transposition Arteries Great Operations Inversion Atrial |
| K48.2 | Transposition Artery Coronary NEC |
| C35.1 | Transposition Eye Muscle NEC |
| W77.7 | Transposition Ligament NEC |
| C35.1 | Transposition Muscle Eye NEC |
| W77.2 | Transposition Muscle NEC |
| B35.1 | Transposition Nipple |
| C08.1 | Transposition Orbit Ligament |
| Q47.1 | Transposition Ovary |
| | |
| B16.1 | Transposition Parathyroid Tissue Modification |
| B14.8 | Transposition Parathyroid Tissue NEC |
| F50.1 | Transposition Parotid Duct |
| F50.- | Transposition Salivary Duct |
| F50.2 | Transposition Submandibular Duct |
| T64.- | Transposition Tendon |
| L82.1 | Transposition Vein Valve |
| C49.2 | Trephine Cornea |
| C55.2 | Trephine Corneoscleral |
| V03.5 | Trephine Cranium |
| | |
| E14.6 | Trephine Ethmoid Sinus |
| E14.6 | Trephine Frontal Sinus |
| | Tube – see also Drainage |
| | Tube – see also Intubation |
| | Tube – see also Prosthesis |
| G08.- | Tube Oesophagus Feeding Open |
| G38.- | Tube Stomach Feeding Open |
| G44.7 | Tube Stomach Removal Endoscopic Fibreoptic |
| M49.- | Tube Suprapubic Attention |
| M38.2 | Tube Suprapubic Insertion |

# U

| | |
|---|---|
| Z71.- | Ulna site NEC |
| Y53.2 | Ultrasonic Control Approach |
| U08.2 | Ultrasound Abdomen NEC |
| U11.1 | Ultrasound Artery Carotid |
| K51.2 | Ultrasound Artery Coronary Intravascular |
| R42.3 | Ultrasound Artery Fetus Cerebral Middle Doppler |
| L72.6 | Ultrasound Artery Intravascular NEC |
| R42.1 | Ultrasound Artery Umbilical Doppler |
| R42.2 | Ultrasound Artery Uterine Doppler |
| M49.7 | Ultrasound Bladder High Intensity Focused |
| | |
| U12.4 | Ultrasound Bladder NEC |
| U13.2 | Ultrasound Bone |
| | Ultrasound Examination – see also Examination |
| U13.2 | Ultrasound Joint |
| U12.3 | Ultrasound Kidneys |
| R43.- | Ultrasound Monitoring Pregnancy |
| U21.6 | Ultrasound NEC |
| R42.- | Ultrasound Obstetric Doppler |
| U09.2 | Ultrasound Pelvis NEC |
| M71.1 | Ultrasound Prostate High Intensity Focused |
| | |
| C87.4 | Ultrasound Retina |
| U12.2 | Ultrasound Scrotum |
| U12.2 | Ultrasound Testes |
| U06.3 | Ultrasound Thyroid Gland |
| U35.3 | Ultrasound Transcranial Doppler Velocimetry |
| Q55.5 | Ultrasound Transvaginal |
| Q20.6 | Ultrasound Uterus Lesion Focused |
| L98.6 | Ultrasound Vessel Microvascular Anastomosis Doppler |
| U11.2 | Ultrasound Vessels Extremities Doppler |
| T29.- | Umbilicus Operations |
| | |
| T29.6 | Umbilicus Operations Plastic |
| Z53.2 | Umbilicus site |
| T29.- | Umbilicus Skin Operations |
| Z53.2 | Umbilicus Skin site |
| | Unblocking – see also Operation |
| L92.- | Unblocking Catheter Access |
| | Unfinished Operations – refer to Tabular List Introduction |
| L69.2 | Unifocalisation Pulmonary |
| Z94.4 | Unilateral Operations |
| | Unspecified Organ – see Organ Unspecified |

| | |
|---|---|
| E85.1 | Ventilation Invasive |
| E85.5 | Ventilation Nebuliser |
| E85.2 | Ventilation Non-invasive NEC |
| E85.- | Ventilation Support |
| Z33.7 | Ventricle Heart site |
| K24.- | Ventricles Heart Operations NEC |
| K24.- | Ventricular Outflow Tract Obstruction Operations |
| K23.5 | Ventriculectomy Left Partial |
| A12.1 | Ventriculocisternostomy |
| A20.2 | Ventriculography Brain |
| | |
| A18.- | Ventriculoscopy Brain |
| A17.2 | Ventriculostomy Third Endoscopic |
| R12.4 | Version Cephalic External |
| Z66.- | Vertebra site |
| V44.4 | Vertebroplasty Spine Fracture |
| N22.3 | Vesiculography Seminal |
| L01.- | Vessel Great Abnormality Combined Operations Open |
| L03.- | Vessel Great Abnormality Operations Transluminal |
| D26.- | Vestibular Apparatus Operations |
| Z21.5 | Vestibular Apparatus site |
| | |
| F11.4 | Vestibuloplasty Mouth |
| Y53.6 | Video Assisted Approach |
| Y74.4 | Video Assisted Thoracoscopic Approach |
| C60.6 | Viscocanulostomy |
| C61.5 | Viscogonioplasty |
| C79.1 | Vitrectomy Anterior Approach |
| C79.2 | Vitrectomy NEC |
| C79.2 | Vitrectomy Pars Plana Approach |
| C79.- | Vitreous Body Operations |
| Z19.2 | Vitreous Body site |
| | |
| P09.- | Vulva Operations NEC |
| Z44.3 | Vulva site |
| P09.- | Vulva Skin Operations NEC |
| Z44.3 | Vulva Skin site |
| P05.- | Vulvectomy |

# W

| | |
|---|---|
| S23.- | W Plasty |
| | Washout – see also Irrigation |
| B16.4 | Washout Parathyroid |
| H42.- | Wiring Perianal Sphincter |
| W20.6 | Wiring Sternum |
| X36.- | Withdrawal Blood |
| M17.3 | Work-up Pre-transplantation Kidney Live Donor |
| M17.2 | Work-up Pre-transplantation Kidney Recipient |
| | Wound – see Operation Skin |
| | Wound – see Operation Subcutaneous Tissue |

# X

| | |
|---|---|
| U08.3 | X-ray Abdomen Plain |
| U13.5 | X-ray Bone Plain |
| U07.3 | X-ray Chest Plain |
| U13.4 | X-ray Joint Plain |
| U21.7 | X-ray Plain NEC |
| U06.4 | X-ray Skull Plain |
| Y27.3 | Xenograft NOC |
| S37.- | Xenograft Skin |
| Y01.3 | Xenoreplacement NOC |
| | Xenotransplantation – see Transplantation |

# Y

| X61.4 | Yoga |
|---|---|

# Z

# Section II

## Alphabetical Index
## of
## Surgical Eponyms

(D) = Device code assigned is the normal code for insertion or replacement.
Tabular List must be consulted for maintenance, removal etc.

Note: If the same operation can be done on different subsites e.g. parts of the spine,
then the surgical eponym is assigned to the unspecified site and reference should
be made to the Tabular List to identify the particular site.

# A

| F04.2 | Abbe | Distant Flap Lip (Two Stage) |
|-------|------|------------------------------|
| G61.1 | Abbe | Jejunal Anastomosis Technique |
| F04.2 | Abbe-Estlander | Local Pedicle Flap Cross Lip (One Stage) |
| X22.9 | Adams | (D) Hip Pin Correction of Cong. Dislocation |
| W27.9 | Adams | (D) Hip Pin for Fixation Epiphysis (Z76.1) |
| E03.8 | Adams | Crushing Nasal Septum |
| W15.6 | Akins | Cuneiform Osteotomy Proximal Phalanx |
| W31.2 | Albee | Graft Tibia (Z77.2) |
| V38.3 | Albee | Interspinous Fusion Lumbar Spine |
| X22.2 | Albee | Osteotomy Pelvis |
| M52.1 | Aldridge-Studdiford | Sling Urethral |
| H14.1 | Allen-Welch | Caecostomy |
| G23.1 | Allison | Repair Oesophageal Hiatus Hernia |
| D12.8 | Almoor | Drainage Petrous Apex Mastoid |
| W40.- | Anametric | (D) Total Replacement Knee (Cemented) |
| W30.1 | Anderson | (D) External Fixator |
| W17.2 | Anderson | Leg Lengthening Procedure (Z90.9) |
| M05.1 | Anderson-Hynes | Pyeloplasty |
| G24.6 | Angelchick | (D) Prosthesis Antireflux Operation |
| D15.1 | Armstrong | (D) Tube Ear |
| C54.4 | Arruga | String Operation for Detached Retina |
| D26.8 | Arslan | Fenestration Inner Ear |
| E43.1 | Asai | Tracheo-oesophagoplasty |
| G11.- | Atkinson | (D) Prosthesis Oesophagus (Code to Procedure) |
| W40.- | Attenborough | (D) Total Replacement Knee (Cemented) |
| W37.- | Aufranc-Turner | (D) Total Replacement Hip (Cemented) |
| W46.- | Austin-Moore | (D) Hemiarthroplasty Hip (Cemented) |
| W47.- | Austin-Moore | (D) Hemiarthroplasty Hip (Uncemented) |
| D14.- | Austin-Shea | Myringoplasty |
| W40.- | Autophor | (D) Total Replacement Knee (Cemented) |

# B

| | | |
|---|---|---|
| L87.4 | Babcock | Subcutaneous Enucleation Varicose Vein |
| M73.5 | Badenoch | Pull Through Urethroplasty |
| V29.4 | Badgeley | Anterior Fusion Cervical Spine |
| W60.1 | Badgeley | Extra-articular Fusion Hip (Z84.3) |
| V29.4 | Bailey | Anterior Fusion Cervical Spine |
| S20.1 | Bakamjian | Flap Deltopectoral (Z49.9) |
| X25.1 | Baker | Osteotomy Os Calcis |
| T70.3 | Baker | Recession Gastrocnemius Muscle (Z58.1) |
| W31.3 | Baldwin | Graft Wrist (Z70.4) |
| G29.2 | Balfour | Excision Gastric Ulcer |
| G28.1 | Balfour | Partial Gastrectomy |
| H49.8 | Ball | Undercutting Perianal Skin |
| G01.1 | Bancroft | Oesophagogastrectomy |
| W77.1 | Bankart | Repair Shoulder (Z81.4) |
| V29.4 | Barbour | Anterior Fusion Cervical Spine |
| C61.4 | Barkan | Goniopuncture |
| C61.3 | Barkan | Goniotomy |
| X49.1 | Barlow | (D) Splintage for Cong. Disloc. Hip (Z90.2) |
| V46.4 | Barr | (D) Skull Traction |
| T64.3 | Barr | Ant. Transfer Tibialis Post. Tendon (Z58.3) |
| W61.1 | Barr | Intra-articular Fusion Ankle (Z85.6) |
| H52.4 | Barron | Band Haemorrhoidectomy |
| R21.3 | Barton | Mid Forceps Rotation Fetal Head |
| P05.1 | Bassett | Vulvectomy (T85) |
| T20.3 | Bassini | Repair Inguinal Hernia |
| T21.3 | Bassini | Repair Recurrent Inguinal Hernia |
| X48.1 | Batchelor | (D) Plaster for Cong. Disloc.Hip (Z90.2) |
| W04.3 | Batchelor | Subtalar Fusion |
| W57.2 | Batchlor-Milch | Excision Arthroplasty Hip (Z84.3) |
| X09.4 | Batch-Spittler-McFaddin | Disarticulation Knee |
| W47.- | Bateman | (D) Hemiarthroplasty Hip (Uncemented) |
| K23.5 | Batista | Partial Left Ventriculectomy |
| W43.- | Beddow | (D) Total Replacement Shoulder (Cemented) (Z81.4) |
| J56.4 | Beger | Subtotal Excision of Head of Pancreas |
| G24.1 | Belsey | Antireflux Operation |
| W12.8 | Benjamin | Double Osteotomy Knee (Z84.6) |
| X07.1 | Berger | Interscapulothoracic Amputation Arm |
| Y82.1 | Biers | Nerve Block IV |
| B31.1 | Biesenberger | Reduction Breast |
| M44.1 | Bigelow | Litholapaxy |
| G28.1 | Billroth I | Partial Gastrectomy & Gastroduodenal Anastomosis |
| G28.3 | Billroth II | Partial Gastrectomy & Gastroenterostomy |
| J07.8 | Binnie | Hepatopexy |
| W58.- | Birmingham | (D) Resurfacing Arthroplasty of Hip (Z84.3) |
| M20.- | Bischoff | Replantation Ureter |
| K29.3 | Bjork-Shiley | (D) Prosthesis Replacement Heart Valve NEC (Normally Code to Valve Replaced) |
| W61.1 | Blair | Intra-articular Fusion Ankle (Z85.6) |

| | | |
|---|---|---|
| K15.1 | Blalock-Hanlon | Creation Defect Atrial Septum |
| L08.3 | Blalock-Taussig | Anastomosis Subclavian to Pulmonary Artery |
| M73.4 | Blandy | Reconstruction Urethra |
| C18.1 | Blascovics | Resection Levator Muscle Eyelid |
| T20.3 | Bloodgood | Repair Inguinal Hernia |
| T21.3 | Bloodgood | Repair Recurrent Inguinal Hernia |
| W19.1 | Blount | (D) Nail Plate Hip |
| W27.3 | Blount | Staple Epiphysiodesis |
| M21.2 | Boari | Creation Flap Bladder |
| J21.1 | Bobb | Cholelithotomy |
| G05.- | Boerema | Button Anastomosis Oesophagus |
| W60.1 | Bosworth | Extra-articular Fusion Hip (Z84.3) |
| X22.2 | Bosworth | Osteotomy Pelvis |
| V38.2 | Bosworth | Posterior Interlaminar Fusion Spine |
| W77.3 | Bosworth | Repair Acromioclavicular Joint (Z81.2) |
| X10.2 | Boyd | Amputation Hindfoot |
| X09.5 | Boyd | Amputation Lower Leg |
| X23.2 | Boyd | Bone Graft Pseudoarthrosis Tibia |
| X09.2 | Boyd | Disarticulation Hip |
| M37.1 | Bradford-Young | Cystourethroplasty |
| T64.2 | Brand | Transfer Tendon Hand (Z56.9) |
| R30.2 | Brandt-Andrews | Expression Placenta |
| M19.1 | Bricker | Ileoureterostomy |
| E06.4 | Brighton | Nasal Balloon Packing |
| W77.1 | Bristow | Repair Shoulder (Z81.4) |
| W60.1 | Brittain | Extra-articular Arthrodesis |
| W61.1 | Brittain | Intra-articular Fusion Elbow (Z81.5) |
| W61.1 | Brittain | Intra-articular Fusion Knee (Z84.6) |
| K32.4 | Brock | Valvulotomy Pulmonary Valve |
| W59.3 | Brockman | Fusion First Metatarsophalangeal Joint |
| G74.3 | Brooke | Ileostomy |
| V37.- | Brooks | Fusion Atlantoaxial Joint |
| L91.1 | Broviac | (D) Central Venous Catheter |
| X49.1 | Browne(Denis) | (D) Splint for Club Foot (Z90.5) |
| M73.2 | Browne(Denis) | Repair Epispadias |
| M73.1 | Browne(Denis) | Repair Hypospadias |
| X49.1 | Browne-Denis | (D) Splint for Club Foot (Z90.5) |
| M73.2 | Browne-Denis | Repair Epispadias |
| M73.1 | Browne-Denis | Repair Hypospadias |
| W19.4 | Brown-Tulloch | (D) Sliding Nail Plate |
| V38.3 | Buck | Fusion Spine for Spondylolisthesis |
| M52.3 | Burch | Colposuspension |
| X09.5 | Burgess | Amputation Lower Leg |
| M37.1 | Burns | Cystourethroplasty |
| T25.1 | Burton | Repair Incisional Hernia |
| X27.4 | Butler | Soft Tissue Release Fifth Toe |
| M73.1 | Byars | Repair Hypospadias |

# C

| | | |
|---|---|---|
| E12.2 | Caldwell-Luc | Sublabial Drainage Maxillary Antrum |
| X09.4 | Callander | Disarticulation Knee |
| W60.1 | Campbell | Extra-articular Fusion Ankle (Z85.6) |
| T64.2 | Campbell-Goldthwait | Transfer Patella Tendon (Z58.8) |
| K29.3 | Carpentier-Edwards | (D) Prosthetic Replacement Heart Valve NEC (Normally Code to Valve Replaced) |
| C03.2 | Castroviejo | (D) Eyeball Prosthesis |
| W43.- | Cavendish | (D) Total Replacement Elbow (Cemented) (Z81.5) |
| W40.9 | Cavendish | (D) Total Replacement Knee (Cemented) |
| W43.- | Cavendish | (D) Total Replacement Shoulder (Cemented) (Z81.4) |
| M73.1 | Cecil | Repair Hypospadias |
| G11.- | Celestin | (D) Prosthesis Oesophagus (Code to Procedure) |
| W60.1 | Chandler | Extra-articular Fusion Hip (Z84.3) |
| T92.2 | Charles | Correction Lymphoedema |
| W62.2 | Charnley | (D) Compression Clamp for Fusion |
| W19.1 | Charnley | (D) Compression Screw Hip |
| W37.- | Charnley | (D) Total Replacement Hip (Cemented) |
| W40.- | Charnley | (D) Total Replacement Knee (Cemented) |
| W62.2 | Charnley | Compression Arthrodesis |
| W37.- | Charnley-Muller | (D) Total Replacement Hip (Cemented) |
| T22.3 | Cheadle-Henry | Repair Femoral Hernia |
| T23.3 | Cheadle-Henry | Repair Recurrent Femoral Hernia |
| X22.2 | Chiari | Osteotomy Pelvis |
| J56.1 | Childs | Pancreaticoduodenectomy |
| J57.1 | Childs | Subtotal Pancreatectomy |
| W60.1 | Cholmeley | Extra-articular Fusion Hip (Z84.3) |
| X10.4 | Chopart | Midtarsal Amputation |
| T08.3 | Clagett | Fenestration Chest Wall |
| V29.4 | Cloward | Anterior Fusion Cervical Spine |
| L83.2 | Cockett | Subfascial Ligation Perforating Varicose Vein |
| D26.8 | Cody | Perforation Footplate |
| G24.5 | Collis | Antireflux Operation |
| X22.3 | Colonna | Arthroplasty Hip |
| W61.1 | Coltart | Intra-articular Fusion Ankle (Z85.6) |
| F22.1 | Commando | Glossectomy & Block Dissection (T85.1) |
| A12.4 | Cordis-Hakim | (D) Valve Ventriculoperitoneal |
| W19.5 | Coventry | (D) Cannulation Screw |
| X23.5 | Coventry (MB) | Osteotomy Tibia |
| K52.6 | Cox Maze | Incision Tissue Atria |
| X49.1 | Craig | (D) Splintage for Cong. Disloc. Hip (Z90.2) |
| C18.3 | Crawford | Tarsofrontalis Sling Eyelid Using Fascia |
| V46.4 | Crutchfield | (D) Skull Traction |
| M05.1 | Culp-Deweerd | Pyeloplasty |
| M05.1 | Culp-Scardino | Pyeloplasty |

# D

| | | |
|---|---|---|
| C45.2 | D'Ombrain | Excision Pterygium & Graft Cornea (C46.2) |
| G04.1 | Dahlman | Excision Diverticulum Oesophagus |
| L06.2 | Damus-Kaye-Stansel | Anastomosis Pulmonary Artery to Aorta |
| W08.5 | Darrach | Distal Excision Ulna (Z71.6) |
| V21.8 | Dautrey | Recurrent Temporomandibular Dislocation |
| P32.2 | Davidov | Reconstruction Vagina Using Peritoneal Graft |
| M23.8 | Davis | Ureterotomy Intubated |
| W40.- | Deane | (D) Total Replacement Knee (Cemented) |
| X19.9 | Debeyre | Reconstruction Soft Tissue Shoulder |
| W43.- | Dee | (D) Total Replacement Elbow (Cemented) (Z81.5) |
| H41.1 | Delorme | Excision Mucosa Rectum |
| K67.9 | Delorme | Pericardiectomy |
| H36.8 | Delorme | Repair Rectum for Prolapse |
| W29.9 | Denham | (D) Bone Pin |
| W40.- | Denham | (D) Total Replacement Knee (Cemented) |
| X49.1 | Denis-Browne | (D) Splint for Club Foot (Z90.5) |
| M73.1 | Denis-Browne | Repair Hypospadias |
| E12.2 | Denker | Radical Antrotomy Maxillary |
| | Denver | Shunt – see nature |
| D14.- | Derlacki | Myringoplasty |
| K34.2 | De Vega | Annuloplasty Tricuspid Valve |
| H15.8 | Devine | Colostomy |
| W19.1 | Deyerle | (D) Pin Hip |
| X22.2 | Dial | Osteotomy Pelvis |
| W03.3 | Dickson-Diveley | Fusion Claw Toe with Transfer Tendon |
| X24.3 | Dillwyn-Evans | Operation for Club Foot |
| E23.2 | Dohlman | Repair Pharyngeal Pouch |
| | Dotter | Transluminal Angioplasty (Code to Vessel) |
| A27.1 | Dragstedt | Subdiaphragmatic Truncal Vagotomy |
| M73.1 | Duckett | Repair Hypospadias |
| H41.8 | Duhamel | Incision Colorectal Septum |
| H41.8 | Duhamel | Pull Through for Hirschsprung Disease |
| X49.1 | Dunlop | (D) Traction System Arm (Z89.9) |
| W27.9 | Dunn | (D) Hip Pin for Fixation Epiphysis (Z76.1) |
| W04.2 | Dunn | Triple Fusion Foot |
| H36.8 | Dunphy | Repair Rectum for Prolapse |
| X19.2 | Durham | Operation for Erbs Palsy |
| T64.4 | Durham-Caldwell | Transfer Biceps Femoris Tendon (Z57.6) |
| W77.3 | Du Toit | Staple Capsulorrhaphy Shoulder (Z81.4) |
| J59.4 | Duval | Pancreaticojejunostomy |
| V41.2 | Dwyer | Anterior Wiring Spine for Scoliosis |
| T54.1 | Dwyer (FC) | Fasciotomy |
| X25.1 | Dwyer (FC) | Osteotomy Os Calcis |

# E

| | | |
|---|---|---|
| D12.8 | Eagleton | Drainage Petrous Apex Mastoid |
| H53.8 | Earle | Haemorrhoidectomy |
| L77.1 | Eck | Side to Side Portocaval Shunt |
| W77.4 | Eden-Hybinette | Block Bone for Recurrent Dislocation |
| W20.1 | Eggers | (D) Fracture Plate |
| W78.3 | Eggers (GWN) | Transfer Tendon Hamstring |
| C55.2 | Elliot | Trephination Sclera |
| W20.1 | Ellis | (D) Fracture Plate |
| W77.2 | Ellison | Soft Tissue Repair Knee (Z84.6) |
| W77.2 | Elmslie | Soft Tissue Stabilisation Ankle (Z85.6) |
| X25.2 | Elmslie | Wedge Tarsectomy |
| T01.1 | Eloesser | Thoracoplasty |
| W19.3 | Ender | (D) Flexible Intramedullary Nail |
| H35.8 | Erickman | Repair Rectum for Prolapse |
| W24.4 | Essex-Lopresti | Operation for Fracture Os Calcis (Z79.2) |
| X24.3 | Evans-Dillwyn | Operation for Club Foot |
| C18.1 | Everbusch | Resection Levator Muscle Eyelid |
| W37.- | Exeter | (D) Total Replacement Hip (Cemented) |

# F

| | | |
|---|---|---|
| X19.2 | Fairbank | Operation for Obstetric Palsy |
| C18.5 | Fasanella-Servat | Tarsomullerectomy |
| P13.2 | Fenton | Perineorrhaphy |
| T20.3 | Ferguson | Repair Inguinal Hernia |
| T21.3 | Ferguson | Repair Recurrent Inguinal Hernia |
| X22.1 | Ferguson (AB) | Open Reduction Congenital Dislocation Hip |
| D26.8 | Fick | Perforation Footplate |
| G40.3 | Finney | Pyloroplasty |
| A27.2 | Finney | Vagotomy & Pyloroplasty (G40.3) |
| W31.1 | Fisk | Graft Scaphoid (Z72.2) |
| X09.2 | Fitzmaurice-Kelly | Disarticulation Hip |
| L71.2 | Fogarty | (D) Catheter Closed Embolectomy Artery (or Code to Artery) |
| L94.8 | Fogarty | (D) Catheter Closed Embolectomy Vein (or Code to Vein) |
| M05.1 | Foley | Pyeloplasty |
| K19.2 | Fontan | Creation Conduit R.Atrium Pulmonary Artery |
| K18.2 | Fontan | Creation Valved Conduit Right Atrium Pulmonary Artery |
| P22.2 | Fothergill | Anterior Colporrhaphy & Amputation Cervix |
| D17.8 | Fowler | Anterior Crurotomy |
| S70.1 | Fowler | Avulsion Nail |
| W03.1 | Fowler (AW) | Reconstruction Forefoot |
| W77.2 | Fowler (SB) | Release Mallet Finger (Z83.5) |
| T64.1 | Fowler (SB) | Transfer Muscle Forearm (Z55.9) |
| V33.3 | Freebody | (D) Anterior Interbody Fusion Lumbar Spine |
| W37.- | Freeman | (D) Total Replacement Hip (Cemented) |
| W38.- | Freeman | (D) Total Replacement Hip (Uncemented) |
| W40.- | Freeman-Swanson | (D) Total Replacement Knee (Cemented) |
| X49.1 | Frejka | (D) Splintage for Cong. Disloc. Hip (Z90.2) |
| D12.8 | Frenckner | Drainage Petrous Apex Mastoid |
| M61.3 | Freyer | Transvesical Prostatectomy |
| W37.- | Furlong | (D) Total Replacement Hip (Cemented) |
| W38.- | Furlong | (D) Total Replacement Hip (Uncemented) |

# G

| | | |
|---|---|---|
| H56.4 | Gabriel | Excision Anal Fissure |
| H33.1 | Gabriel | Resection Rectum |
| W77.2 | Galeazzi | Tenodesis Semitendinosis Patellofemoral Joint (Z84.4) |
| T20.1 | Gallie | Repair Inguinal Hernia Fascia Lata |
| T21.1 | Gallie | Repair Recurrent Inguinal Hernia |
| W04.3 | Gallie (WE) | Arthrodesis Subtalar Joint |
| V37.- | Gallie (WE) | Fusion Atlantoaxial Joint |
| T64.4 | Garceau | Transfer Tibialis Anterior Muscle (Z58.4) |
| W24.1 | Garden | (D) Cannulated Screw Hip |
| W12.9 | Gariepy | Osteotomy Upper Tibia (Z77.1) |
| W40.- | Geomedic | (D) Total Replacement Knee (Cemented) |
| W40.- | Geometric | (D) Total Replacement Knee (Cemented) |
| W61.1 | Ghormley | Intra-articular Fusion Hip (Z84.3) |
| H14.1 | Gibson | Caecostomy |
| T92.4 | Gibson-Tough | Correction Lymphoedema |
| W61.1 | Gill (AB) | Intra-articular Fusion Shoulder (Z81.4) |
| X22.2 | Gill (AB) | Osteotomy Pelvis |
| V43.- | Gill (GG) | Excision Spondylolisthesis |
| Q54.1 | Gilliam | Suspension Uterus |
| V09.3 | Gillies | Reduction Fracture Zygomatic Complex |
| W61.1 | Gill-Stein | Intra-articular Fusion Wrist (Z82.1) |
| W57.2 | Girdlestone | Excision Arthroplasty Hip (Z84.3) |
| T64.2 | Girdlestone | Transfer Flexor Tendon Toe (Z59.2) |
| T64.4 | Girdlestone | Transfer Pectoralis Major Tendon (Z54.3) |
| V27.1 | Girdlestone (GR) | Laminectomy & Fusion Spine |
| T64.2 | Girdlestone-Taylor | Transfer Flexor Tendon Toe (Z59.2) |
| W25.9 | Gissane | (D) Spike Fixator |
| L09.1 | Glenn | Anast. Superior Vena Cava R.Pulmonary Artery |
| W15.2 | Golden | Osteotomy Base First Metatarsal Hallux Valgus |
| W04.3 | Goldthwait | Stabilisation Hindfoot |
| W77.2 | Goldthwait | Transfer Infrapatellar Tendon (Z84.4) |
| X09.1 | Gordon-Taylor | Hindquarter Amputation |
| | Gortex | Prosthetic Material (Code to Procedure) |
| W04.3 | Grice | Subtalar Fusion |
| X09.4 | Gritti-Stokes | Disarticulation Knee |
| G74.8 | Gross | Exteriorisation Operation Intestine |
| W19.2 | Grosse-Kempf | (D) Intermedullary Nail Trochanter Femur  (Z76.3) |
| X23.5 | Gruca | Bifurcation Tibia |
| L71.5 | Grunzig | (D) Catheter for Transluminal Dilation Artery (or Code to Artery) |
| W40.- | Guepar | (D) Total Replacement Knee (Cemented) |
| D17.1 | Guildford | Stapedectomy |
| W40.- | Gunston | (D) Total Replacement Knee (Cemented) |
| X09.5 | Guyon | Amputation Lower Leg |

# H

| | | |
|---|---|---|
| B34.1 | Hadfield | Excision Subareolar Duct Breast |
| W27.8 | Hagie | (D) Hip Pin for Fixation Epiphysis (Z76.1) |
| A12.4 | Hakim | Insertion Ventriculoperitoneal Shunt |
| A12.2 | Halber | (D) Valve for Spina Bifida |
| B27.1 | Halsted | Mastectomy (T85.2) |
| T20.8 | Halsted | Repair Inguinal Hernia |
| T21.3 | Halsted | Repair Recurrent Inguinal Hernia |
| L23.2 | Hamilton | Flap Repair Coarctation Aorta |
| M05.1 | Hamilton-Stewart | Pyeloplasty & Plication Kidney (M05.4) |
| H05.1 | Hampton | Ileorectal Anastomosis |
| V41.1 | Harrington | (D) Instrumentation Spine |
| V46.2 | Harrington | (D) Rod Fixation Fracture Spine |
| W62.- | Harrison Nicholle | (D) Prosthetic Peg for Joint Fusion |
| H33.5 | Hartmann | Resection Rectum |
| V41.1 | Hartshill | (D) Instrumentation Spine |
| W46.- | Hastings | (D) Hemiarthroplasty Hip (Cemented) |
| T64.4 | Hauser | Transfer Infrapatellar Tendon (Z57.3) |
| E95.1 | Heaf | Tuberculosis test |
| Q08.9 | Heaney | Vaginal Hysterectomy |
| G40.3 | Heinecke-Mickulicz | Pyloroplasty |
| A27.2 | Heinecke-Mikulicz | Vagotomy & Pyloroplasty (G40.3) |
| W56.- | Helal | (D) Arthroplasty Metatarsophalangeal Joint |
| W03.2 | Helal | Osteotomy Metatarsal Bone |
| G09.1 | Heller | Cardiomyotomy |
| L41.5 | Hellstrom | Translocation Renal Vessel |
| M43.2 | Helmstein | Prolonged Hydrostatic Overdistension Bladder |
| C19.8 | Henderson | Incision Muller Muscle Eyelid |
| W61.1 | Henderson (MS) | Intra-articular Fusion Hip (Z84.3) |
| W19.5 | Herbert | (D) Small Fragment Screw |
| W40.- | Herbert | (D) Total Replacement Knee (Cemented) |
| X10.9 | Hey | Amputation Foot |
| W74.2 | Hey-Groves | Reconstruction Ant.Cruciate Ligament (Z84.6) |
| W27.2 | Heymann-Herndon | Clearance Joint (Z76.1) |
| W03.8 | Heymann-Herndon | Correction Metatarsus Varus |
| V38.2 | Hibbs | Fusion Lumbar Spine |
| W61.1 | Hibbs | Intra-articular Fusion Hip (Z84.3) |
| L91.1 | Hickman | (D) Central Venous Catheter |
| W20.1 | Hicks | (D) Fracture Plate |
| G24.4 | Hill | Gastropexy Antireflux Operation |
| T64.4 | Hitchcock | Transposition Biceps Brachii (Z54.4) |
| W30.1 | Hoffmann | (D) External Fixator |
| G28.3 | Hofmeister | Valved Gastrectomy |
| W15.1 | Hohmann | Osteotomy Neck First Metatarsal Hallux Valgus |
| W04.2 | Hoke | Fusion Hindfoot |
| W19.1 | Holt | (D) Nail Hip |
| A20.1 | Holter | (D) Valve Drainage Ventricle |
| T92.4 | Homan | Correction Lymphoedema |
| E14.4 | Horgan | Transantral Ethmoidectomy |
| D17.1 | Hough | Stapedectomy |
| D17.1 | House | Stapedectomy |

| | | |
|---|---|---|
| E14.1 | Howarth | External Frontoethmoidectomy |
| W37.- | Howse | (D) Total Replacement Hip (Cemented) |
| T64.2 | Huber | Transfer Thenar Muscle (Z56.2) |
| W19.2 | Huckster | (D) Intermedullary Nail & Screw |
| M20.- | Hutch | Replantation Ureter |
| E21.1 | Hynes | Pharyngoplasty |
| M05.1 | Hynes-Anderson | Pyeloplasty |

# I

| | | |
|---|---|---|
| W58.- | Ilch | (D) Surface Replacement Hip (Z84.3) |
| W37.- | Ilch | (D) Total Replacement Hip (Cemented) |
| W40.- | Ilch | (D) Total Replacement Knee (Cemented) |
| X49.1 | Ilfield | (D) Splintage for Cong. Disloc. Hip (Z90.2) |
| W43.- | Irving | (D) Total Replacement Ankle (Cemented)(Z85.6) |
| W40.- | Irving | (D) Total Replacement Knee (Cemented) |
| T83.2 | Irwin | Myotomy |
| | Ivalon | Sponge Prosthetic Material (Code to Procedure) |
| G01.1 | Ivor-Lewis | Oesophagogastrectomy |

# J

| N11.3 | Jaboulay | Eversion Hydrocele Sac |
|-------|----------|------------------------|
| X09.1 | Jaboulay | Hindquarter Amputation |
| G31.3 | Jabouley | Gastroduodenostomy |
| A32.4 | Janetta | Microvascular Decompression Facial Nerve |
| E14.4 | Jansen-Horgan | Transantral Ethmoidectomy |
| C35.1 | Jensen | Transposition Muscles Eye |
| W19.1 | Jewett | (D) Nail Plate Hip |
| M73.4 | Johanson | Reconstruction Urethra |
| C25.1 | Jones | Canaliculodacryocystorhinostomy |
| Q09.5 | Jones | Metroplasty |
| T67.8 | Jones | Repair Peroneal Tendon (Z58.2) |
| W74.2 | Jones (KG) | Reconstruction Ant. Cruciate Ligament (Z84.6) |
| W57.2 | Jones (L) | Resection Head Humerus (Z69.1) |
| W03.3 | Jones (R) | Operation for Claw Toe |
| W03.4 | Jones (R) | Transfer Tendon to First Metatarsal |
| W12.2 | Jones (R) | Valgus Osteotomy Hip (Z76.2) |
| W60.1 | Jones (W) | Extra-articular Fusion Shoulder (Z81.4) |
| W61.1 | Jones (W) | Intra-articular Fusion Hip (Z84.3) |
| W77.2 | Jones (W) | Stabilisation Ankle (Z85.6) |
| T64.4 | Joplin | Sling Procedure Muscle Foot (Z59.-) |
| W79.1 | Joplin | Soft Tissue Operation for Hallux Valgus |
| X19.1 | Josserand | Scapulopexy |
| W47.- | Judet | (D) Hemiarthroplasty Hip (Uncemented) |
| T64.4 | Judet | Pedicle Graft Gluteus Muscle (Z57.1) |
| T79.2 | Judet | Quadricepsplasty |

# K

| J29.1 | Kasai | Hepatojejunostomy |
|---|---|---|
| W03.1 | Kates-Kessel | Reconstruction Forefoot |
| M75.2 | Kaufman | (D) Prosthesis Male Incontinence |
| T25.3 | Keel | Repair Incisional Hernia |
| N08.3 | Keetley-Torek | Bilateral Orchidopexy First Stage |
| N08.4 | Keetley-Torek | Bilateral Orchidopexy Second Stage |
| N09.3 | Keetley-Torek | Unilateral Orchidopexy First Stage |
| N09.4 | Keetley-Torek | Unilateral Orchidopexy Second Stage |
| J07.8 | Kehr | Hepatopexy |
| W32.1 | Keil | (D) Prepared Graft Bone |
| W57.1 | Keller | Excision Arthroplasty First MTP Joint |
| M53.1 | Kelly-Kennedy | Urethrovesical Plication |
| W43.- | Kessel | (D) Total Replacement Shoulder (Cemented) (Z81.4) |
| W03.1 | Kessel-Kates | Reconstruction Forefoot |
| W61.1 | Key | Intra-articular Fusion Knee (Z84.6) |
| R21.3 | Kielland | Mid Forceps Rotation Fetal Head |
| E14.1 | Killian | External Frontoethmoidectomy |
| F29.1 | Kilner-Wardill | Repair Cleft Palate |
| X09.1 | King-Steelquist | Hindquarter Amputation |
| X09.3 | Kirk | Amputation Thigh |
| X09.4 | Kirk | Disarticulation Knee |
| W29.1 | Kirschner | (D) Wire Fixation |
| J72.4 | Kirschner | Repair of Spleen |
| V41.1 | Knodt | (D) Spinal Distraction Rod |
| G74.1 | Koch | Continent Ileostomy |
| T92.8 | Kondoleon | Correction Lymphoedema |
| K37.6 | Konno | Aortoventriculoplasty |
| A75.9 | Krause | Sympathetic Denervation |
| C06.9 | Kroenlein | Lateral Orbitotomy |
| X07.5 | Krukenberg | Amputation Below Elbow |
| C15.1 | Kuhnt-Szymanowski | Repair Ectropion |
| W19.2 | Kuntschner | (D) Intramedullary Fixation |
| S22.4 | Kutler | Local Flap Closure Finger Tip (750.3) |

# L

| | | |
|---|---|---|
| G53.6 | Ladd | Correction Malrotation Duodenum |
| W04.2 | Lambrinudi | Triple Fusion Joints Hindfoot |
| F29.1 | Langenbeck | Repair Cleft Palate |
| W59.3 | Lapidus | Arthrodesis M.T.P. Joint for Hallux Valgus |
| T71.1 | Lapidus | Synovectomy Peroneal Tendon (Z58.2) |
| X27.4 | Lapidus | Transplantation Tendon Fifth Toe |
| X07.2 | Larry | Disarticulation Shoulder |
| P18.2 | Latzko | Partial Colpocleisis |
| M73.4 | Leadbetter | Reconstruction Urethra |
| M19.2 | Leadbetter | Ureterosigmoidostomy |
| M20.- | Leadbetter-Politano | Replantation Ureter |
| K06.2 | Lecompte | Direct Ventriculo-arterial Connection |
| P18.1 | Le Fort | Complete Colpocleisis |
| V10.4 | Le Fort | Osteotomy Maxilla |
| F03.1 | Lemesurier | Repair Cleft Lip |
| A75.4 | Leriche | Perivascular Sympathectomy |
| C25.3 | Lester-Jones | (D) Dacryocystorhinostomy Tube |
| L81.1 | Le Veen | (D) Peritoneovenous Shunt |
| S27.- | Limberg | Random Pattern Local Flap Skin |
| W74.1 | Lindemann | Muscle Transfer Knee (Z84.6) |
| T67.9 | Lindholm | Repair Rupture Tendon |
| W54.- | Link | Arthroplasty Joint |
| L87.8 | Linton | Interruption Perforating Varicose Vein |
| L83.2 | Linton | Subfacial Ligation Perforating Vein Leg |
| T64.4 | Lippman | Transportation Biceps Brachii (Z54.4) |
| T72.3 | Lipscomb-Duvries | Tenosynoplasty Peroneal Tendon (Z58.2) |
| X07.2 | Lisfranc | Disarticulation Shoulder |
| X10.3 | Lisfranc | Tarsometatarsal Amputation |
| X07.1 | Littlewood | Forequarter Amputation |
| W40.- | Liverpool | (D) Total Replacement Knee (Cemented) |
| H33.1 | Lloyd-Davis | Resection Rectum |
| H51.1 | Lockhart-Mummery | Haemorrhoidectomy |
| T22.3 | Lockwood | Repair Femoral Hernia |
| T23.3 | Lockwood | Repair Recurrent Femoral Hernia |
| J29.- | Longmire | Biliary Bypass |
| W38.- | Lord | (D) Total Replacement Hip (Uncemented) |
| N11.2 | Lord | Plication Hydrocele Sac |
| W12.2 | Lorenz | Osteotomy Hip (Z76.2) |
| T23.3 | Lotheissen | Repair Recurrent Femoral Hernia |
| T22.3 | Lothiessen | Repair Femoral Hernia |
| W19.3 | Lottes | (D) Intramedullary Nail Tibia (Z77.2) |
| W77.8 | Lowman | Transfer Tendon Tibialis Anterior (Z86.2) |
| W55.- | Luck | (D) Interposit. Cup Arthroplasty Hip (Z84.3) |
| E14.1 | Luc-Ogston | External Frontoethmoidectomy |
| X22.1 | Ludloff | Open Reduction Congenital Dislocation Hip |
| V41.1 | Luque | (D) Instrumentation Spine |

# M

| W55.- | Macintosh | (D) Plateau Prosthesis Tibia Knee (Z84.6) |
|---|---|---|
| W77.2 | Macintosh | Plastic Stabilisation Tenodesis Knee (Z84.6) |
| W38.- | Madreporique | (D) Total Replacement Hip (Uncemented) |
| W77.2 | Magnuson-Stack | Op. for Recur. Dislocation Shoulder (Z81.3) |
| T25.3 | Maingot | Repair Incisional Hernia |
| G28.8 | Maki | Partial Gastrectomy Preserving Pylorus |
| T20.2 | Maloney | (D) Nylon Darn Repair Inguinal Hernia |
| T21.2 | Maloney | Repair Recurrent Inguinal Hernia |
| W40.- | Manchester | (D) Total Replacement Knee (Cemented) |
| P22.9 | Manchester | Colporrhaphy |
| T70.3 | Maquet | Elevation Tubercle Tibia (Z57.3) |
| W40.- | Marmor | (D) Total Replacement Knee (Cemented) |
| M52.2 | Marshall-Marchetti-Krantz | Retropubic Suspension Urethra |
| G30.2 | Mason | Gastric Partitioning |
| G23.1 | Mason | Repair Oesophageal Hiatus Hernia |
| W19.1 | Massie | (D) Nail Plate Hip |
| W47.- | Matchett-Brown | (D) Hemiarthroplasty Hip (Uncemented) |
| W31.1 | Mattie-Russe | Graft Scaphoid (Z72.2) |
| H41.8 | Maunsell-Weir | Proctectomy |
| W43.- | Mayo | (D) Total Replacement Elbow (Cemented)(Z81.5) |
| H35.4 | Mayo | Repair Rectum for Prolapse |
| T24.3 | Mayo | Repair Umbilical Hernia |
| L87.3 | Mayo | Stripping Varicose Vein |
| W57.1 | Mayo (CH) | Excision Arthroplasty First MTP Joint |
| G33.1 | Mayo-Ward | Gastroenterostomy |
| X09.4 | Mazet | Disarticulation Knee |
| W20.1 | McAtee | (D) Fixation Olecranon (Z71.1) |
| W79.1 | McBride | Soft Tissue Operation for Hallux Valgus |
| P23.4 | McCall | Repair Enterocele |
| V20.9 | McCarthy | Arthroplasty Temporomandibular Joint |
| R12.1 | McDonald | Encirclement Suture Cervix Gravid Uterus |
| T22.3 | McEvedy | Repair Femoral Hernia |
| T23.3 | McEvedy | Repair Recurrent Femoral Hernia |
| X23.2 | McFarland | Bone Graft Pseudoarthrosis Tibia |
| D16.8 | McGee | Malleostapediopexy |
| P21.1 | McIndoe | Construction Vagina |
| T52.1 | McIndoe (A) | Fasciectomy Palm |
| W40.- | McKee | (D) Total Replacement Knee (Cemented) |
| W37.- | McKee-Farrer | (D) Total Replacement Hip (Cemented) |
| G02.2 | McKeown | Oesophagectomy |
| B31.1 | McKssock | Reduction Breast |
| W19.1 | McLaughlin | (D) Nail Plate Hip |
| W77.1 | McLaughlin | Repair Shoulder (Z81.3) |
| W13.3 | McMurray | Osteotomy Hip (Z76.2) |
| T20.3 | McVay | Repair Inguinal Hernia |
| T21.3 | Mcvay | Repair Recurrent Inguinal Hernia |
| W40.- | Melbourne | (D) Total Replacement Knee (Cemented) |
| J05.3 | Menghini | (D) Biopsy Liver (Open) |
| J13.2 | Menghini | (D) Biopsy Liver (Percutaneous) |
| S42.- | Michel | (D) Clip Skin Closure |

| | | |
|---|---|---|
| W57.2 | Milch-Batchelor | Excision Arthroplasty Hip (Z84.3) |
| H33.1 | Miles | Resection Rectum |
| F03.1 | Millard | Repair Cleft Lip |
| W03.8 | Miller | Fusion Midtarsus |
| H51.1 | Milligan-Morgan | Haemorrhoidectomy |
| M61.2 | Millin | Retropubic Prostatectomy |
| M52.1 | Millin-Reed | Suspension Urethrovesical |
| W37.- | Minneapolis | (D) Total Replacement Hip (Cemented) |
| W38.- | Minneapolis | (D) Total Replacement Hip (Uncemented) |
| H53.8 | Mitchell | Haemorrhoidectomy |
| W15.1 | Mitchell | Osteotomy Neck First Metatarsal Hallux Valgus |
| M19.2 | Mitrofanoff | Urinary Diversion |
| V38.- | Moe | Posterior Joint Fusion Spine |
| S05.- | Mohs | Chemosurgical Excision Skin |
| C60.5 | Molteno | (D) Implantation Tube Anterior Chamber Eye |
| W46.- | Monk | (D) Hemiarthroplasty Hip (Cemented) |
| W47.- | Monk | (D) Hemiarthroplasty Hip (Uncemented) |
| W37.- | Monk | (D) Total Replacement Hip (Cemented) |
| W38.- | Monk | (D) Total Replacement Hip (Uncemented) |
| W27.9 | Moore | (D) Hip Pin for Fixation Epiphysis (Z76.1) |
| W46.- | Moore-Austin | (D) Hemiarthroplasty Hip (Cemented) |
| K24.6 | Morrow | Left Ventricular Myectomy & Myotomy |
| P23.4 | Moschowitz | Repair Enterocele |
| H19.8 | Moschowitz | Sigmoid Colonopexy (Z28.6) |
| G28.3 | Moynihan-Mayo | Partial Gastrectomy |
| W43.- | Mueli | (D) Total Replacement Wrist (Cemented) (Z82.1) |
| W37.- | Muller | (D) Total Replacement Hip (Cemented) |
| K05.- | Mustard | Reconstruction Transposition Great Arteries |
| T64.4 | Mustard | Transplant Iliopsoas (Z57.2) |
| C11.3 | Mustarde | Canthoplasty for Correction Epicanthus |
| D03.3 | Mustarde | Pinnaplasty |

# N

| | | |
|---|---|---|
| A47.1 | Nashold | Needling Substantia Gelatinosa Cervical Reg. |
| W49.- | Neer | (D) Hemiarthroplasty Shoulder (Cemented) |
| W50.- | Neer | (D) Hemiarthroplasty Shoulder (Uncemented) |
| N28.3 | Nesbitt | Plication Corpora of Penis |
| W19.1 | Neufield | (D) Nail Plate Hip |
| W77.1 | Neviaser | Repair Shoulder (Z81.2) |
| W77.2 | Nicola | Tenodesis Shoulder (Z81.4) |
| W01.3 | Nicolandi | Osteoplastic Reconstruction Thumb |
| W45.- | Nicolle | (D) Total Replacement MCP Joint (Z83.2) |
| W55.- | Niebauer | (D) Prosthetic Replacement MCP Joint (Z83.-) |
| G24.3 | Nissen | Abdominal Antireflux Operation |
| G24.1 | Nissen | Thoracic Antireflux Operation |
| G76.4 | Noble | Plication Intestine |
| K17.3 | Norwood | Aortopulmonary Reconstruction Procedure |
| | Nottingham | (D) Prosthesis Oesophagus (Code to Procedure) |
| T25.3 | Nuttall | Repair Incisional Hernia |

# O

| | | |
|---|---|---|
| W75.1 | O'Donoghue | Repair Ligament Knee (Z84.6) |
| W78.2 | O'Malley | Release Capsule Hip for Osteoarthritis |
| W77.2 | Ober | Operation for Recur. Disloc. Patella (Z84.4) |
| T55.3 | Ober-Yount | Gluteoiliotibial Fasciotomy |
| V16.2 | Obwegeser | Osteotomy of Mandible |
| F11.4 | Obwegeser | Vestibuloplasty Mouth |
| N08.2 | Ombredanne | Bilateral Orchidopexy One Stage |
| M73.1 | Ombredanne | Repair Hypospadias |
| N09.2 | Ombredanne | Unilateral Orchidopexy One Stage |
| E21.3 | Orticochea | Pharyngoplasty |
| T64.4 | Osmond-Clark | Transfer Peroneus Brevis Tendon (Z58.2) |
| M79.4 | Otis | Internal Urethrotomy |
| W30.1 | Oxford | (D) External Fixator |

# P

| | | |
|---|---|---|
| T70.3 | Page | Muscle Slide Forearm (Z55.1) |
| L83.1 | Palma | Cross Over Saphenous Graft |
| Q55.- | Papanicolau | Cervical Smear |
| M20.- | Paquin | Replantation Ureter |
| W20.2 | Parham | (D) Cerclage Band |
| H04.2 | Parks | Creation Ileal Pouch |
| H51.8 | Parks | Submucosal Haemorrhoidectomy |
| B27.3 | Patey | Mastectomy (T85.2) |
| D08.2 | Pattee | Reconstruction External Auditory Canal |
| H15.- | Paul-Mickulicz | Colostomy |
| H10.5 | Paul-Mickulicz | Resection Colon |
| W12.9 | Pauwels | Osteotomy Upper Femur (Z76.2) |
| X49.1 | Pavlik | (D) Splintage for Cong. Disloc. Hip (Z90.2) |
| G61.3 | Payne-Dewind | Jejunocolostomy |
| X49.1 | Pearson | (D) Splint Knee (Z84.6) |
| A75.5 | Peet | Resection Splanchnic Nerve |
| X22.2 | Pemberton | Osteotomy Ilium |
| M51.2 | Pereyra | Endoscopic Suspension Bladder Neck |
| X49.1 | Perkins | (D) Traction System Leg (Z90.-) |
| X24.3 | Perkins | Operation for Club Foot |
| D15.1 | Perlee | (D) Tube Ear |
| J59.3 | Peustow | Pancreaticojejunostomy |
| M53.8 | Peyera-Raz-Gitter | Colposuspension Vaginal |
| W31.9 | Phemister | Bone Graft |
| W27.1 | Phemister | Epiphysiodesis |
| X10.1 | Pirogoff | Amputation Ankle |
| W40.- | Platt | (D) Total Replacement Knee (Cemented) |
| M20.- | Politano-Leadbetter | Replantation Ureter |
| G28.3 | Polya | Partial Gastrectomy |
| W40.- | Polycentric | (D) Total Replacement Knee (Cemented) |
| Q27.1 | Pomeroy | Bilateral Ligation Fallopian Tubes |
| T70.5 | Poncet | Lengthening Tendo Achillis (Z58.1) |
| W91.2 | Ponsetti Treatment | Manipulation Joint (Z86.9) |
| D16.8 | Portman | Malleostapediopexy |
| L06.4 | Potts-Smith | Anast. Descending Aorta L. Pulmonary Artery |
| W37.- | Pretoria | (D) Total Replacement Hip (Cemented) |
| W40.- | Pretoria | (D) Total Replacement Knee (Cemented) |
| W71.3 | Pridie | Forage Knee (Z84.6) |
| G33.1 | Printer-Mason | Gastroenterostomy |
| W43.- | Pritchard-Walker | (D) Total Replacement Elbow (Cemented) (Z81.5) |
| W19.1 | Pugh | (D) Nail Plate Hip |
| X49.1 | Pugh | (D) Traction System |
| W60.1 | Putti | Intra-articular Fusion |
| W77.1 | Putti-Platt | Repair Shoulder (Z81.3) |

# R

| | | |
|---|---|---|
| D12.8 | Ramadier | Drainage Petrous Apex Mastoid |
| G40.1 | Rammstedt | Pyloromyotomy |
| H11.9 | Rankin | Colectomy |
| H33.1 | Rankin | Resection Rectum |
| V22.8 | Ransford | Decompression Cervical Spine |
| K16.1 | Rashkind | Balloon Atrial Septostomy |
| K18.3 | Rastelli | Creation Valved Conduit Pulmonary Artery |
| W62.2 | Ratliff | Compression Fusion Ankle (Z85.6) |
| X08.4 | Ray | Amputation of Finger |
| X10.4 | Ray | Transmetatarsal Amputation |
| K06.2 | Rev | Direct Ventriculo-arterial Connection |
| W19.1 | Richards | (D) Screw Hip |
| W38.- | Ring | (D) Total Replacement Hip (Uncemented) |
| X20.3 | Riordan | Operation for Congenital Absence Radius |
| W01.5 | Riordan | Transfer Opponens Thumb |
| H35.4 | Ripstein | Repair Rectum for Prolapse NEC |
| H35.2 | Ripstein | Repair Rectum for Prolapse Using Teflon |
| V29.4 | Robinson-Smith | Discectomy & Fusion Cervical Spine |
| J57.1 | Rodney-Smith | Distal Pancreatectomy |
| J29.1 | Rodney-Smith | Hepatojejunostomy |
| J56.2 | Rodney-Smith | Pancreaticoduodenectomy |
| W06.8 | Roos | Excision First Rib (Z74.3) |
| H36.1 | Roscoe-Graham | Repair Rectum for Prolapse |
| M75.2 | Rosen | (D) Prosthesis Male Incontinence |
| K33.1 | Ross | Pulmonary Autograft Aortic Root Replacement |
| W19.1 | Ross-Brown | (D) Nail Hip |
| K33.2 | Ross-Konno | Aortoventriculoplasty Pulmonary Autograft |
| M10.4 | Rosving | Deroofing of Multiple Cysts of Kidney |
| J19.3 | Roux-en-Y | Cholecystojejunostomy |
| J30.2 | Roux-en-Y | Choledochojejunostomy |
| G01.2 | Roux-en-Y | Oesophagogastrectomy |
| J59.- | Roux-en-Y | Pancreaticojejunostomy |
| W77.2 | Roux-Goldthwaite | Stabilisation Knee By Transplant. Tendon (Z84.4) |
| G02.3 | Roux-Herzen-Judine | Oesophagectomy |
| X27.4 | Ruiz-Mora | Excision Proximal Phalanx Fifth Toe |
| W19.3 | Rush | (D) Intramedullary Nail |
| X49.1 | Russell-Hamilton | (D) Traction System Leg (Z90.9) |

# S

| | | |
|---|---|---|
| X22.2 | Salter | Osteotomy Pelvis |
| J29.1 | Sawaguchi | Hepatojejunostomy |
| W12.2 | Schanz | Osteotomy Hip (Z76.2) |
| Q08.- | Schauta | Radical Vaginal Hysterectomy – refer to Tabular List Introduction |
| T01.1 | Schede | Thoracoplasty |
| C55.8 | Scheie | Cautery Incision Sclera |
| G27.- | Schlatter | Total Gastrectomy |
| W19.2 | Schnieder | (D) Nail for Forearm Fracture (Z71.3) |
| P14.1 | Schuchardt | Episiotomy Non Obstetrical |
| D16.8 | Schuknecht | Malleostapediopexy |
| D10.3 | Schwartze | Cortical Mastoidectomy |
| T64.1 | Schwarzmann-Crego | Transfer Hamstring (Z57.7) |
| G61.3 | Scott | Jejunocolostomy |
| T64.8 | Seddon-Brooks | Transfer Pectoralis Major Tendon (Z54.3) |
| L72.1 | Seldinger | Arteriography (Or Code to Artery) |
| G21.- | Sengstaken | (D) Intubation Oesophagus |
| G21.- | Sengstaken-Blakemore | (D) Intubation Oesophagus |
| K05.- | Senning | Reconstruction Transposition Great Arteries |
| X19.2 | Sever | Operation for Erbs Palsy |
| W77.2 | Sharrard | Transfer Iliopsoas Muscle (Z57.2) |
| D16.8 | Shea | Malleostapediopexy |
| D16.8 | Shea-Guilford | Malleostapediopexy |
| J05.3 | Sheeba | (D) Biopsy Liver (Open) |
| J13.2 | Sheeba | (D) Biopsy Liver (Percutaneous) |
| W40.- | Sheehan | (D) Total Replacement Knee (Cemented) |
| W40.- | Shiers | (D) Total Replacement Knee (Cemented) |
| R12.1 | Shirodkar | Encirclement Suture Cervix Gravid Uterus |
| Q05.1 | Shirodkar | Repair Internal Os Cervix Uteri |
| T20.3 | Shouldice | Repair Inguinal Hernia |
| T21.3 | Shouldice | Repair Recurrent Inguinal Hernia |
| W79.2 | Silver | Bunionectomy |
| T70.3 | Silver | Recession Gastrocnemius Muscle (Z58.1) |
| T70.3 | Silverskoild | Recession Gastrocnemius Muscle (Z58.1) |
| D15.1 | Silverstein | (D) Tube Ear |
| B10.1 | Sistrunk | Excision Thyroglossal Cyst |
| X09.4 | Slocum | Disarticulation Knee |
| W77.2 | Slocum | Transfer Pes Anserinus (Z84.6) |
| W21.3 | Smillie | (D) Intra-articular Fragment Pin |
| W55.- | Smith-Petersen | (D) Interposition Arthroplasty |
| W62.1 | Smith-Petersen | Intra-articular Fusion Hip (Z84.3) |
| W24.1 | Smith-Petersen (M) | (D) Nail Hip |
| A75.1 | Smithwick | Cervical Sympathectomy |
| H41.8 | Soave | Operation for Hirschsprung Disease |
| W16.1 | Sofield | Multiple Osteotomy & Fixation |
| W13.1 | Somerville | Rotation Osteotomy Femur (Z76.3) |
| X09.1 | Sorondo-Ferre | Hindquarter Amputation |
| W13.3 | Southwick | Osteotomy Femur (Z76.2) |
| G11.- | Souttar | (D) Prosthesis Oesophagus (Code to Procedure) |
| W78.2 | Soutter | Soft Tissue Release Hip |

| X07.2 | Spence | Disarticulation Shoulder |
|---|---|---|
| M58.8 | Spence | Vaginal Urethrocystostomy |
| D10.1 | Stacke | Radical Mastoidectomy |
| M51.2 | Stamey | Endoscopic Suspension Bladder Neck |
| W13.2 | Stamm | Osteotomy Glenoid (Z68.4) |
| W37.- | Stanmore | (D) Total Replacement Hip (Cemented) |
| W40.- | Stanmore | (D) Total Replacement Knee (Cemented) |
| W43.- | Stanmore | (D) Total Replacement Shoulder (Cemented) (Z81.4) |
| W61.1 | Staples | Intra-articular Fusion Elbow (Z81.5) |
| X20.3 | Starr | Operation for Congenital Absence Radius |
| K29.3 | Starr-Edwards | (D) Caged Prosthetic Replacement Heart Valve NEC (Normally Code to Valve Replaced) |
| X22.2 | Steez | Osteotomy Pelvis |
| T54.2 | Steindler | Release Plantar Fascia |
| W61.1 | Steindler (A) | Intra-articular Fusion Elbow (Z81.5) |
| W61.1 | Steindler (A) | Intra-articular Fusion Shoulder (Z81.4) |
| T64.1 | Steindler (A) | Transfer Flexor Muscle Forearm (Z55.1) |
| W29.9 | Steinmann | (D) Traction System |
| M05.1 | Stewart-Hamilton | Pyeloplasty & Plication Kidney (M05.4) |
| W58.- | St Georg | (D) Resurfacing Arthroplasty Knee (Z84.6) |
| H51.1 | St Mark | Haemorrhoidectomy |
| H33.1 | St Mark | Resection Rectum |
| H50.9 | Stone | Anoplasty |
| Q09.5 | Strassman | Metroplasty |
| T70.5 | Strayer | Recession Gastrocnemius Muscle (Z58.1) |
| B31.1 | Strombeck | Reduction Breast |
| J05.8 | Stromeyer-Little | Hepatotomy |
| Q03.1 | Sturmdorf | Conisation Cervix Uteri |
| G60.1 | Surmay | Jejunostomy Operation |
| X22.2 | Sutherland | Osteotomy Pelvis |
| K65.2 | Swan-Ganz | (D) Catheter Heart |
| W54.- | Swanson | Arthroplasty Joint |
| H41.8 | Swenson | Operation for Hirschsprung Disease |
| T24.3 | Swenson | Repair Umbilical Hernia |
| X10.1 | Syme | Amputation Ankle |
| M75.3 | Syme | External Urethrotomy |

# T

| | | |
|---|---|---|
| T36.8 | Talma-Morison | Omentopexy |
| M73.4 | Tanagho | Reconstruction Urethra |
| G10.8 | Tanner | Gastric Transection |
| T20.3 | Tanner | Repair Inguinal Hernia |
| T21.3 | Tanner | Repair Recurrent Inguinal Hernia |
| F03.1 | Tenison-Randall | Repair Cleft Lip |
| G24.5 | Thal | Stricturoplasty Antireflux Operation |
| G24.5 | Thal-Nissen | Stricturoplasty Antireflux Operation |
| W58.- | Tharies | (D) Resurfacing Replacement Hip (Z84.3) |
| S35.- | Thiersch | Split Autograft Skin |
| H42.1 | Thiersch | Wire for Prolapse Rectum |
| X40.1 | Thomas | (D) Intravascular Shunt for Dialysis |
| X49.1 | Thomas | (D) Splint Leg (Z90.9) |
| T92.3 | Thompson | Correction Lymphoedema |
| W46.- | Thompson (Fr) | (D) Hemiarthroplasty Hip (Cemented) |
| W47.- | Thompson (FR) | (D) Hemiarthroplasty Hip (Uncemented) |
| T79.2 | Thompson (TC) | Quadricepsplasty |
| J18.5 | Thorek | Partial Cholecystectomy |
| W19.1 | Thornton | (D) Nail Plate Hip |
| O10.- | Tikhoff Linberg | Complex Reconstruction of Shoulder (W) |
| Q09.5 | Tompkins | Metroplasty |
| N08.2 | Torek-Bevan | Bilateral Orchidopexy One Stage |
| N09.2 | Torek-Bevan | Unilateral Orchidopexy One Stage |
| A12.1 | Torkildsen | Ventriculocisternostomy |
| L38.2 | Touroff | Ligation Subclavian Artery |
| L85.1 | Trendelenburg | High Ligation Long Saphenous Vein |
| L12.4 | Trendelenburg | Pulmonary Embolectomy |
| W60.1 | Trumble | Extra-articular Fusion Hip (Z84.3) |
| X24.1 | Turco | Soft Tissue Release for Club Foot |
| M73.4 | Turner-Warwick | Reconstruction Urethra |

# U

W40.-          Uci                                    (D) Total Replacement Knee (Cemented)

# V

| Q10.8 | Vabra Aspiration | Biopsy Endometrium |
|---|---|---|
| M73.1 | Van Der Meulen | Repair Hypospadias |
| X23.6 | Vannes | Rotationplasty Leg |
| P21.5 | Vecchietti | Construction of Vagina |
| F11.3 | Visor-Sandwich | Augmentation Alveolar Ridge |
| L88.2 | VNUS Closure | Radiofrequency Ablation of Varicose Vein of Leg |
| X49.1 | Von Rosen | (D) Splintage for Cong. Disloc. Hip (Z90.2) |
| W78.2 | Voss | Release Capsule Hip for Osteoarthritis |
| T70.5 | Vulpius | Elongation Tendo Achillis (Z58.1) |

# W

| | | |
|---|---|---|
| W30.1 | Wagner | (D) External Fixator |
| W17.2 | Wagner | (D) Lengthening Leg (Z90.9) |
| W58.- | Wagner | (D) Surface Replacement Hip (Z84.3) |
| W40.- | Walldius | (D) Hinge Arthroplasty Knee (Cemented) |
| F29.1 | Wardill | Repair Cleft Palate |
| L81.2 | Waterhouse | Glanscorpora Shunt for Priapism |
| L06.3 | Waterston | Anastomosis Aorta to Right Pulmonary Artery |
| W77.2 | Watson-Jones | Tenodesis Stabilisation Ankle (Z58.2) |
| T67.9 | Watson-Jones | Tenoplasty |
| W61.1 | Watson-Jones (R) | Intra-articular Fusion Ankle (Z85.6) |
| W77.1 | Weaver & Dunn | Repair Shoulder (Z81.2) |
| H14.8 | Weir | Appendicostomy |
| E02.8 | Weir | Correction Nostril |
| H35.2 | Wells | Repair Rectum for Prolapse |
| Q07.- | Wertheim | Radical Hysterectomy – refer to Tabular List Introduction |
| T64.9 | Westminster | Relocation Tendon |
| C15.2 | Wheeler | Repair Entropion |
| J56.2 | Whipple | Pancreaticoduodenectomy |
| T70.5 | White | Lengthening Tendo Achillis (Z58.1) |
| H51.1 | Whitehead | Haemorrhoidectomy |
| T79.8 | Whitman | Repair Serratus Anterior Muscle (Z60.8) |
| W06.8 | Whitman | Talectomy (Z79.1) |
| F50.1 | Wilke | Bilateral Diversion Parotid Duct |
| P21.1 | Williams | Construction Vagina |
| T01.1 | Wilms | Thoracoplasty |
| W15.1 | Wilson | Osteotomy Neck First Metatarsal Hallux Valgus |
| V38.3 | Wiltse | Posterior Fusion Lumbar Spine |
| J19.4 | Winiwater | Cholecystoenterostomy |
| L81.2 | Winter | Glanscorpora Shunt for Priapism |
| G75.- | Witzel | Temporary Enterostomy |
| S36.- | Wolfe | Full Thickness Skin Graft |
| U40.2 | Wood's light | Diagnostic Ultraviolet Skin Test |
| X19.1 | Woodward | Reconstruction Soft Tissue Shoulder |
| D14.- | Wullstein | Myringoplasty |

# Y

| H40.2 | York-Mason | Excision Lesion Rectum |
| H40.8 | York-Mason | Repair Fistula Rectum |
| M73.1 | Young | Repair Hypospadias |
| T64.9 | Young | Transfer Tendon |
| M73.2 | Young-Dees | Repair Epispadias |
| W78.3 | Yount | Soft Tissue Release Knee |

# Z

| | | |
|---|---|---|
| M51.1 | Zacharin | Abdominoperineal Suspension Urethra |
| P24.1 | Zacharin | Repair Vault Vagina |
| T64.1 | Zachary | Transfer Flexor Muscle Forearm (Z55.1) |
| X19.2 | Zachary-L'Episcopo | Operation for Obstetric Palsy |
| S64.1 | Zadik | Excision Nail Bed |
| W01.5 | Zancolli | Opponensplasty Thumb |
| T64.1 | Zancolli | Transfer Flexor Muscle Forearm (Z55.1) |
| W19.1 | Zickel | (D) Intramedullary Nail Plate Hip |
| W20.1 | Zuezler | (D) Hook Fixation Plate Olecranon (Z71.1) |

# Section III

Alphabetical Index
of
Surgical Abbreviations

| Code | Abbreviation | Description |
|---|---|---|
| W71.4 | ACI | Autologous Cartilage Implantation |
| M55.6 | ACT | Adjustable Continence Therapy |
| X09.3 | AKA | Above Knee Amputation |
| O19.1 | AMIC | Autologous Matrix Induced Chondrogenesis (W) |
| H33.1 | AP | Abdominoperineal Resection Rectum |
| | | |
| D13.- | BAHA | Bone Anchored Hearing Aid |
| E13.6 | BAWO | Bilateral Antral Washout |
| E95.2 | BCG | Bacillus Calmette-Guerin Vaccination |
| X09.5 | BKA | Below Knee Amputation |
| W34.- | BMT | Bone Marrow Transplant |
| E85.2 | BPAP | Bilevel Positive Airway Pressure |
| | | |
| E85.2 | CNP | Continuous Negative Airway Pressure |
| E85.2 | CPAP | Continuous Positive Airway Pressure |
| U21.2 | CT | Computed Axial Tomography Scanning |
| | | |
| Y94.1 | DATSCAN | Dopamine Transporter Scan |
| C25.- | DCR | Dacryocystorhinostomy |
| U13.1 | DEXA | Dual Emission X-Ray Absorptiometry Scan |
| W24.2 | DHS | Dynamic Hip Screw Closed |
| W24.1 | DHS | Dynamic Hip Screw Closed Intracapsular |
| W19.1 | DHS | Dynamic Hip Screw Open |
| B39.3 | DIEP | Deep Inferior Epigastric Perforator Flap |
| L06.2 | DKS | Anastomosis Pulmonary Artery to Aorta |
| Y94.4 | DTPA | Diethylenetriamine Pentacetic Acid Imaging |
| | | |
| E63.2 | EBUS-TBNA | Endobronchial Ultrasound Guided Transbronchial Needle Aspiration |
| X58.1 | ECMO | Extracorporeal Membrane Oxygenation |
| A83.- | ECT | Electroconvulsive Therapy |
| R12.4 | ECV | External Cephalic Version |
| M10.5 | ENDOBRST | Endoscopic Endoluminal Balloon Rupture Stenosis Pelviureteric Junction Kidney |
| M27.6 | ENDOBRST | Endoscopic Endoluminal Balloon Rupture Stenosis Ureter |
| L27.- | EVAR | Endovascular Aneurysm Repair |
| L88.1 | EVLT | Endovascular Laser Therapy of Saphenous Varicose Vein |
| L88.3 | EVLT | Endovascular Laser Therapy of Varicose Vein NEC |
| | | |
| O11.1 | GOJ | Gastro-oesophageal Junction site (Z) |
| | | |
| M49.7 | HIFU | High Intensity Focused Ultrasound Bladder |
| M71.1 | HIFU | High Intensity Focused Ultrasound Prostate |
| | | |
| K59.- | ICD | Implantable Cardioverter Defibrillator |
| Y96.- | ICIS | Intracytoplasmic Injection of Sperm |
| B38.2 | IGAP | Inferior Gluteal Artery Perforator Flap |
| Q13.1 | IVF | In Vitro Fertilisation |
| L72.6 | IVUS | Intravascular Ultrasound Artery |
| K51.2 | IVUS | Intravascular Ultrasound Coronary Artery |

| | | |
|---|---|---|
| C44.5 | LASEK | Laser Subepithelial Keratomileusis |
| C44.2 | LASIK | Laser in Situ Keratomileusis |
| | | |
| U12.6 | MAG3 | Mercaptoacetyltriglycine Renogram |
| L69.- | MAPCAs | Major Systemic to Pulmonary Collateral Arteries |
| N34.4 | MESA | Microsurgical Epididymal Sperm Aspiration |
| Y94.3 | MIBG | Metaiodobenzylguanidine Imaging |
| U16.2 | MRCP | Magnetic Resonance Cholangiopancreatography |
| U21.1 | MRI | Magnetic Resonance Imaging Scanning NEC |
| U10.7 | MUGA | Multiple Gated Acquisition Scan |
| | | |
| E85.2 | NIPPV | Non-Invasive Positive Pressure Ventilation |
| U21.1 | NMR | Nuclear Magnetic Resonance Scanning NEC |
| E98.- | NRT | Nicotine Replacement Therapy |
| | | |
| W83.7 | OATS | Osteoarticular Transfer System |
| E91.3 | ODI | Oxygen Desaturation Index Measurement |
| | | |
| H41.2 | PART | Peranal Resection Tumour |
| X33.- | PBSCT | Peripheral Blood Stem Cell Transplant |
| H15.7 | PEC | Percutaneous Endoscopic Sigmoid Colostomy |
| E93.1 | PEF | Peak Expiratory Flow Rate Study |
| G44.5 | PEG | Percutaneous Endoscopic Gastrostomy |
| N34.5 | PESA | Percutaneous Epididymal Sperm Aspiration |
| U21.3 | PET | Positron Emission Tomography |
| L99.7 | PICC | Percutaneous Transluminal Insertion Central Catheter |
| C44.4 | PRK | Photorefractive Keratectomy |
| J77.1 | PTVS | Percutaneous Transhepatic Portal Venous Sampling |
| | | |
| O29.1 | SAD | Subacromial Decompression (Open) (W) |
| U17.2 | SeHCAT | Selenium-75-Homocholic Acid Taurine Study |
| B38.1 | SGAP | Superior Gluteal Artery Perforator Flap |
| J12.3 | SIRT | Selective Internal Radiotherapy with Microspheres Lesion Liver |
| W84.7 | SLAP | Superior Labrum Anterior Posterior Repair |
| U21.4 | SPECT | Single Photon Emission Computed Tomography |
| U28.- | SST | Serum Skin Test |
| U29.7 | SST | Short Synacthen Test |
| Q11.- | STOP | Suction Termination of Pregnancy |
| | | |
| X65.1 | TBI | Total Body Irradiation |
| A70.7 | TENS | Transcutaneous Electrical Nerve Stimulator |
| N34.6 | TESE | Testicular Sperm Extraction |
| J11.4 | TIPS | Transjugular Intrahepatic Portosystemic Shunt |
| U20.2 | TOE | Transoesophageal Echocardiography |
| M53.6 | TOT | Introduction Transobtruator Tape |
| B39.- | TRAM | Transverse Rectus Abdominis Myocutaneous Flap |
| U20.1 | TTE | Transthoracic Echocardiography |
| R07.- | TTTS | Twin to Twin Transfusion Syndrome |
| R08.- | TTTS | Twin to Twin Transfusion Syndrome |

| | | |
|---|---|---|
| Q48.1 | TUDOR | Transurethral Ultrasound Directed Oocyte Recovery |
| M70.7 | TUNA | Transurethral Radiofrequency Needle Ablation |
| M65.- | TURP | Transurethral Resection Prostate |
| M53.3 | TVT | Introduction Tension-Free Vaginal Tape |
| | | |
| F32.6 | UVP | Uvulopalatoplasty |
| F32.5 | UVPP | Uvulopalatopharyngoplasty |
| | | |
| Y74.4 | VATS | Video-Assisted Thoracoscopic Surgery |
| U15.3 | VQ | Ventilation Perfusion Quotient Scan |

# Section IV

Alphabetical Index
of
Common Surgical Suffixes

| Suffix | Meaning |
| --- | --- |
| anastomosis | Connection |
| -centesis | Puncture |
| -clasis | Fracture |
| -cleisis | Shutting In |
| -clysis | Rectal Injection |
| -desis | Binding |
| dialysis | Cleaning |
| | Compensation |
| -ectasia | Dilation |
| | Fusion |
| | Stabilisation |
| | Stretching |
| -ectomy | Excision |
| -exeresis | Removal |
| | Stripping Off |
| -graphy | Visual Display |
| -lysis | Freeing from Adhesions |
| | Loosening |
| -ostomy | Opening |
| -otomy | Incision |
| | Opening |
| -paxy | Crushing |
| | Washout |
| -pexy | Fixing |
| | Suspension |
| -plasty | Moulding |
| | Reformation |
| -plexy | Weaving |
| -rrhaphy | Suturing |
| -schisis | Division |
| -scopy | Inspection |
| -stasis | Positioning |
| | Stopping |
| -stomy | Making A Mouth |
| | Opening |
| -tasis | Stretching |
| -taxis | Arranging |
| -tome | Cutting Instrument |
| -tomy | Cutting (Not Puncture) |
| | Section |
| -tripsy | Crushing |
| -trity | Crushing |